The Devil's Pleasure Palace

*The Cult of Critical Theory
and the Subversion of the West*

The Devil's Pleasure Palace

*The Cult of Critical Theory
and the Subversion of the West*

Michael Walsh

Encounter Books
New York • London

First American edition published in 2015 by Encounter Books, an activity of Encounter for Culture and Education, Inc., a nonprofit, tax exempt corporation.
Encounter Books website address: www.encounterbooks.com

Manufactured in the United States and printed on acid-free paper. The paper used in this publication meets the minimum requirements of ANSI/NISO Z39.48-1992 (R 1997) (*Permanence of Paper*).

FIRST AMERICAN EDITION

Library of Congress Cataloging-in-Publication Data

Walsh, Michael, 1949–
The devil's pleasure palace : the cult of critical theory and the subversion of the West / by Michael Walsh.
pages cm
Includes bibliographical references and index.
ISBN 978-1-59403-768-9 (hardcover : alk. paper)—ISBN 978-1-59403-769-6 (ebook)
1. Critical theory—United States. 2. Nihilism (Philosophy) 3. United States—Civilization—194– I. Title.
HM480.W35 2015
149′.8—dc23

2015002549

For Ann Patricia Walsh, my mother,
who taught me to love words

Philosophers have only interpreted the world in various ways; the point is to change it.

— Marx, *Theses on Feuerbach*

But I can't listen to music often, it affects the nerves. One wants to say pleasant stupidities and stroke on the head the people who, living in this dirty hell, can create such beauty. And today it is impossible to stroke anyone on the head—they bite off your hand, and it is necessary to beat heads, beat them ruthlessly, although we, ideally, are against any sort of violence against people. Hmmm, the task is diabolically difficult.

— Vladimir Lenin, as recounted by Maxim Gorky in *Days with Lenin*

Only a humanity to which death has become as indifferent as its members, which has died to itself, can inflict it administratively on innumerable people.

— Theodor Adorno, *Minima Moralia: Reflections on a Damaged Life*

You can discover what your enemy fears most by observing the means he uses to frighten you … Take away hatred from some people, and you have men without faith.

— Eric Hoffer, *The Passionate State of Mind*

It is true that storytelling reveals meaning without committing the error of defining it, that it brings about consent and reconciliation with things as they really are, and that we may even trust it to contain eventually by implication that last word which we expect from the "Day of Judgment."

— Hannah Arendt, *Men in Dark Times*

At the core of liberalism is the spoiled child—miserable, as all spoiled children are, unsatisfied, demanding, ill-disciplined, despotic, and useless. Liberalism is a philosophy of sniveling brats.

— P. J. O'Rourke, *Give War a Chance*

The champions of socialism call themselves progressives, but they recommend a system which is characterized by rigid observance of routine and by a resistance to every kind of improvement. They call themselves liberals, but they are intent upon abolishing liberty. They call themselves democrats, but they yearn for dictatorship. They call themselves revolutionaries, but they want to make the government omnipotent. They promise the blessings of the Garden of Eden, but they plan to transform the world into a gigantic post office. Every man but one a subordinate clerk in a bureau. What an alluring utopia! What a noble cause to fight for!

— Ludwig von Mises, *Bureaucracy*

The crisis of the West consists in the West's having become uncertain of its purpose.

— Leo Strauss, *The City and Man*

Contents

THE ARGUMENT

In the aftermath of World War II, America—the new leader of the West—stood alone as the world's premier military power. Yet its martial confidence contrasted vividly with its sense of cultural inferiority. Still looking to a defeated and dispirited Europe for intellectual and artistic guidance, a burgeoning transnational elite in New York City and Washington, D.C., embraced not only the war's refugees but also many of their resolutely nineteenth-century "modern" ideas as well.

Few of these ideas have proven more pernicious than those of the so-called Frankfurt School and its reactionary philosophy of "critical theory." At once overly intellectualized and emotionally juvenile, Critical Theory—like Pandora's Box—released a horde of demons into the American psyche. When everything could be questioned, nothing could be real, and the muscular, confident empiricism that had just won the war gave way, in less than a generation, to a fashionable Central European nihilism that was celebrated on college campuses across the United States. Seizing the high ground of academe and the arts, the new nihilists set about dissolving the bedrock of the country, from patriotism to marriage to the family to military service. They have sown (as Cardinal Bergoglio—now Pope Francis—has written of Satan, who will play a large role in our story) "destruction, division, hatred, and calumny"—and all disguised as a search for truth that will lead to human happiness here on earth.

Of course, what has resulted is something far from that. Were any of the originators of Critical Theory sill among us, they might well say, quoting Sir Christopher Wren: *Si monumentum requiris, circumspice.* Look about your daily lives here in early twenty-first-century America and Western Europe, and see the shabbiness, hear the coarseness of speech and dialogue, witness the lowered standards not only of personal behavior but also of cultural norms, savor the shrunken horizons of the future.

The Frankfurt School sucker punched American culture right in its weak solar plexus. Americans have always been sympathetic to an alternative point of view, sympathetic to the underdog, solicitous of strangers, especially foreign refugees fleeing a monster like Hitler. Largely innocent of the European battles over various forms of socialism, and softened up to a certain extent by the Roosevelt administration's early, frank admiration of Mussolini as it tried to solve the economic crisis of the Depression, the American public was open to self-criticism.

The problem with the Frankfurt School scholars was that they arrived with ideological blinders—men of the Left fighting other men of the Left back in the old *Heimat*—and were unable to see that there was another, different world welcoming them in the United States if only they would open their eyes. (How, for example, could they hate California?) They appear not so much scholarly as simple, viewing American capitalism as a vast, deliberate, conspiracy against their own socialist ideas, when, in fact, their ideas were simply wrong, their analysis flawed, and their animus ineradicable. They were creatures of their own time and place, with no more claim to absolute truth than the man on a soapbox in Speakers' Corner in Hyde Park or the lunatic staggering down Market Street in San Francisco talking to himself. Everybody's got a beef.

One thing they did get right, though: Popular culture lay at the heart of the American experience. It was hugely influential in a way that surpassed the understanding of European academics; without official sanction, it spoke for the people in a way that state-sponsored Socialist Realist art never could. They knew pop culture was potent, very potent, but they had no idea how to create more of it, or control it. They were so obsessed with their crude and unsophisticated Marxism, so devoted to their paradigm of the class struggle, that they worried about pop culture's destructive top-down effect on the gullible proletariat and viewed

Hollywood and the mass media as, naturally, a capitalist plot to seduce the rubes. (Seduction, they believed, was their socialist birthright, not capitalism's.) They desired self-improving, consciousness-raising art to be a matter for the State, and they disdained the profit motive, though they certainly had no objection to making money. But their successors had no such quibbles with mass culture. They grasped that the "long march through the institutions" (as the Marxists characterized it) would be the ticket to ideological hegemony and even greater wealth—evolution, not revolution.

This is a book about how we got here. It is also a book about good and evil; about creation and destruction; about capitalism and socialism; about God, Satan, and the satanic in men; about myths and legends and the truths within them; about culture versus politics; about the difference between story and plot. It is about Milton versus Marx, the United States versus Germany, about redemptive truth versus Mephistophelean bands of illusion and the Devil's jokes. It concerns itself with the interrelation of culture, religion, sex, and politics—in other words, something herein to offend nearly everybody.

And, I hope, to inspire. For the taboos of our culture are also its totems, and the political arguments that rage around them are symptomatic of both disease and good health, of infection and immunity. They are not simply battlefields in the larger contemporary culture war—they *are* the culture war, a war that has been raging since the Garden of Eden but that manifests itself today in the unceasing attack of cultural Marxism (which molts and masquerades under many names, including liberalism, progressivism, social justice, environmentalism, anti-racism, etc.) upon what used to be called the Christian West.

Although this battle is simply the latest front in an ancient war, this critical struggle—"the Fight" or "the Struggle" (or *der Kampf*), as leftists call it—is the defining issue of our time. It will determine not only what kind of country the United States of America will become but also whether the Western world will continue the moral, cultural, and technological dominance it shares with the larger Anglophone world, or finally succumb to a relentless assault on its values and accept the loss of its cultural vigor. In other words, will it—will we—repel the invaders, organize sorties, ride out and crush them—or wearily open the gates to the citadel and await the inevitable slaughter?

The aggressors include the Frankfurt School of (mostly German) Marxist philosophers, theoreticians, and writers, as well as their intellectual descendants and acolytes in the U.S., including the followers of Saul Alinsky, the Marxist "community organizer" whose influence has only waxed in the years since his death in 1972 and has extended even to the Oval Office. Throughout, I refer to this cabal as the Unholy Left, a term unapologetically both descriptive and judgmental. It is a term I suspect they would dearly like to embrace but can't quite bring themselves to yet, if only for electoral reasons.

I am not talking of garden-variety "liberals" (actually, big-government statists, so long as that big government does not come down on them), who see Washington as a kind of taxpayer-funded supra-charity, dispensing goodies to the deserving poor and making sure chemicals aren't dumped in the drinking water. Rather, I refer to the hard Left, the radicals, many of whom are now in power, who would remake ("fundamentally transform")—*wreck*—the United States of America and, by extension, the civilization of the West.

On the other side are not conservatives per se, but those who see themselves in the role of *conservators*—preservers of the Western legacy who recognize that we should not lightly abandon a long, shared cultural tradition that, whatever its real or perceived faults, has been the primary engine of human moral, spiritual, social, scientific, and medical progress.

Therefore, I propose to look at the history of the Left–Right conflict (to put it in its simplest terms) not only in terms of politics but in terms of art and culture as well. If the Paleolithic cavemen who painted the walls of Lascaux kept precise, detailed, written astronomical records, we don't know about them. But their symbols and images of animals and people, left on the walls of ancient caves in France, might well contain astronomic information—preserved via the medium of art. Via their paintings, they left us a nearly indelible image of their world. Looking at the vivid illustrations of bulls, stags, and horses—and even other human beings—we can begin to understand who we are in a way that science cannot teach us. The cave paintings are not only evidence; they are *human interpretations* of evidence, part of our shared heritage. Their artists were who we still are today. They are trying to tell us something.

Similarly, the worldview of the ancient Greeks comes down via the medium of poetry and oral narrative, later preserved in written form;

and this slender reed of happenstance, subject to the vagaries of selection and preservation, is, together with Jerusalem, one of the pillars upon which rests the entire edifice of Western civilization. Legends they seem to us, but like the cave paintings, they are interpretations of phenomena, internalized by the artists and then re-externalized in the form of narrative—our ur-Narrative, or founding myth, from which all that is human in our society flows. We ignore the philosophical and moral significance of this patrimony at our peril and should never dismiss it as mere superstition or storytelling, somehow inferior to the philosophy of Socrates, Plato, and Aristotle. The writings are all of a piece, clues to our essence, messages in sacred bottles, washed ashore upon the sands of time.

They are stories of gods and goddesses and titans, but mostly they are stories of heroes. Humanity is inconceivable without heroes; we are not egalitarian members of an ant farm, shuttling from cradle to grave, indistinguishable from one another and easily replaceable. Not everyone can be a hero, but everyone can dream of heroism. Bravery has always been a cardinal human virtue, so great that it was embodied by none other than Jesus Christ, another foundational cultural pillar of the West.

In his book *Christ: A Crisis in the Life of God,* the Pulitzer Prize–winning author Jack Miles looks at the story of Jesus of Nazareth as the tale of the hero of the New Testament, complete with the happy ending of the Resurrection. As Miles write in his prologue:

> *All mankind is forgiven, but the Lord must die. This is the revolutionary import of the epilogue that, two thousand years ago, a group of radical Jewish writers appended to the sacred scripture of their religion. Because they did so, millions in the West today worship before the image of a deity executed as a criminal, and—no less important—other millions who never worship at all carry within their cultural DNA a religiously derived suspicion that somehow, someday, "the last will be first, and the first last." (Matt. 20:16)*

The humbly heroic Christ—born into straitened circumstances of a virgin mother, a precocious teacher and rabbi who undertook a brief, three-year ministry that was both populist and political, who was captured through treachery, unfairly tried, tortured, and executed, and who returned in triumph over death—is the archetypal Christian hero, supplanting the Homeric heroes (Achilles, Odysseus) who did not give their lives for something larger than themselves, their families, or their tribes. But Christ, the Lamb of God, the Redeemer, Messiah, willingly fails in order to succeed, bestowing a gift upon a humanity that is still not sure whether it wants to accept it. His story—what used to be unapologetically called "The Greatest Story Ever Told"—resonates down through two thousand years of Western history, touching nearly ever major subsequent tale of heroism, from the *Chanson de Roland* to *The Little Mermaid.*

For what we—in an increasingly secular West—misread as a political argument is, in reality, nothing of the sort. It is a *literary* argument, if we define literature properly not as "fiction" but as the expression of the soul of a people, in this case, of all people. Politics (which for many has come to replace sports as the subject of rooting interest par excellence) is merely its secondary manifestation, the generally tiresome litany of regurgitated policy prescriptions and bogus campaign promises that residents of the Western democracies routinely encounter today. But where once in our culture raged religious arguments (whose moral underpinnings were never in doubt), today we are concerned not simply with the details of a system of governance and social organization, but with the very nature of that system itself. In fact, at issue is the essence of Western civilization and how it may be subverted to achieve a vastly different—indeed, opposite—end than originally intended. For one side has changed the meaning of the principal words in the debate, including "democracy," "culture," "civilization," and "justice," among others. The two sides speak different languages, but with a superficially shared vocabulary that serves as a means of deceit for one and confusion for the other.

Seduction, subversion, sedition—these are the tools of a creature we once called Satan, the Father of Lies, the loser of the Battle in Heaven. Yet he continues the fight here on earth with the only weapons at his disposal: man's inherent weaknesses and zeal to be duped if the cause seems appealing enough. Chief among the weaknesses of Western man today are his fundamental lack of cultural self-confidence, his willingness to open his ears to the siren song of nihilism, a juvenile eagerness to believe the worst about himself and his society and to relish, on some level, his own prospective destruction.

Whether one views the combatants in the struggle between God and Satan ontologically, mythically, or literarily, God created man in his own image and likeness but chose to give him free will—a force so powerful that not even God's infinite love can always overcome it. Thus given a sporting chance to ruin God's favorites, the fallen Light-Bringer, Lucifer, picked himself and his fellows off the floor of the fiery lake into which they were plunged by the sword of St. Michael, and endeavors each day not to conquer Man but to seduce and destroy him. As Satan observes in Book One of Milton's *Paradise Lost*:

> *The mind is its own place, and in itself*
> *Can make a Heav'n of Hell, a Hell of Heav'n.*
> *What matter where, if I be still the same ...*
> *To reign is worth ambition though in Hell:*
> *Better to reign in Hell than serve in Heav'n.*

Satan himself, however, has no need for servants in Hell, as God does in Heaven; he is instead satisfied with corpses on earth. As modern history shows, the Devil has had great success and ample reward in that department. But he cannot be satisfied with his infernal kingdom. As in a Hollywood sequel, the body count must be ever higher, just to keep the antagonist interested. Damnation consists not in consignment to the netherworld, but in the rejection of the ur-Narrative—a willful separation of oneself from the heroic path for which history and literature provide a clear signpost.

As Milton writes in the *Areopagitica*, the poet's seminal essay on freedom of speech and, more important, freedom of thought: "I cannot praise a fugitive and cloistered virtue, unexercised and unbreathed, that never sallies out and sees her adversary, but slinks out of the race where that immortal garland is to be run for, not without dust and heat." For Milton, the very absence of conflict was in itself contemptible, unmanly—inhuman.

This eternal conflict, then, is the essence of my religio-cultural argument, which I will view through the triple prisms of 1) atheist cultural Marxism that sprang up amid the physical and intellectual detritus of Europe after the calamity of World War I, and its practical, battering-ram application, Critical Theory; and 2) the Book of Genesis, from which our cultural self-understanding flows, and Milton's great explicative epic poem, in which a God who reigns supreme is also a strangely absent and largely offstage Prime Mover; and 3) Johann Wolfgang von Goethe's emblematic reworking of the man caught in the middle between Heaven and Hell, between God and Mephistopheles: *Faust.*

It is the story of humanity's journey, of roads taken and not taken, and about the choices we must make. Let us begin, then, in Hell.

OF THE DEVIL'S PLEASURE PALACE

In 1813, the sixteen-year-old Viennese composer Franz Peter Schubert began work on his first opera, *Des Teufels Lustschloss* (*The Devil's Pleasure Palace*), with a libretto by August von Kotzebue. The work remained unperformed until 1978, when it finally was staged in Potsdam, outside of Berlin. To say that Schubert was young when he composed this youthful but culturally seminal work partially obscures that he also proved middle-aged, dying at thirty-one in 1828. People got older younger then, grew up faster, and perhaps lived life more fully. In any case, the creative force embodied by Schubert was in a hurry to meet its negation, which is to say, its completion.

In *Des Teufels Lustschloss*, Oswald, a poor knight, marries Luitgarde, an aristocrat's niece who is promptly disinherited. Heading for a new life, they are caught in a raging storm and take refuge in a nearby inn. When superstitious villagers tell of a strange, haunted castle in the vicinity, Oswald and his faithful squire, Robert, set off to investigate the manor house, which indeed turns out to be bristling with terrors and temptations. One of the latter takes the form of a shapely Amazon who tries to seduce Oswald, warning him of dire consequences should he not succumb. (He does not.) The more adamantly faithful Oswald is, though, the more terrors rise up to threaten him. He is finally saved by the timely arrival of Luitgarde, who, when threatened with death herself, stands fast—and suddenly the castle crumbles.

In the end, it all turns out to have been an illusion. The spirits were the villagers in disguise, hired by Luitgarde's uncle to test Oswald's courage under fire and prove him worthy of Luitgarde.

Conventional musical wisdom has long held that Kotzebue's libretto is the principal reason for the opera's neglect—an explanation applied to all Schubert operas, as it happens. More likely, the cause is Schubert's inexpert handling of the dramatic necessities inherent in operatic composition; what works so brilliantly for him in songs and song cycles failed him as a composer in the larger forms of vocal compositions (although, curiously, not in his symphonies, each of which grew in sophistication and scope).

But, seen in another light, Kotzebue's work is entirely in line with European philosophical thought of the time as expressed through art. Recall that this is the early nineteenth century, not the twentieth; the horrors of 1914 and 1939 are still far in the future. The happy ending (a victory of love over death) is not a cop-out but the proof of the promise of redemption—that we must suffer the temptations and travails of Christ and face our worst fears in order to win in the end. That its conclusion ("And then I woke up … and it was all a dream!") has since become a groan-worthy cliché is not Kotzebue's fault, given that he wrote in a less cynical age, but anyone ever tempted to throw a shoe at the end of Fritz Lang's 1944 film noir, *The Woman in the Window*, knows what I mean. Not to mention *Alice's Adventures in Wonderland*.

And who represents the saving power of divine grace? Almost invariably, the woman, whose own self-sacrifice rescues and transfigures the flawed male hero. In Goethe's famous words from the second part of *Faust*: "*Das Ewig-Weibliche zieht uns hinan*," or, "the Eternal Feminine draws us onward." The Eternal Feminine, a sexually anti-egalitarian concept that feminists of both sexes today would regard as laughable, is one of the organizing principles of the cosmos, and a crucial factor in the hero's journey. Even the pansexuality of today, try though it might, cannot replace this naturally primal force: the union of opposites into a harmonious, generative whole.

Crucially, then, Oswald is saved by the love of a good woman; so is the Flying Dutchman in Wagner's opera; so is Robert le diable in

Meyerbeer's opera of the same name; so is Max the *Freischütz* in Weber's masterpiece. And so, in another Wagner work, is Parsifal, whose sexual rejection of Kundry (the Magdalene figure) and her alluring Flower Maidens ultimately releases Kundry from Klingsor's curse; without her compelled attempt at seduction, Parsifal could never have found strength through sexual sublimation, a potency that allows him to conquer the evil magician and regain the Spear, thus causing Klingsor's own infernal pleasure palace to crumble into dust.

In short, in these tales, the twentieth-century cynicism of the inter-war generation does not yet hold sway in the larger culture. The age of anxiety, alienation, nihilism, and anomie still lies in the future. But it will come, creating along the way its own secular Xanadu, another poetic *Lustschloss*, to tempt and seduce Western civilization into self-destruction, with shame and self-doubt its principal snares.

Two years after this ambitious but abortive effort, Schubert wrote the song that made his reputation, "Erlkönig," based on a text by Goethe. The hammering octaves and rolling bass line in the piano would later inspire silent-movie pianists around the world, but they perfectly express the song's terrifying tale of a desperate father, his deathly ill son in his arms, riding furiously on horseback to bring the boy to safety, and chased by the *Erlkönig*, the Elf King, the figure of Death, who sings beguilingly to the boy in a voice that only the child can hear:

> *Du liebes Kind, komm, geh' mit mir!*
> *Gar schöne Spiele, spiel ich mit dir,*
> *Manch bunte Blumen sind an dem Strand,*
> *Meine Mutter hat manch gülden Gewand.*
>
> *(Darling child, come away with me!*
> *Such beautiful games I can play with you,*
> *So many colorful flowers on the beach,*
> *My mother has many a golden robe.)*

The music grows in intensity as the father speeds for safety, but Death's seductive song is faster, his blandishments richer, and the boy is so desirable. The child cries that the Elf King has grabbed him, the anguished father arrives at his destination, and ... *"in seinem Armen das*

Kind war tot" ("in his arms, the child was dead"). In one stroke of youthful genius, Romanticism in music had begun.

Des Teufels Lustschloss may never have found its place in the operatic repertory (nor has any other Schubert stage work). It is important nevertheless for what it tells us about the state of European theatrical thinking at the beginning of the philosophically tumultuous, watershed nineteenth century—what the taste of the audience was and what effect the work had upon later generations of creative artists. A straight line runs from the penultimate sequence of Mozart's *Don Giovanni*, with its whiff of the diabolical, and the entirety of *The Magic Flute,* with its battle between good and evil, through Schubert's youthful works to Meyerbeer's Parisian spectacular, *Robert le diable*, and Marschner's supernatural *Hans Heiling*, and ahead to the spooky German landscapes of Carl Maria von Weber's *Der Freischütz,* the haunted seacoast of Wagner's *Flying Dutchman*, and right through to the end of Wagner's *Ring of the Nibelung* cycle—which is to say, the end of the world.

Or, to put it another way, these operas convey mankind's innate desire to come face to face with the hidden forces behind our origins: good and evil, Heaven and Hell, God and Satan. From this primal conflict emerges our yearning for dramatic narrative and the daemonic in art ("daemonic" in the sense of uncanny or supernatural)—signposts pointing the way toward a meaning of life that science (which rejects the daemonic) cannot provide, if only we pay attention and follow where they lead.

The more the hero tries to avoid his fate, the more it rushes toward him. This paradox is the dilemma of modern Western man emerging from the abattoir of the twentieth century's battlefields, understandably shell-shocked and conflict-averse, and it is also one of the central themes of every tale from Gilgamesh to Disney's animated version of *Tarzan.* Only by embracing his doom—to use the old English word—and facing down his greatest fears, fears far more terrifying than the actual combat will eventually prove, can he overcome his broken humanity and become godlike.

We like to think that, as Aristotle teaches in his doctrine of mimesis, art imitates life, that our all-too-human creations of drama, poetry, theater, and literature are reflections of the human condition, scenes glimpsed through the glass darkly of imperfect understanding. But what if the opposite is true? That far from being mere *imitation*s of deeper truths, art is born deep in the unconscious and shaped according to historical principles of structure and expression, and is God's way of leading humanity to a deeper understanding of its own essential nature and potential, and of its own fate? What if art is not so much imitation or reflection as it is revelation and pathway? What if it reveals deeper truths about the essence of humanity than narrow science ever could; and that the twentieth century's belief in the primacy of materialism (invested with such explanatory numen as to become indistinguishable from faith) has misaligned the natural order and imbued us with a false consciousness of reality (to use a Marxist term)?

Art, as I will argue in these pages, is *the* gift from God, the sole true medium of truth. The nineteenth-century German biologist Ernst Haeckel famously declared that "ontogeny recapitulates phylogeny," meaning that in growing from embryo to adult, the individual organism goes through stages that mimic the evolutionary stages of the species. The stages that an individual passes through in his lifespan from fertilized egg to maturity (ontogeny), will "recapitulate," Haeckel theorized, all the stages that the species itself passed through in the course of evolution (phylogeny). But perhaps it is, in an artistic and religious sense, precisely the opposite: It is phylogeny that recapitulates ontogeny. The evolutionary development of the species—its teleology—was adumbrated in the first moment of life. Think of art, therefore, as the Big Bang Theory applied to the soul instead of the body; by imagining the creative process in reverse, we can approach the instant of our origins and then beyond.

The key to time travel is to move faster than the speed of light, for from the movement of light (at 186,000 miles per second) comes our notion of time; to travel faster than light moves us not through space but back in time. Rolling the Big Bang all the way back would end, at least temporarily, in the winking out of a spark, and then nothing: infinite, eternal void, no space, no time, no being. But if that is true, then where did the spark come from? Or has the universe, as current theory is now beginning to favor, existed eternally, raising the possibility that the universe is itself God?

It's a question that artists have been trying to answer longer than scientists have. "*Ich schreite kaum, doch wähn' ich mich schon weit*" ("I've hardly taken a step, yet it seems I've already traveled far"), observes the "perfect fool" Parsifal to Gurnemanz in the first act of Wagner's eponymous opera. "*Du siehst, mein Sohn, zum Raum wird hier die Zeit*," replies Gurnemanz ("You see, my son, here time becomes space"). The context is Parsifal's search for the Holy Grail—the lasting symbol of man's quest for truth and something that he can attain only in a transcendental dimension where time and space are one and the same thing.

The search for the originating spark of creation lies at the center of the human experiment, in just about every facet of study, whether called religion, philosophy, science, or art. It sits at the heart of every human culture, no matter how primitive or sophisticated. Indeed, cultures at the fringes of each extreme resemble one another in at least one salient way: They reject other forms of knowledge in an attempt to believe in *something*. A cargo cult on a remote Pacific island bears a very close resemblance to, say, the global-warming cult of the Western sophisticates; both believe passionately in simplistic cause and apparent effect, and neither wants to hear contradictory evidence, even of the plainest kind.

Nor is it any accident that the quest myth is basic to every society, whether told around tribal campfires or in Hollywood tentpole movies. In *The Hero with a Thousand Faces,* Joseph Campbell limns the universal "monomyth" (what I am calling the ur-Narrative) this way: "A hero ventures forth from the world of common day into a region of supernatural wonder: Fabulous forces are there encountered and a decisive victory is won: The hero comes back from this mysterious adventure with the power to bestow boons on his fellow man." The quest has many apparently different objectives, but in reality there is only one: salvation.

The quest for the Grail—the chalice that held Christ's holy blood, the physical manifestation of the sacrifice on the cross and the redemption of God's promise—is the theme of one of Western civilization's most venerable narratives, essential to every redemptive fantasy. Whether it is a physical object or an abstract idea, a thing or person—and it is instructive that Parsifal asks Gurnemanz "*Wer ist der Gral?*" or, "Who [not *what*] is the Grail?"—the Grail is that which may be sought but never fully understood, a goal receding at speeds faster than light the closer we approach it, a secret knowledge that can be revealed only at a later time, often at the price of the hero's own personal sacrifice, in the imitation of Christ.

But there is another important aspect to Campbell's heroic quest, the obstacles that the "fabulous forces" of darkness must throw at the hero in order to frighten him from his mission. From the time of Aristotle, the quest has been expressed in what Hollywood today calls the three-act structure, which I might summarize thus: The hero is called away from his normal existence, usually against his will or despite his unworthiness; he encounters all manner of setbacks, dangers, and temptations, which imperil him so greatly that it seems to the audience he can never escape; and, finally, he overcomes, accomplishes the mission, and returns as best he can to the status quo ante—but he is irrevocably changed.

(It is instructive to note that the tale of Christ's Passion conforms exactly to this structure: the entry into Jerusalem to confront his destiny; the Agony in the Garden and the Crucifixion; and, at last, the triumph of the Resurrection.)

One of the Aristotelian conditions of storytelling is that the story must have a beginning, a middle, and an end. This arc is so fundamental to the Western way of design that the entire history of drama and literature is unthinkable without it. Obviously, such is not the case with the ongoing struggle between Right and Left, but that is only because we are experiencing the story as it is occurring, having been born into it, and we will almost certainly depart from it before the outcome is clear. We are merely the Rosencrantzes and Guildensterns of the plot. But outcome there must certainly be.

A good example of this structure from the Homeric era is the figure of Ulysses. In love with his wife, Penelope, he (in the non-Homeric versions of the story) feigns madness in order to escape his call to duty in the Trojan War (Act One). When that fails, he fights bravely and victoriously alongside his legendary comrades, breaking the stalemate with the invention of the Trojan Horse (Act Two, Part One); he then must endure a decade of wandering and many dangers (Act Two, Part Two). He finally manages to return home to Ithaca and oust the suitors who, like locusts, have descended on his wife and property in his absence (Act Three). It is a rare tale that does not follow this intuitive narrative structure.

What the West has experienced since the end of the Second World War has been the erection of a modern Devil's Pleasure Palace, a Potemkin village built on promises of "social justice" and equality for all, on visions of a world at last divorced from toil and sweat, where every man and woman is guaranteed a living, a world without hunger or want or cold or fear or racism or sexism (or any of the many other "isms" the Left is forever inventing—Linnaeus had nothing on the Left in the taxonomy department).

A world, in other words, that sounds very much like Heaven. It is the world promised us by Critical Theory and by the principal figures of the Frankfurt School: the music critic Theodor Adorno; the sex theorist Wilhelm Reich (whose theories and writings I shall examine in detail); as well as founding fathers Antonio Gramsci and Georg Lukács.

Instead, as empirical evidence proclaims, this world has become Hell. The world sought by the Frankfurt School and its Critical Theory disciples is all an illusion, just as surely as the *Teufels Lustschloss* was. The corpses of the untold millions who have died in the attempts of the literally Unholy Left to found the Kingdom of Heaven here on earth, divorced from God, surely testify. Our pleasure palaces are many and varied, ranging from the creature comforts of modern civilization and its nearly endless opportunities for self-abnegating entertainment to our gleeful, olly-olly-oxen-free abjuration of formal religion, and to our false sense of enduring cultural security, which was only partly dented by the events of September 11, 2001. And yet our pleasure palaces can and will fall, as have those of all civilizations before ours. And unlike in Schubert's opera, this time there is no guaranteed happy ending.

Something wicked this way has come, and we are in the fight of our lives. How, or even whether, we choose to fight it is not the subject of this book. The subject is why we must.

CHAPTER ONE

WHOSE PARADISE?

And fast by hanging in a golden Chain
This pendant world, in bigness as a Star
Of smallest Magnitude close by the Moon.
Thither full fraught with mischievous revenge,
Accursed, and in a cursed hour he hies.
— *Paradise Lost*, Book Two

Rage is the salient characteristic of Satan and of the satanic in men. There are others, including guile, deceit, and temptation. But at the heart of Satan's mission is an overwhelming animus against God and the godly. In the second book of Milton's epic poem, Satan has a conference with his fellow demons, determined to loose the bonds of Hell, where he has been chained, and carry the fight to the Principal Enemy (the name, let us recall, that the Communist Soviets gave to the capitalist United States during the Cold War) in the only battlefield that remains open to him: Earth.

Miraculously, God lets him do it. Passing the twin guardians of Hell's gate—Satan's offspring, Sin and Death—he launches himself upward "like a pyramid of fire." Directed by Chaos, Lucifer traverses the void, leaving in his wake a bridge from Hell to Earth, to provide a pathway for the demons who will surely follow upon its completion.

Since this poetic moment—itself derived from the oldest Western foundational narrative of them all, Genesis—the war, the fight, the struggle, the *Kampf* has raged essentially uninterrupted. It is Genesis that first lays out the *ur-Kampf*, the primal conflict, with which we are dealing even to this day. One may deny the specifics of Genesis; the cult of "science" has made that easy to do. But what one cannot do is deny its poetry, which resonates deeply within our souls. And poetry clearly precedes science, so which is more likely to be truer to the human soul?

Please note that I am not making an "anti-science" argument here but merely questioning the modern notion of the supremacy of science over its antecedents, poetry and drama. Science has much to teach us, but its primary function is incremental, not universal (no serious scientist pretends that it is). There is no "settled science," but there is a settled ur-Narrative, no matter how much or how often the Left may inveigh against it and try to substitute new norms for it. Before we were aware of the movements of the sun, moon, and stars, we were aware of the movements of our hearts.

Conflict is the essence of history, but also of drama. Without conflict, there can be no progress, without progress there can be no history, without history there can be no culture, without culture there can be no civilization. And—since nothing in this world, or any other possible world in the universe, is or can be static—without the cultural artifact of drama, there can be no civilization. The least dramatic place on earth was the Garden of Eden. Then Eve met the Serpent, and the rest is history. From Genesis, Chapter Three:

> 1 *Now the serpent was more subtil than any beast of the field which the LORD God had made. And he said unto the woman, Yea, hath God said, Ye shall not eat of every tree of the garden?*
> 2 *And the woman said unto the serpent, We may eat of the fruit of the trees of the garden:*
> 3 *But of the fruit of the tree which is in the midst of the garden, God hath said, Ye shall not eat of it, neither shall ye touch it, lest ye die.*
> 4 *And the serpent said unto the woman, Ye shall not surely die:*
> 5 *For God doth know that in the day ye eat thereof, then your eyes shall be opened, and ye shall be as gods, knowing good and evil.*
> 6 *And when the woman saw that the tree was good for food, and that it was pleasant to the eyes, and a tree to be desired to make one wise, she took of the fruit thereof, and did eat, and gave also unto her husband with her; and he did eat.*

In other words, to Eve's question "Why?" the Serpent responded, in classic Frankfurt School/Critical Theory fashion: "Why not?" All our troubles stem from this crucial moment, this crucial choice, this key "plot point," when the protagonist (in this instance, Eve) must make a choice—but, crucially, at this point in the story, without enough information and backstory (Who is this Serpent? How does he speak like a human being?) to make an informed choice. So she takes a bite. Why not? *Ye shall be as gods, knowing good and evil.*

This is, to put it bluntly, one hell of a claim, delivered right at the beginning of our recorded history. Satan is promising Eve, the ur-Mother, that she can transcend her human perfection (sinless, immortal) and become godlike by knowing both good and evil. One might observe that Satan ought to know, since evil comes into the world through his rebellion. And yet, paradoxically, it is her transgression—her Original Sin in reaching for the Godhead—that makes her, and us, fully human. Would we want it any other way?

As Milton reminds us in the *Areopagitica*:

> *Good and evil we know in the field of this world grow up together almost inseparably; and the knowledge of good is so involved and interwoven with the knowledge of evil, and in so many cunning resemblances hardly to be discerned, that those confused seeds which were imposed upon Psyche as an incessant labour to cull out, and sort asunder, were not more intermixed. It was from out the rind of one apple tasted that the knowledge of good and evil, as two twins cleaving together, leaped forth into the world. And perhaps this is that doom which Adam fell into of knowing good and evil, that is to say of knowing good by evil.*

What, after all, was wrong with the Garden? It was perfect. But its very perfection made it imperfect. Would you, as a human being, rather be human or angelic? Surely, the angels could not have been jealous of a subspecies such as *Homo sapiens* if humans were not potentially superior to the angels, precisely because of their free will, which endows them with the capacity to live a heroic narrative. (Is St. Michael a hero or merely the instrument of God's divine will? And, if so, does that make him less heroic than, say, Cincinnatus or Horatius?) Is worshipping God at the foot of his throne, as the angels do, the true destiny of humans? Or does Milton's Satan make a valid point when he says that it is better—*more human*—to reign in Hell than serve in Heaven? Is Satan's assertion not one of the most human statements ever penned?

(The compellingly heroic Satan of Arrigo Boito's opera *Mefistofele* could not have put it better.)

To the Devil his due; he won a kingdom; he has a purpose. He even appears heroic, with one crucial exception: He cannot die fighting. He has no real skin in the game. His war with God—which by definition he cannot win—is an illusion. Is it therefore a test? Of whom? God? Satan? Us?

The yearning for a prelapsarian state of grace is present in all cultures; the Fall of Man is one of our most potent stories. It is at once retroactively aspirational (a restoration of the status quo), religious (Jesus saves), and comfortingly childlike (was the Garden of Eden really filled with ever-ripe fruit trees?). Did we, via Eve and the apple, bring the Fall upon ourselves, or was it engineered by satanic forces; and, if so, why did God not stop it? The simple answer to the last question is: because then there would be no freedom, no drama. No *choice* (to use a current leftist buzzword).

Thus, this primal drama becomes the hallmark of civilizational self-awareness. Recall that it is only after eating the fruit of the Tree of Knowledge that Adam and Eve realize they are naked and thus sexual beings. And self-awareness is far more essential to human advancement than are the creature comforts of science. We consider the civilization of the ancient Greeks great—indeed, foundational—because of Homer, Plato, Euripides, and Aristotle, not because of their modes of transport or their health-care system.

And not, one should note, because of their political system either, from which the Western democracies draw much of their inspiration. The Greek political system was an outgrowth of Greek culture, with its sophisticated sense of self, not the other way around. Societies cannot create a political system from the top down (as opposed to one that grows organically) any more than they can create a truly living language from the top down, as shown with Esperanto and Volapük, languages that linguists constructed but that failed to take hold. Languages are plastic and evolutionary, but they are never random. Neither are the cultures to which they give rise.

This is not a trivial issue. As bilingual speakers know, one thinks slightly differently, depending on the language one is using, not simply in matters of vocabulary, but in sentence structure, even conceptualization of both concrete and abstract ideas. "Evening" or "twilight," for instance, evokes one image in English (the fading of the light), while the German

"*Abendrot*" conjures up something richer, more colorful, even poignant; the English "gloaming" probably comes closest. Richard Strauss chose "Im Abendrot," based on the poem by Eichendorff, as one of his ineffable *Four Last Songs*, and a more affecting evocation of day turning to night has never been written.

The situation becomes even more complex when the two languages are not members of the same family of tongues. Obviously, it is possible to switch smoothly between, say, English and Chinese, but that does not mean it is easy, and much imagery will inevitably be lost in translation. No matter how much or how often the egalitarian Left tries to argue in favor of its one-size-fits-all ideology, empirical evidence and experience tell us that this is simply wishful thinking, advanced for a political purpose. Not all languages or cultures are the same; nor do they have the same value. But despite the plain evidence of your senses, the Left has ways of making you toe the line.

"Who is the Tolstoy of the Zulus? The Proust of the Papuans? I'd be glad to read him," ventured the Nobel Prize–winning author Saul Bellow in 1988, thus setting off a firestorm of feigned outrage among the bienpensant readers of the *New Yorker*—an early violation of the repressive strictures we have come to know as political correctness.

"The scandal is entirely journalistic in origin," Bellow later explained in a 1994 piece for the *New York Times*, defending himself. "Always foolishly trying to explain and edify all comers, I was speaking of the distinction between literate and preliterate societies. For I was once an anthropology student, you see.... My critics, many of whom could not locate Papua New Guinea on the map, want to convict me of contempt for multiculturalism and defamation of the third world. I am an elderly white male—a Jew, to boot. Ideal for their purposes."

Bellow concluded with this remarkably prescient passage:

Righteousness and rage threaten the independence of our souls. Rage is now brilliantly prestigious. Rage is distinguished, it is a patrician passion. The rage of rappers and rioters takes as its premise the majority's admission of guilt for past and present injustices, and counts on the admiration of the repressed for the emotional power of the uninhibited and "justly" angry. Rage can also be manipulative; it can be an instrument of censorship and despotism. As a one-time anthropologist, I know a taboo when

I see one. Open discussion of many major public questions has for some time now been taboo. We can't open our mouths without being denounced as racists, misogynists, supremacists, imperialists, or fascists. As for the media, they stand ready to trash anyone so designated.

In other words, celebration of diversity stops where any possible cultural superiority or inferiority might begin. But, to use leftist cant, isn't diversity our strength? And if so, where did that diversity begin?

Seen in this light, the incident in the Garden takes on a new meaning: Eve is not the cause of the Fall of Man, but its enabler. The Serpent's Temptation of Eve is not only the first great satanic crime—although, to be sure, Adam and Eve had free will before the First Mother encountered the Snake—it is also the liberating act, the *felix culpa*, or happy fault that freed Man to fulfill his destiny as something other than God's humble, obedient servant. As St. Augustine wrote in the *Enchiridion*, "For God judged it better to bring good out of evil than not to permit any evil to exist."

Paradise may have been lost, but what was gained may have been something far more valuable, something, when you stop to think about it, that more closely comports with God's stated plan for humanity: creatures endowed with free will and thus potentially superior to the angels. Eve's first bite of the apple is not, then, simply Original Sin—it is the inciting incident of mankind's own drama. Something was lost, to be sure, but something was gained as well, implanted in our breasts from the beginning: a sense of where we are going. Evil, sin, change, flux, drama, and death itself are the means to get there.

As poets and authors have known since the time of the ancient Greeks, a world without conflict cannot exist. And, by our lights, accustomed to this world, if it did, it would be a very dull place indeed. For here, outside the Garden, without God available for direct consultation, it is only in the clash of conflicting ideas that truth—furtively, hesitantly—emerges, however unwelcome that truth might ultimately be. Oedipus's search for his father's killer first drives him into the arms of his mother and later, when the truth is revealed, to his own self-blinding and exile.

So the modern American tendency to regard peace as man's natural state and war as its aberration has it exactly backward. We intuit this about man's nature, and history validates this insight recurrently and bloodily. To be human is to be Fallen. But to be satanic—that is to say, to accept uncritically the legitimacy of Critical Theory's anti-human argument—is to have no chance at redemption at all. For how can nihilism be redemptive?

A world at peace, absent the arrival of the Second Coming, would surely be a very dull and unproductive place, perhaps possible only through a universal tyranny. While no one wishes war, sometimes war must come; war is an inevitability, and peace is the outcome of its successful, if temporary, sorting-out. Hobbes was right, although he failed to allow for man's nature, divine as well as human. Though red in tooth and claw, nature occasionally calls for, and sometimes obtains, a temporary state of balance, out of which the world promptly spins and begins the cycle again. This is not pessimism, this is realism. Free, we differ, argue, fight, and sometimes kill. Enforced peace ends in slavery and the grave—as one of the world's major religions promises and, in its *Dar al-Islam* (house of Islam), tries to practice. Trying, testing, questioning, pushing: These are man's true natural attributes, and trouble, his natural state.

A world without conflict, or post-conflict, however, is exactly what various all-encompassing political systems have promised. But the path to this utopia has been paved with much misery and death. In our time, the main retailer of such a myth has been socialism, in two forms: German National Socialism and Soviet Marxism—especially the latter.

The two prime movers of the Frankfurt School, Antonio Gramsci and Georg Lukács, sought to overturn the existing order—first the moral order and then the political order—like the the nineteenth-century radicals that they were. (Except for their outsized influence, there is nothing "modern" about either thinker.) More akin to anarchists such as Proudhon, Bakunin, Kropotkin, and Luigi Lucheni (who assassinated the Empress Elisabeth of Austria in 1898), Gramsci and Lukács had no interest in any compromise that could be the result of the Hegelian formula of thesis, antithesis, and synthesis. For them, there were only winners and losers—and in this, we must grudgingly admit they were right. To compromise is to negate the validity of one's own position and succumb to the temptation to see reason at work, when the true radical knows that reason is only a tool, put to base uses. In the *ur-Kampf*, both sides seek a lost Paradise, and it is clear from both cultural and religious tradition whose side each is on. The forces of good seek a kind of Edenic restoration, with man this time taking his place alongside and above the angels at the throne of God, while the vengeful revolutionaries dream of a new, better Paradise that they themselves control, one from which God is entirely absent.

Which raises this important question: Just *whose* Paradise has been lost? The conventional interpretation of our Genesis-based foundational myth is that it is *our* paradise, the Garden of Eden, that has been lost. But man's heroic post-lapsarian quest is not to return to Eden, but to get to Heaven—something that is explicitly denied forever to Satan and his minions. They made their choice when they allied themselves with the seductive and beautiful angel Lucifer, and now they (save only Abdiel, the angel who was tempted by the satanic but in the end returned to God) must suffer eternally in the realm of the hideous, deformed Satan into whom the angel Lucifer has been transformed.

The Paradise that has been irrevocably lost is not ours but *Satan's*. No wonder those who advocate the satanic position fight for it so fiercely; it is not Eden they seek to restore but Heaven itself, albeit under new management. Bent on revenge, it is Satan who, in the form of the Serpent, tempts Eve to taste of the fruit of the Tree of Knowledge. (Satan, it should be noted, is extremely sexually attracted to the gorgeous Eve.) In Milton's poem, it is Satan whose journey we follow. For some divine reason, he has been given a sporting chance for revenge, and, by God, or somebody, he is going to take it.

The roots of the intractable political conflict that currently plagues Western societies lie almost entirely in our rejection of myth, legend, and religion as "unscientific" and in our embrace of barren "process" to deliver solutions to the world's ills. Whether it goes by the name of "global warming" or "climate change" or "social science," this worldview claims to be all-encompassing, eternal, and grounded in "settled science," which boasts remarkable successes in empirical, experimental endeavors. With these technological achievements as cover and camouflage, this ideology brooks no rivals to its monopoly of knowledge; it dogmatically excommunicates all competing truth claims. *Nulla salus extra scientiam*, it thunders. Outside science, there is no salvation.

Let us call this Lenin's Wax Dummy Effect. During the Cold War, critics in the West remarked that the Soviet Union and its doctrine of Marxism-Leninism resembled nothing so much as a new religion, complete with scripture (the writings of Marx and Engels), charismatic prophets (Lenin and Stalin) with the aura of demigods, a Church Militant (the Party), a mother church (the Kremlin), and a clerical caste (the Politburo and Soviet apologists in the West). The religion also had, tellingly, a funerary temple to the mummified corpse of the Founder lying in eternal state just outside the Kremlin's walls, where tourists and Soviet citizens alike would wait in the cold of a Russian winter to shuffle past the bier and gaze upon the embalmed body of the Leader, Teacher, Beacon, Helmsman, the Immortal Guide, V.I. Lenin (whose relics were gathered at the Lenin Institute and Lenin Museum immediately upon his death).

Having officially outlawed religion in the name of state atheism—or, rather, mandated the replacement of the Deity with the State—the Soviets nevertheless needed to create a faux Christianity, a grotesque and parodic wax dummy, in order to make a successful transition from the Church (the opiate of the masses) to dialectical materialism. In the Hegelian dialectic of thesis, antithesis, and synthesis, the thesis was the Church, the antithesis was Lenin's wax dummy, and the synthesis was to be the triumphant materialism of Marx. But if they truly believed in the principles of Marxism-Leninism (a modification of German Communism with Russian overtones), why did they need the wax dummy, the faux religion?

Deception. Full fraught with mischievous revenge, the ghost of Karl Marx, via his vicar on earth, Lenin, demanded that his deeply anti-human prescriptions for human happiness be obscured with the trappings of old Mother Russia's traditional culture. But this had things exactly backward: an attempt to create Marxism's foundational myth both ex nihilo and as a false-flag operation. That Soviet Communism collapsed in a smoldering heap less than seventy years after its founding should have come as no surprise to anyone—it had not a leg to stand on—but the fact that its demise surprised so many in the West tells us a lot about the weakened state of Western culture as well.

True, "deception" is a loaded word. It has a whiff of conspiracies, of lurkers behind the arras, of plots hatched in the dead of night in clandestine safe houses, of dead drops in pumpkin patches. The act of deception has two goals. The first is to confuse and mislead the enemy, while the second is to secretly communicate with one's own side, safely passing along information so as not to raise suspicion and bring unwelcome attention and consequences.

Deception, however, can work for good and ill. Many of our cultural narratives feature a hero in disguise: the undercover cop, bravely penetrating a criminal organization; the spy behind enemy lines; the codewriters and encryption experts, signaling to on-the-ground agents and triggering acts of sabotage. In Puccini's *Turandot*, the hero Calàf arrives in Peking as the Unknown Prince in order to tackle the life-or-death riddles posed by the ice-maiden Princess Turandot and thus win her hand. Turandot's recondite puzzles collide with Calaf's hidden identity: In the often-unremarked twist at the heart of the opera, Calàf must turn his own heart to ice and reject the love of his faithful slave girl, Liù, in order to warm the heart of Turandot and win both her love and her kingdom—the hero as a cold bastard.

For heroes can be morally compromised. Think of John le Carré's world-weary spies, evolving into the very monsters they fight. Think of the nonviolent worm finally turning at the conclusion of Sam Peckinpah's *Straw Dogs*, when the nerdy mathematician (Dustin Hoffman) at last goes on a homicidal rampage. Recall Shane, who reluctantly resumes his past role as a gunslinger to save the family he loves, only to ride off at the end into the gathering darkness, knowing he has broken his compact with himself. Not even the pitiful cries of the boy who has adopted him as a surrogate father—"Come back, Shane!"—can make him change his mind.

All these heroes embody what we might call the satanic in men, the flirtation with the dark side, by which so many of us are tempted. In itself, there is nothing wrong with this. The Fall freed man from the shackles of a deathless Paradise and allowed him to assist in his own salvation by facing up to evil, not by avoiding it. Eve unknowingly, innocently, confronted evil for the first time in human history—an evil that God has allowed to exist—and accepted its implicit invitation to begin the struggle anew, this time on the turf of human souls.

But perhaps the first real hero of the creation ur-Narrative is not Eve but the angel Abdiel, who faces down the rebellious Lucifer in Book Five of *Paradise Lost* and warns his angelic cohort of the doom that is fast approaching:

Unshaken, unseduced, unterrified
His Loyalty he kept, his Love, his Zeal...
And with retorted scorn his back he turn'd
On those proud Towers to swift destruction doom'd.

The "dreadless angel," as Milton calls Abdiel, is one of the most fascinating minor characters in the poem, and were it a television series, he would no doubt eventually have had his own spin-off. For it is Abdiel, a seraph in Lucifer's legion in Heaven, who first ponders Lucifer's revolution—brought on by God's announcement that he had begotten a Son—and then rejects it, returning to the divine fold, even though his former comrades reward his faithfulness with scorn and threats. He stands in for all thinking members of humanity, who must face, or flirt with, evil in order to know it, who must hear its siren song in order to resist it, and who must at least briefly contemplate or perhaps even embrace it before rejecting and destroying it. "Unshaken, unseduced, unterrified"—what better description of a true hero can there be?

As readers have often remarked, Milton's God—"Heaven's awful Monarch"—is a morally complex character, more akin to the stern God of the Israelites in the Old Testament than to the loving God in the New; "Messiah," his Son, is the Hero-to-Come. Love does not seem to be one of the prime attributes of Milton's God. Indeed, one way to interpret his actions during the Fall of Man—given his omnipotence and omnipresence—is that he foresaw and willed the fate of Adam and Eve, created (or allowed) the test he at least knew they *could* fail, and issued the demand for obedience with the absolute knowledge that they *would* fail through his poisoned gift of free will.

"The reason why the poem is so good is that it makes God so bad," writes the English literary critic William Empson in *Milton's God*. "[Milton] is struggling to make his God appear less wicked, as he tells us he will at the start, and does succeed in making him noticeably less wicked than the traditional Christian one, though, after all, owing to his loyalty to the sacred text and the penetration with which he makes its story real to us, his modern critics still feel, in a puzzled way, that there is something badly wrong about it all. That his searching goes on in *Paradise Lost*, I submit, is the chief source of its fascination and poignancy."

For Abdiel, there is no Paradise to be lost, since he eventually returns to the side of God. He had a choice, and he made it. But humanity's choice never ends. At multiple moments in our lives, we are forced to choose between good and evil—indeed, we are forced to define, or provisionally redefine, both terms, and then choose. But what are we to do with an example such as God? God frees Satan from his chains at the bottom of the Lake of Fire, God allows Satan's unholy issue, Sin and Death, to emerge, and then he gives Sin the key to the gates of Hell. God stands idly by as Satan flings himself toward Earth, bent on humanity's seduction and destruction. Does God therefore require evil for the working out of his plan? Small wonder that a third of God's angels, as the story begins, hate him already and are very willing to heed Lucifer's call to take up arms against him.

In Milton, God seems to deny his own complicity. Of the first couple's disobedience, God says in Book Three:

> *They, therefore, as to right belonged*
> *So were created, nor can justly accuse*
> *Their Maker, or their making, or their fate,*
> *As if Predestination overruled*
> *Their will, disposed by absolute decree*
> *Or high foreknowledge. They themselves decreed*
> *Their own revolt, not I. If I foreknew,*
> *Foreknowledge had no influence on their fault,*
> *Which had no less proved certain unforeknown.*

Easy for him to say, one might observe, since he's God—opening up the awful possibility that the buck stops nowhere.

I have spent some time on the first few books of Milton's great poem—books focused on Satan and his revenge plot—for several reasons. The first is the work's cultural influence. Hard as it may be to believe in our post-literate age, *Paradise Lost* was once a fixture of the American household, not only a work of art but also a volume of moral instruction to be kept alongside the Bible as clarification, explication, and inspiration. Many could quote from it by heart, as they could from scripture and the works of Shakespeare.

The second reason is to frame the moral argument for the political argument that is to come. I make no apologies for the explicitly Christian context of my analysis; as a Catholic, I would be foolish to try to tackle the subject from any other perspective. Nevertheless, I am not relying on the fine points of dogma or any particular set of teachings (other than right = good, wrong = bad). The moral principles from which I shall proceed are found across all cultural divides. Make no mistake: The crisis in which the United States of America currently finds itself enmeshed is a *moral* crisis, which has engendered a crisis of cultural confidence, which in turn has begotten a fiscal crisis that threatens—no, guarantees—the destruction of the nation should we fail to address it.

Third, I focus on Milton because the archetypal biblical characters limned first in Genesis and expanded upon by Milton—we call them "God," "Satan," "Adam," "Eve," and the "Son" (Jesus)—are fundamental to the ur-Narrative and have served as templates and models for countless subsequent characters in the literature and drama that followed. Call them what you will: the stern father, the rebellious son and the good son, the hapless but oddly empowered bystanders caught up in the primal conflict of the first family. What, after all, is Wagner's *Ring of the Nibelung* cycle but (as the late Dietrich Fischer-Dieskau famously described it) a "family tragedy" in which Wotan's greed and arrogance force him to beget a morally uncompromised son (Siegfried) to wash away both Wotan's sins and the entire ancien régime, redeeming humanity into the bargain.

This is, I hope, a helpful and even novel way of looking at politics. Left to the wonks, political discussions are almost entirely program-and-process, the realm of lawyers, MBAs, and the parasite journalist class that feeds on both of them. It's the reason that congressional bills and their attendant regulations now run to thousands of pages, as opposed to the terse, 4,543-word U.S. Constitution, whose meaning was plainly evident to an average literate citizen of the late eighteenth century. Contrast that with the inaptly named Patient Protection and Affordable Care Act, whose word count, with regulations, is nearly twelve million and counting, with new regulations being added along the way. When it comes to lawmaking, brevity may be the soul of wit, but complexity is the very essence of "trickeration."

Who is to say which makes for the best political analysis? Rather than getting down in the weeds with the increasingly specialized schools of government (whose mission effectively is to churn out more policy wonks), perhaps it is better to pull back and look at our political history for what it really is: a narrative, with a beginning, a middle, and an end that is yet to come. It may at times be a tale told by an idiot; as passions sweep away reason, bad laws are enacted and dire consequences ensue. At other times, it may be a story told by a master craftsman, with twists and turns and reversals and plot points that surprise, delight, enthrall, and appall.

Most of all, it is a story with heroes and villains. And this brings us back full circle, to the foundational myth of our polity—Satan's rebellion, which led to the Fall of Man, and to the Devil's Pleasure Palace erected to seduce and beguile humanity while the war against God, as ever, continues, and with no material help from the Deity apparently in sight.

CHAPTER TWO

THESIS

What is *The Godfather* about? Ask almost anyone and he or she will tell you it's the story of a Mafia don, Vito Corleone, and his three sons who are battling other Italian crime families for control of the rackets in post–WWII New York. But that is not what *The Godfather* is about. And therein lies the crucial distinction between plot and what screenwriters call story. Plot is the surface, story is the reality. Plot is the ordering of events: This happens and then that happens, and the next thing happens, and on to the end. Plot is what we tell each other when we describe what the movie or novel is about. Plot is what hangs on the narrative framework. Plot … doesn't matter.

What matters is *story*—the deeper, underlying significance of the events of the plot. This happens and then, *because of* that, something else happens; and *because of* that, the next thing happens: the force of destiny. Thus, *The Godfather* is about a man who loves his family so much and tries so hard to protect it that he ultimately destroys it.

There are many plots, but few stories. Earlier I touched on what Joseph Campbell described as "the hero's journey," but here I should note that that journey need be neither successfully completed nor happily ended. Don Corleone's all-American tale is the rise of a monster whose true face remains hidden until his very last moments, when he stuffs a piece of an orange (a symbol of imminent death) in his mouth and grimaces at his grandson, terrifying the boy with the sudden revelation of his grandfather's true nature.

Still, we might tell the same story—about a man who loves his family so much that he destroys it—in many different ways and in many different times and places. In *The Searchers*, Ethan Edwards, the character played by John Wayne, goes on a monomaniacal mission to rescue his niece who has been abducted by Comanches and turned into a squaw. He aims not to bring her home (most of her family was murdered by the Indians) but to kill her, though in the end he does not kill her but returns her to her remaining relatives. The movie's last image—the cabin door slowly swinging shut on Ethan, condemning him to a lifetime of bitter loneliness—was later borrowed by Coppola for the final scene of *The Godfather*. In this, the door to Michael's inner sanctum is closed against his wife, Kay—except that it is Michael who is being penned in to the life of crime to which his father has condemned him, and Kay who is being shut out. Stories about families are among our most primal, which is why they have such tremendous power.

Therefore, it's no accident that one of the chief targets of the Unholy Left is the family—just as the nascent family of Adam and Eve was Satan's target. The family, in its most basic biological sense, represents everything that those who would wish "fundamental change" (to use a famous, curdling phrase) on society must first loathe. It is the cornerstone of society, the guarantor of future generations (thus obeying nature's first principle of self-preservation via procreation), the building block of the state but superior to it, because the family is naturally ordained, whereas the state is not. Against the evidence of millennia, across all cultures, the Left hurls the argument that the family is nothing more than a "social construct" that we can reengineer if we choose.

Like Satan, the modern leftist state is jealous of the family's prerogatives, enraged by its power, and it seeks to replace this with its own authority; the satanic condition of "rage," in fact, is one of the Left's favorite words (e.g., in 1969, the "Days of Rage" in Chicago) as well as one of its chief attributes. The ongoing, expansive redefinition of what constitutes a "family" is part of the Left's assault. If any group of two or more people, no matter how distant their biological relation, or even if they are entirely unrelated, can be called a "family," then there is no such thing. But see how it has been accomplished: As lustful Satan ("involved in rising mist") comes to Milton's Eve in the body of a snake in order to appeal to her vanity and curiosity while at the same time calming her fears at his sudden apparition in the Garden, so does "change" cloak itself in euphemism, disguising its real intentions, appealing to the transgressive impulse in nearly everyone, and promising a better tomorrow if only we compromise on this one tiny little stricture.

Soviet Communism (along with its evil twin, National Socialism, as pure an expression of the satanic in man as one can imagine) understood this well: Destroy the family, seize the children, and give the insupportable notion of a Marxist post-Eden replacement paradise a purchase on power for at least one more generation. American youth who grew up in the 1950s, as I did, heard numerous horror stories of Russian children who informed on their own parents, mini-vipers in the bosom of the families that sheltered them. Probably the most famous was the thirteen-year-old Pavlik Morozov, an instantly mythologized Soviet Young Pioneer who informed on his father to the secret police and was in turn murdered by "reactionary" members of his own family, who were later rounded up and shot. Whether the story is actually true—and post-Soviet scholarship suggests that it was largely fabricated—the Soviet myth required just such an object lesson and just such a martyr to the Communist cause.

The crucial importance of narrative to the leftist project cannot be overstated. Storytelling—or a form of it in which old themes are mined and twisted—sits at the center of everything the Left does. Leftists are fueled by a belief that in the modern world, it does not so much matter what the facts are, as long as the story is well told. Living in a malevolent, upside-down fantasy world, they would rather heed their hearts than their minds, their impulses than their senses; the gulf between empirical reality and their ideology-infused daydreams regularly shocks and surprises them, even as it discomforts or kills millions who suffer the consequences of their delusions.

And what, precisely, is the point of their twisted narrative? Simply this: It, like scripture, contains all the themes and clichés deemed necessary to sell a governing philosophy that no one in his right mind would actually vote for absent deception and illusion. No matter how evil, the leftist story must seem to have a positive outcome; it must appeal to the better angels of our nature; it must promise a greater good, a higher morality, a new and improved tomorrow. In short, it must do what Milton's Tempter ("with show of zeal and love / To man, and indignation at his wrong") does in the Garden: lie. Thus spake Lucifer to Eve, in the same words that come out of the culturally Marxist mouth of every cajoling leftist. We might well refer to this passage in Book Nine of *Paradise Lost* as the Left's very own foundational myth:

> *Queen of this Universe! do not believe*
> *Those rigid threats of Death. Ye shall not die.*
> . . . .
> *... will God incense his ire*
> *For such a petty Trespass, and not praise*
> *Rather your dauntless virtue, whom the pain*
> *Of Death denounced, whatever thing Death be...*
> *Why then was this forbid? Why but to awe,*
> *Why but to keep ye low and ignorant...*
> . . . .
> *... ye shall be as Gods,*
> *Knowing both Good and Evil as they know.*

This speech by Satan is perhaps the most perfect embodiment of wheedling Leftism ever written, combining nearly all the tactics we still see in use today. The Tempter, in a nutshell, asks: Why not? Besides, what's the big deal? God is lying to you. He wants to keep you naked and ignorant. Look at me: I ate the apple, and now I, a mere serpent, can speak human language with wisdom and compassion. And you—just one small "transgression" against a stupid and arbitrary edict, and you, too, shall be as God is.

Eve bites. In that instant, true, Paradise is lost to humanity (Adam's loving acquiescence is at this point a fait accompli); but also in that instant, Eve becomes not godlike but fully human. The Fall is the central paradox of human existence and the root of all mankind's misery and opportunity. How we react to it—or even if we react against the very notion of it and dismiss it as a fairy tale produced by a hegemonic culture—determines just about everything about us. Are we the independent heroes of our own stories, battling to make our way in the world? Or are we mere stick figures being pushed through a plot? Are we strong or are we weak? Destined for glory or already fallen and sure to be condemned? Is freedom a gift or an illusion?

For Milton—as it should be for us—the knowledge of good and evil is a fundamental aspect of our human nature. It is the basis of free will, and our (God-given) ability to freely choose between them. It can make us better or worse, lead us to salvation or damnation.

This is the argument for the *felix culpa*, the Fortunate Fall celebrated in the Catholic Easter proclamation: "O felix culpa ... O happy fault that won for us so great a Savior." The Fall, in this light, is the best thing that ever happened to humanity. Of course, people argue about this endlessly, and there are compelling arguments on both sides: Since God is the Author of all, did he therefore engineer the Fall? (Milton's God denies it.) If God created Lucifer, and the fallen Lucifer (Satan) then sired, directly or indirectly, both Sin and Death, is God therefore responsible for evil? Does God somehow require sin, as Calvin would have it? Can there ever be a true Hegelian-Marxist synthesis between Good and Evil, and if so, what would it be? As former president Herbert Hoover—to this day, one of the Unholy Left's most useful cartoon villains—wrote in a posthumously published memoir of the New Deal: "The world is in the grip of a death struggle between the philosophy of Christ and that of Hegel and Marx."

In stories of heroes, there is never a synthesis; indeed, there cannot be. The satanic Left understands this all too well, no matter what lip service they pay to "synthesis." The hero must not—and ultimately cannot—cooperate with the villain. Even if it appears that he does so, it is merely deception on his part, allowing him to wield the villain's weapon against him. (The hero very often does require sin—in some cases, he can win the day only at the cost of his soul.) Similarly, the antagonist (who, remember, is the hero of his own story) cannot compromise with the hero in any real sense. If he did, he would lose.

Which brings us back to the political argument at the heart of this book. We frequently hear terms such as "bipartisanship" and "compromise" in the halls of Congress, especially coming from the Unholy Left whenever it finds itself on the short end of an electoral decision. But, according to the dictates of narrative, such "compromise" cannot hold, except in the short term—and not even then, I would argue, since compromise, even in the smallest things, leads to synthesis, and there can be no synthesis between Good and Evil. As the crude metaphor goes, one part ice cream mixed with one part dog poop is dog poop, not ice cream.

The objection now will come that mine is a Manichaean view of the world: black and white, with no shade of gray between, much less fifty. Critics will label my notion—in a term much favored by adherents of the Left—"simplistic" and cry that it fails to allow for the subtleties and nuances of the human condition.

But so what? That is akin to observing that firearms are bad because they are designed to kill people—when no one would disagree that killing is precisely their object, which is, far more often than not, a force for good. There is no nuance in a handgun. It is either loaded or unloaded. Its safety, should it have one, is either on or off. It is either pointed at the target or it is not pointed at the target. The bullet is either fired or it is not.

A hero given to inaction while he studies the subtleties and nuances of a critical situation is not much of a hero. We remember Hamlet not for his heroism but for his inability to act. His most famous soliloquy is a paean to omphaloskepsis—navel-gazing. And yet, we can put even that—"to be or not to be"—within a Manichaean frame, because Hamlet's inability to come down on one side or the other until it is too late gets a lot of people killed.

Far from being admirable, Hamlet is an archetype of the contemptible fence-sitter, and he pops up again and again in popular storytelling. Take for example, the character of the mapmaker Corporal Upham in Steven Spielberg's *Saving Private Ryan*. Hastily assigned to Captain Miller's rescue operation after the carnage of the Normandy landing, Upham at first argues for the release of a captured German soldier ("Steamboat Willie"); later he fatally hesitates in a ruined stairwell while one of his comrades, Private Mellish, is overcome and stabbed through the heart with his own souvenir Hitler Youth dagger on the floor above. Near the end of the film, Steamboat Willie returns to kill Captain Miller in the final battle on the bridge and, after he surrenders, is shot in cold blood by Upham—freed at last of his nuances, Upham commits a war crime as a retributive act for his own earlier cowardice and foolishness. There is something to be said for recognizing good and evil after all.

And yet how often in real life we fail, including the statesmen among us. Neville Chamberlain botched Munich when he failed to take the measure of Hitler. George W. Bush failed with Vladimir Putin ("I looked the man in the eye. ... I was able to get a sense of his soul"). Collectively, the West is confounded by Islam because it fails to credit the plain words of Islamist animus against the West; how much interpretation, after all, does the slogan "Death to America" actually require?

We know this thanks to our ur-Narrative, our primal story, the divine spark hidden deep within us that gives our lives meaning. Critical Theory seeks to undermine this self-knowledge at its root by insisting that everything is a "construct," a plot by the "privileged."

Once again, phylogeny recapitulates ontogeny instead of the reverse: The primal, universal, species-wide story (phylogeny) is buried deep within each individual organism (ontogeny), within the heart, soul, and psyche of every human being. Story is not a reflection of the world but its engine and essence. Story alone will not achieve the final triumph of Good over Evil, but it propels the way.

CHAPTER THREE

ANTITHESIS

"For Germany, the *criticism of religion* has essentially been completed, and the criticism of religion is the prerequisite of all criticism," wrote Marx in *A Contribution to the Critique of Hegel's Philosophy of Right*, published in 1844. "*Religious* suffering is at one and the same time the *expression* of real suffering and a *protest* against real suffering. Religion is the sigh of the oppressed creature, the heart of a heartless world, just as it is the spirit of a spiritless situation. It is the *opium* of the people.

"The abolition of religion as the *illusory* happiness of the people is the demand for their *real* happiness. To call upon them to give up their illusions about their condition is to call upon them to *give up a condition that requires illusions*. The criticism of religion is, therefore, *in embryo, the criticism of that vale of tears* of which religion is the *halo*." (Emphases are Marx's.)

These are the demented ravings of a dangerous idiot, given a claim to legitimacy by the facile turns of phrase, the insistence on having it both ways (for the Unholy Left, something can be itself and its exact opposite at the same time), and the rage against reality, in this case the "vale of tears."

Goethe's Mephistopheles—a literary adumbration of Marx if ever there was one—could not have said it better, for it takes a Father of Lies to convince others to rebel against the evidence of their hearts and their senses, not to mention their own self-interest. If we simply analyze the words of Marx's famous statement about the opium of the masses, what do we get? References to "protest," of course—that would become a staple of leftist agitation for more than a century afterward—as well as "illusion." This recalls the scene in *Faust*, Part One, outside the venerable Auerbachs Keller in Leipzig, in which Mephisto frees a group of students from a spell with these words: "*Irrtum, laß los der Augen Band! Und merkt euch, wie der Teufel spaße.*" ("O Error, let loose their eyes' bond! / And heed how the Devil jokes.")

Lying is the centerpiece of both the satanic and the leftist projects. Since few people would willingly consign themselves to Hell, the rebels (for so they always reflexively think of themselves) must mask their true intentions. Reviewing François Furet's 2014 book, *Lies, Passions, and Illusions,* Brian Anderson, editor of the Manhattan Institute's *City Journal,* wrote in *National Review*:

> *Communism's power to seduce, Furet begins, was partly based on the mendacity of Marxist regimes and their followers. "Communism was certainly the object of a systematic lie," he writes, "as testified to, for example, by the trips organized for naïve tourists and, more generally, by the extreme attention the Soviet regime and the Communist parties paid to propaganda and brainwashing." Yet these lies were exposed quickly and often, almost from October 1917 on. They wouldn't have remained so effective for so long without the emotional pull of the grand illusions that they served: that the Bolsheviks were the carriers of history's true meaning, and that Communism in power would bring about true human emancipation.... Describing Communism as a secular religion isn't an exaggeration.*

Faust's famous bargain with the Devil (made at Easter, let us recall), was not simply for perfect wisdom (he expresses his frustration with imperfect, earthly modes of study in the poem's famous opening), but also for a brief moment of perfect happiness, a moment to which he can say, "tarry a while, thou art so fair"—something he believes to be impossible. To Faust, this seems like a good bet:

FAUST
Were I to lay me down, becalmed, on a idler's bed,
It'd be over for me in a trice!

If you can fawningly lie to me,
Until I am pleased with myself,
If you can deceive me with gaiety,
Then that will be my last day!
This bet I offer you.

MEPHISTOPHELES
You're on!

FAUST
And you're on!
Were I to say to the moment:
"Abide with me! You are so beautiful!"
Then you may clap me in irons,
Then will I wish to go to perdition!

Faust, so very German, is also the perfect modern man: born in the nineteenth century, wreaking havoc in the twentieth, and still battling against both God and the Devil in the twenty-first, often while denying the existence of both. He is the essence of the daemonic, if not quite the satanic. After all, in Goethe's telling, Faust is ultimately saved, in part by Gretchen's sacrifice—saved, that is, by the Eternal Feminine, the sexual life force greater than the power of Hell, which pulls men ever onward and closer to the Godhead—and also by God's infinite grace, which can even overcome a bargain with the Devil, if man only strives hard enough.

What would the Unholy Left do without illusion? It is the cornerstone of their philosophical and governing philosophy, a desperate desire to look at basic facts and plain meanings and see otherwise, to see, in fact, the very opposite. From this standpoint, nothing is ever what it seems (unless it comports with quotidian leftist dogma), and everything is subject to challenge. At the same time, the Left's fondness for complexity over simplicity betrays its affection for obfuscation and misdirection. The reason the leftist program dares not show its true face in an American election is that it would be overwhelmingly rejected (even today, after a century of constant proselytism from its redoubts in academia and the media). But in an age when credentialism is disguised as supreme, practically Faustian knowledge, and when minutiae are elevated to the status of timeless universal principles (even as the existence of such principles is otherwise denied), Leftism masquerades as sophistication and expertise. But the mask conceals only intellectual juvenile delinquency gussied up in Hegelian drag. The coat might be too small and the shoes too big, but if you don't look too closely and really wish to believe—as in Billy Wilder's *Some Like It Hot*—the illusion might pass for reality.

Which brings us back to Critical Theory and the Frankfurt School, the embodiment of the antithetical, whose adherents elevated this delinquent doublespeak into an art form, brought it to the U.S. via Switzerland after fleeing the Nazis, and—wittingly or unwittingly—injected into American intellectual society an angry, defeatist philosophy alien to the Anglo-American and Enlightenment traditions. The Frankfurt School thinkers were the cream of German philosophical society—which is to say the cream of the restive European intellectual society of the period—who had made international reputations for themselves at the University of Frankfurt and then received a warm welcome into the American Ivy League.

The work of the Frankfurt scholars—among them, Theodor Adorno, Walter Benjamin, Erich Fromm, Max Horkheimer, Herbert Marcuse, and Wilhelm Reich—was grounded in an ideology that demanded (as Marx would say), for philosophical reasons, an unremitting assault on Western values and institutions, including Christianity, the family, conventional sexual morality, nationalistic patriotism, and adherence in general to any institution or set of beliefs that blocked the path of revolution. Literally nothing was sacred. Some representative samples:

Herbert Marcuse:
*Freedom of enterprise was from the beginning not altogether a blessing. As the liberty to work or to starve, it spelled toil, insecurity, and fear for the vast majority of the population. If the individual were no longer compelled to prove himself on the market, as a free economic subject, the disappearance of this freedom would be one of the greatest achievements of civilization (*The One-Dimensional Man, *1964).*

Max Horkheimer:
Although most people never overcome the habit of berating the world for their difficulties, those who are too weak to make a stand against reality

have no choice but to obliterate themselves by identifying with it. They are never rationally reconciled to civilization. Instead, they bow to it, secretly accepting the identity of reason and domination, of civilization and the ideal, however much they may shrug their shoulders. Well-informed cynicism is only another mode of conformity (Eclipse of Reason, *1947).*

Theodor Adorno:
A German is someone who cannot tell a lie without believing it himself (Minima Moralia, *1951).*

Who were these people? Marxists all, first and foremost, sent fleeing from their think-tank roost at the *Institut für Sozialforschung* (Institute for Social Research) at the Goethe University in Frankfurt (where else?). The Third Reich hounded them out in part because they were Jews and in part because they were Communists. Ambivalent regarding the achievements of the Enlightenment—in other words, the society that had given them birth, nurture, shelter, and prestige—they rejected the notion of the individual as all-important, preferring to see history as Marx did, as a dialectical battle of opposing historical forces from which a non-teleological perfection would somehow eventually emerge. Adorno and Horkheimer liked to imagine their works as "a kind of message in a bottle" to the future. Unfortunately for posterity, several of those bottles washed up on the eastern bank of the Hudson River near Columbia University in New York City, changing the course of American history.

Among the Frankfurt School's members was the half-Russian Richard Sorge, who became a spy for the Soviet Union. While he contributed little in the way of cultural theory to Communism, his work as a traitor and double agent is worth remarking upon. After serving in World War I, Sorge—the name means "worry" in German—became a Communist in 1919, but he joined the Nazi Party in 1933 to burnish his German bona fides. Under journalistic cover, he was the first to report to Stalin that Hitler was planning Operation Barbarossa, the invasion of the Soviet Union in June 1940, a report that Stalin disbelieved. While undercover in Japan as a reporter, Sorge informed the Soviets that the Japanese would not open up an eastern front with the Soviet Union, thus allowing Stalin to transfer military assets to the east to combat Hitler. Sorge was discovered by the Japanese in late 1941 and hanged three years later. In honor of his service to the Motherland, he was declared a Hero of the Soviet Union in 1964.

The Frankfurt School included both Marxists and Freudians in its ranks, which was crucial to its later success in the United States (and a more toxic combination of nineteenth-century voodoo can hardly be imagined). As the website Marxists.org proudly puts it:

> *In 1931/32, a number of psychoanalysts from the Frankfurt Institute of Psychoanalysis and others who were acquainted with members of the* Institut [für Sozialforschung] *began to work systematically with the* Institut.... *In joining what was predominantly a "Hegelian-materialist" current of Marxists, these psychologists gave the development of Marxist theory an entirely new direction, which has left its imprint on social theory ever since.... The intellectuals who founded the Frankfurt* Institut *deliberatively cut out a space for the development of Marxist theory, inside the "academy" and independently of all kinds of political party [sic]. The result was a process in which Marxism* merged *with bourgeois ideology. A parallel process took place in post–World War Two France, also involving a merging with Freudian ideas. One of the results was undoubtedly an enrichment of bourgeois ideology.*

Thanks a lot. To this day, we can chart the *Institut's* baleful effects through the prisms of artistic narrative (including literature, poetry, music, and opera) and the Hegelian-Marxist dialectic, minus the illusory synthesis.

It was the Berlin-born Marcuse—who taught at Columbia, Harvard, Brandeis, and the University of California, San Diego—whose political influence was, on balance, the greatest of them all, owing to his voguish popularity among college students in the 1960s (he was the flip side of Eric Hoffer, the "longshoreman philosopher," who had nearly as great an influence on young conservatives of the period). Marcuse came up with the particularly nasty concept of "repressive tolerance," a notion that has guided the Unholy Left since the publication of his essay by the same name in 1965 in *A Critique of Pure Tolerance*, by Marcuse, Robert Paul Wolff, and Barrington Moore Jr. It might be best described as "tolerance for me, but not for thee." But let Marcuse explain:

The realization of the objective of tolerance would call for intolerance toward prevailing policies, attitudes, opinions, and the extension of tolerance to policies, attitudes, and opinions which are outlawed or suppressed. … Surely, no government can be expected to foster its own subversion, but in a democracy such a right is vested in the people (i.e., in the majority of the people). This means that the ways should not be blocked on which a subversive majority could develop, and if they are blocked by organized repression and indoctrination, their reopening may require apparently undemocratic means. They would include the withdrawal of toleration of speech and assembly from groups and movements which promote aggressive policies, armament, chauvinism, discrimination on the grounds of race and religion, or which oppose the extension of public services, social security, medical care, etc. … Liberating tolerance, then, would mean intolerance against movements from the Right and toleration of movements from the Left.

This casuistry is deception in its purest form. In the half-century since Marcuse's essay, "tolerance" has taken on the status of a virtue—albeit a bogus one—a protective coloration for the Left when it is weak and something to be dispensed with once it is no longer required. It is another example of the Left's careful strategy of using the institutions of government as the means for its overthrow. Saul Alinsky precisely articulated this as Rule No. 4 in his famous *Rules for Radicals*: "Make the enemy live up to its own book of rules. You can kill them with this, for they can no more obey their own rules than the Christian church can live up to Christianity." By casting human frailty as hypocrisy, Alinsky and his fellow "community organizers" executed a nifty jujitsu against the larger culture, causing it to hesitate when it should have been forcefully defending itself. And the shot at Christianity (there is no one "Christian church") is a characteristic touch as well.

Today, we can see the damage of such cheap sophistry all around us—in our weakening social institutions, the rise of the leviathan state, and the decline of primary, secondary, and college education. But destruction was always the end, not just the means. As Marcuse noted in "Reflections on the French Revolution," a talk he gave in 1968 on the student protests in Paris: "One can indeed speak of a cultural revolution in the sense that the protest is directed toward the whole cultural establishment, including the morality of the existing society."

In the same year, in a lecture titled "On the New Left," he went into greater detail:

> *We are faced with a novelty in history, namely with the prospect of or with the need for radical change, revolution in and against a highly developed, technically advanced industrial society. This historical novelty demands a reexamination of one of our most cherished concepts.... First, the notion of the seizure of power. Here, the old model wouldn't do anymore. That, for example, in a country like the United States, under the leadership of a centralized and authoritarian party, large masses concentrate on Washington, occupy the Pentagon, and set up a new government. Seems to be a slightly too unrealistic and utopian picture. (Laughter.) We will see that what we have to envisage is a type of diffuse and dispersed disintegration of the system.*

Marcuse, by reason of both his longevity and residence in the U.S., spoke directly to the counterculture of the late '60s, and his words fell on fertile ground, sprouting like the dragon's teeth sewn by Cadmus to create a race of super warriors, the *Spartoi*. They still dwell among us.

Even more important, however, is the Frankfurt School's literary role as antagonist to what we might characterize as heroic Judeo-Christian Western culture—which was formed from Greco-Roman civilization, the conservative impulse of the Thomistic Middle Ages, the Renaissance and the Enlightenment (whose ultimate expression was the Constitution of the United States)—as well as Victorian and Edwardian high culture (perhaps the apogee of Western civilization). That civilization, in the classic literary fashion of the hero's subconsciously pursuing his own destruction, gave birth to the resentful philosophy of Marxism-Leninism, the destructive First World War, the various socialist revolutions (some, such as Russia's, successful and others, as in Bavaria's, unsuccessful), the Cold War, and the short interregnum of "the End of History" before the long-dormant Muslim assault on the West resumed in earnest on September 11, 2001. Obviously, this list of world-historical events is not exhaustive, no more so than a plot synopsis can stand in for, say, James Joyce's *Ulysses* or Thomas Mann's *Der Zauberberg* (*The Magic Mountain*).

It does, however, establish the framework for a discussion in which I seek to demonstrate that far from being a natural outgrowth of a strain of Western political philosophy that culminated in Marxism and, worse, in Marxism-Leninism, the cultural philosophy of the Frankfurt School was itself aberrational in that it was profoundly anti-religious as well as anti-human. While substituting its own rituals for religion and unleashing its murderous wrath on the notion of the individual, it masqueraded as a force both liberating and revolutionary, when in fact its genesis is as old as the Battle in Heaven.

Consider the death toll alone. Yes, the European wars of religion—including the Thirty Years War between 1618 and 1648 and Cromwell's invasion of Catholic Ireland in 1649—inflicted a horrible loss on the population, and we cannot underestimate the Great War's toll on the cultural confidence of European civilization. Moreover, with German connivance, WWI opened Russia to Communist revolutionaries. But the twentieth-century wars unleashed by Marxism-Leninism took wartime slaughter to a new, mechanistic level, both domestically—Stalin's forced starvation of Ukrainians, the Maoist revolution in China, the Stalinist purges, Pol Pot's Cambodia, the repressive society of North Korea, and the wholesale slaughter that followed the American collapse in Southeast Asia—and internationally, from World War II through Korea and Vietnam, Angola and Afghanistan. If Satan needs corpses, the Marxist-Leninists have been only too happy to provide them.

Further, the dissolution of the Soviet Union, brought about by its own internal contradictions (as the Marxists might say) opened up the U.S.S.R.'s southern flank to the forces of Islamic extremism, itself in part a reaction to the Soviets' ill-fated invasion of Afghanistan and poorly executed attempt to subvert Iran (after the fall of the Shah in 1979) via the Communist, pro-Soviet Tudeh Party. Osama bin Laden battled the Soviets in Afghanistan and wrongly concluded that he and his "holy warriors" had beaten the Red Army. In fact, the Soviet defeat in Afghanistan was more attributable to the Russians' loss of cultural self-confidence brought on by the decadent, self-discrediting Marxism-Leninism of the Brezhnev era than it was owing to the losses inflicted by a ragtag band of mujahideen armed with Stinger missiles. The army that had bulldozed Hitler from Stalingrad to Berlin had nothing to support it after the Soviets had hollowed out Russian society and morals with their imported philosophy. After that, of course, Bin Laden turned his sights upon the United States, seeing America as another "weak horse."

A wonderful illustration to *Faust* by Eugène Delacroix depicts Mephistopheles in winged flight over Wittenberg, one of several "*Lutherstädte*" (Luther towns) in Germany associated with the events of the Protestant Reformation. As a depiction of the sacred (the church spires) and the profane (the fallen angel, his wings still intact, flying impudently naked above the symbols of the Principal Enemy), it vividly expresses the ongoing battle between good and evil. It also unites many of the images—innate images, as I have argued, the embedded ur-Narrative we all share—about which we have been speaking, including the divine, the daemonic, and the satanic, the Battle in Heaven, the Fall of Man, and the Faustian bargain.

For Satan, as for Marx, religion was an impediment to the grand design of transforming humanity from a collection of free-willed, autonomous individuals into a mass of self-corralling slaves who mistake security for liberty and try to keep the cognitive dissonance to a minimum in order to function.

The Marxist view of religion has gone through an evolution, to the point where some of the Frankfurt School's defenders argue that cultural Marxism did, in fact, make a place for "religion" (or at least transcendence) in its weltanschauung. It "evolved," they say, past the official atheism of Marxism-Leninism as practiced by a backward society like the Union of Soviet Socialist Republics.

It is worth a moment to reflect on the use of this word. "Evolution" is most closely associated with Darwin, thus affording it a patina of "science" as far as the Marxists are concerned, but whenever the word is used by the Left, it takes on an added, quasi-teleological meaning: We are evolving toward something, a "higher state." Thus, Supreme Court justices are said to have "grown in office" or "evolved" as they make their way from right to left during the course of their lifetime tenures. And politicians are said to have "evolved" whenever they switch positions from something more conservative to something rather more liberal (as with gay marriage). As Rob Clements noted on the blog The Other Journal (which has the tagline "an intersection of theology and culture"):

> In its most prolific phase, from the 1930s to the 1950s, the [Frankfurt
> School] consisted mainly of dissident Marxists who believed that orthodox
> Marxist theory could not adequately explain the turbulent development

of capitalist societies in the twentieth century, particularly with regard to the rise of fascism as a working-class movement. This led many of these dissident Marxists to take up the task of re-appropriating Marxism in light of conditions that Karl Marx himself had never considered. The school has a clear genealogy, appropriating elements of Marxist materialism, Hegelian philosophy, German idealism, Gestalt psychology, and atheistic Jewish Messianism. This synthesized analysis gave expression to a trans-disciplinary, anticapitalist intellectual tradition with both immanent (material) and transcendent (metaphysical or spiritual) themes.

In a nutshell, here we see the problem with nontraditional theory and dogma: It must constantly change the terms of the debate to accommodate, however reluctantly, reality, as much as the Marxists would like to ignore it. T.H. Huxley (the quotation has been attributed to others) spoke of the "murder of a beautiful theory by a brutal gang of facts." Cultural Marxist theory is always getting used to such brutal facts and twisting its theory to fit them—thus, the necessity for "evolution" as part of its unholy eschatology.

Dubbing revision "evolution" also gives a patina of "science" to Marxist theory, something it desperately seeks, having largely abandoned its claims to economic "science" in the wake of a century of failure. Having co-opted, if not actually invented, the "social sciences" (the inherent oxymoron generally goes unremarked), cultural Marxism and Critical Theory seek to legitimize their attempted murder of beautiful facts with a gang of brutal theorems, each one more beguiling that the last, iron fists in velvet gloves, grimacing skulls beneath seductive skins.

Something that has "evolved" is better than something that has not. New and improved is better, fitter than the old and diminished. Whether this is true, at least in the sociopolitical realm, is very much open to debate. Rhetorically, the point is to establish the inevitable teleology of "progressivism," always moving "forward" into a bright and shining future and casting off the vestigial physical and moral attributes of the past.

Thus is born Critical Theory, the hallmark of the Frankfurt School's "progressive" (in reality, ultra-regressive) guerrilla assault on Western and American culture—Critical Theory, which essentially holds that there is no received tenet of civilization that should not either be questioned (the slogan "question authority" originated with the Frankfurt School) or attacked. Our cultural totems, shibboleths, and taboos are declared either completely arbitrary or the result of a long-ago "conspiracy," steadfastly maintained down through the ages—as degenerate modern feminism blames male "privilege" and other forms of imaginary oppression. If the feminists have an argument, it is with God, not men; but since few of them believe in God, it is upon men that they turn their harpy ire.

In its purest form, which is to say its most malevolent form, Critical Theory is the very essence of satanism: rebellion for the sake of rebellion against an established order that has obtained for eons, and with no greater promise for the future than destruction.

"Satanism" is a strong word, but for the purposes of our discussion, it is a vital one. With no artificial Hegelian synthesis at our disposal—as there was none for Milton or Goethe or any other storyteller of stature who has pierced the veil of darkness—we are left with a stark, elemental choice. If the myth of the Fall is correct—and either it is, or it is a mass hallucination that somehow, against all odds, has sprung up and endured—then there can be only good and evil, with no accommodation between them possible.

Further: God seeks no accommodation with Satan. There is no divine principle worth compromising, no request from the heavenly side of the conflict to meet Hades halfway on matters of faith and morals. No, all the requests for compromise and pleas for negotiation come exclusively from Satan. As Antonio says in Shakespeare's *Merchant of Venice*:

> *Mark you this, Bassanio,*
> *The devil can cite Scripture for his purpose.*
> *An evil soul producing holy witness*
> *Is like a villain with a smiling cheek.*
> *A goodly apple rotten at the heart.*
> *O, what a goodly outside falsehood hath!*

Goodly indeed. Throughout literature, the Devil is frequently portrayed as sincere, earnest, reassuring and cajoling, slow to reveal his terrifying face. Deception is his stock-in-trade, and human beings who give him the slightest benefit of the doubt end up unhappily, and worse. To doubt the accuracy of these portrayals—no matter whence they originate, whether from folk tradition or (as I argue) some deep, Jungian wellspring of primal memory and collective unconscious—is to doubt nearly the entire course of human history (although Critical Theory presumes to do just that). It is to believe that only in the past century and a half or so have we been able to penetrate religion's veil of illusion and see reality for what it is: nothing.

This is nihilism, which often poses as sophisticated "realism," and I argue that it is just another form of satanism. Denial of the eternal becomes a way of temporal life; and, by extension, Death is embraced as a way of Life. En passant, it is amusing to note that the practitioners of nihilism are often the same people who denounce "denialism" in other aspects of everyday life (various psychological conditions, "climate change," etc.), just as those who describe themselves as "pro-choice" with regard to abortion are anti-choice in just about every other facet of their political lives, including health care, school choice, and so forth.

In the movie *Independence Day*, the scientist played by Jeff Goldblum realizes shortly after alien ships appear over the world's great cities that their intentions are far from benign—that, in fact, the aliens are coordinating a massive attack using earthling technology. "They're using our own satellites against us," he explains, making a hasty sketch to illustrate his point. So does Satan—or the satanic forces, or the iron laws of history, or *la forza del Destino*, call it what you will—use our own best qualities and noblest intentions against us, pervert them to his own ends in order to accomplish his singular mission, which is the moral destruction of humanity.

Pascal's famous wager—What is the downside to betting on the existence of God?—comes into play here, and in its most basic form. Let us posit that there exists neither God nor Satan, Heaven nor Hell, that human oral, religious, and literary tradition is one long primitive misapprehension of reality, that we emerged accidentally, ex nihilo, and to eternal *nihil* shall we return. (Note the implied belief in eternity, no matter which side of the argument you take.) But why then would any self-respecting individual wish to cast his or her lot in with the dark side of the proposition? Is Nothing more attractive than Something? Is Nothing a goal devoutly to be sought, a prize fiercely and joyously to be won? Again, we turn to storytelling.

Aside from a brief flurry of nihilistic films from the late 1960s and early '70s, few are the movies that offer a hero who doesn't care if he lives or dies, and who doesn't fight death with all his power in order to win the particular battle we see him waging during the course of his story. (Even film noir heroes do that, though they usually lose.) One that comes to mind might (*might*) be an exception: *To Live and Die in L.A.*, written by former Secret Service agent Gerald Petievich and directed by William Friedkin. The movie's hero, Chance (William Petersen), plays fast and loose with life (we first meet him bungee-jumping off a high bridge), inadvertently leads his partner to his death at the hands of the counterfeiter Rick Masters (Willem Dafoe), and vows to get Masters by any means necessary—means that wind up getting a federal agent killed. Near the end of the film, in a shootout in a locker room, Chance is killed with a shotgun blast to the face, his life's work left unfulfilled.

Or maybe not unfulfilled after all: His mania to get Masters has been passed on to his new, straight-arrow partner, who kills the villain in a final, flaming confrontation and then takes Chance's informant mistress as his own. "You're working for me now," he coldly informs her. Temporary victory has been achieved, and the cycle goes on.

Progressives like to throw around the phrases "the arc of history" and "the wrong side of history." Martin Luther King Jr., quoting the abolitionist Theodore Parker, formulated it this way: "The arc of the moral universe is long, but it bends toward justice." But when you stop to think about this, it's simply a wishful assertion with no particular historical evidence to back it up. Such sloganeering emerges naturally from the Hegelian-Marxist conception of capital-H History. The only teleology they can allow has to do with abstract, ostensibly "moral" pronouncements of a chimerical, ever-receding horizon of perfect "justice." The moral universe must not and will not ever admit of amelioration in our lifetimes, or indeed any lifetimes, they insist. It is a Faustian quest, at once admirable and yet a fool's errand; no means will ever suffice to achieve the end.

What evidence is there that there is an arc of history and that it bends in any particular direction? One would think that the Unholy Left would be the last to assert such a grand pattern, given their disbelief in the Deity. Whence comes this "arc"? Who created it? Where did its moral impulse toward "justice" come from? What is "justice" anyway, and who decides? And if the word "justice" bears a bien-pensant modifier (as in "environmental justice"), the only "justice" is likely to be the "justice" of revenge. The word "justice," in the hands of the Left, has come to mean pretty much any policy goal they desire.

None of this matters, however, when the purpose of the assertion is not to offer an argument but to shut down the opposition via the timely employment of unimpeachable buzzwords and to advance a political agenda that has little or nothing to do with the terms deployed for its advancement. Indeed, martial metaphors, not moralistic catchphrases, are the key to understanding the modern Left and its "scientific" dogma of Critical Theory: Theirs is a Hobbesian war of all against all (*bellum omnum contra omnes),* of every man's hand against every other man's. As Orwell, who knew a thing or two about the intellectual fascism of the Left, wrote in *1984:* "War is peace, freedom is slavery, ignorance is strength." These three aphorisms are the official slogans of the Ministry of Truth in *1984,* and the truth is whatever the Ministry says it is. Truth is malleable and fungible, a function of day and date. The Devil will say what he has to say and will quote such scripture as he requires in order to achieve the sole objective remaining to him: the ruination of Man and his consignment to Hell.

CHAPTER FOUR

THE SLEEP OF PURE REASON PRODUCES MONSTERS

At the end of the eighteenth century, the Spanish artist Francisco Goya produced a suite of etchings called "Los Caprichos," the most famous of which was *El sueño de la razón produce monstruos.* The Age of Enlightenment was receding as Romanticism took hold, Kant had issued his *Critique of Pure Reason,* and the publication of Goethe's *Faust* was less than ten years away. By the third decade of the nineteenth century, the Romantic monsters had broken through the steel of the Enlightenment's rational faculties, unleashed first by Goethe in *The Sorrows of Young Werther* (1774), Weber in *Der Freischütz* (1821), Berlioz in the *Symphonie Fantastique* (1830), and, soon enough, in the music of Liszt and Wagner.

Goya expanded upon the etching's caption in some editions: "Fantasy abandoned by reason produces impossible monsters: United with her, she is the mother of the arts and the origin of their marvels." It is at once a statement and a warning: The Romantic spirit, in a kind of Newtonian equal-and-opposite reaction, would now impel men to probe the depths of their thoughts and hearts, to go deeper than even Enlightenment science (or the science of today, for that matter) had ever hoped to go. But what might be revealed was not guaranteed to be beautiful; in fact, it was almost certain to not be.

Romanticism gave birth to much great art, but it also gave birth to—as Peter Viereck argues in *Metapolitics: The Roots of the Nazi Mind* (1941)—Hitler, by way of Father Jahn, Johann Fichte, Hegel, and Wagner, from whose coinage Viereck derived his title. "How shall we classify Wagner's ideas and his psychological development?" asks Viereck. "On this score his biographers and critics of all schools are for once unanimous. His fiercest enemy, Nordau, calls him 'the last mushroom on the dung-hill of romanticism.' His ablest admirer, Thomas Mann, finds 'the concept of the romantic is still the best label for him.' " Viereck goes on: "Quite correctly, Wagner himself stresses his kinship to the German romantic school by his terminology, operatic themes, literary allusions, and basic postulates. He worships the first romantics, be it noted, for 'arousing the Volk spirit in the War of Liberation.' "

"The Volk spirit in the War of Liberation"—these words, slightly updated, apply today. Now, however, they are acted upon with the full force of a political party and the devotion of many millions of people who have bought into the notion of Critical Theory, especially as applied to the law—a new enormity called Critical Legal Theory.

Writing of the events in Ferguson, Missouri, which occasioned ready-made riots and protests across the nation in the fall of 2014, the scholar and military historian Victor Davis Hanson wrote:

> *Ferguson illustrated many of the problems of postmodern liberalism: the anti-empirical insistence that the facts of the shooting of Michael Brown did not matter much; critical legal theory, which ignored the time-honored role of a disinterested grand jury; the tolerance of illegality as some sort of acceptable protest against the system; and the liberal media's hyping a crisis on the understanding that the ramifications of the violence were safely distant from their own schools, neighborhoods, and restaurants.*

Critical Theory, applied to the law, is little more than mob rule and anarchy; like everything else it touches, it is the negation of what it purports to examine. No one any longer pretends it is anything else. "Sentence first, verdict afterwards" is no longer regarded as a perversion of the ideal of blind justice but, in fact, is understood as justice itself. Indeed, it is a "higher" form of justice that is meant to rectify a long litany of past wrongs: justice as payback, capital punishment that is not only deserved but welcomed by the victim.

This is the dark side of the Romantic impulse, the drive to right wrongs (whether perceived or real), to crush the hated foe and, if necessary (if possible?), die in the attempt. It is why Byron chose to perish, quixotically, fighting the Ottoman Turks in Greece. The last lines of his poem "January 22nd, Missolonghi," written on his thirty-sixth, and last, birthday, are instructive:

> *If thou regret'st thy Youth, why live?*
> *The land of honourable Death*
> *Is here:—up to the Field, and give*
> *Away thy breath!*
>
> *Seek out—less often sought than found—*
> *A Soldier's Grave, for thee the best;*
> *Then look around, and choose thy Ground,*
> *And take thy rest.*

This is how the Romantics saw themselves. The academics and theoreticians of the Frankfurt School may not have looked much like Lord Byron, but they *felt* like Lord Byron in their sense of mission. For them, the Western world—which had given them its complex, poetic, and scientific languages as their birthright—was the moral equivalent of the Ottoman Empire. It stood for everything they opposed. It was crushing, dogmatic, aggressive, arbitrary, unjust, and it had to be destroyed—to use a current favorite phrase of the Left—*by any means necessary*. There was no time for, and no point to, "morality." In order to right the monstrous wrongs of the West, its reason must be put to sleep. The monsters (from the id!) must be set free.

Only an unholy combination of artist and sadist could do that. As Viereck notes in *Metapolitics*: "Hitler's wound as a rejected artist never healed. ... The disciplined militarist and the arty bohemian co-existed in Hitler. The mix enhanced his sadistic brutality. The mix also enhanced the air of mystery needed for his charisma."

The Frankfurt School, some of them artists manqués themselves, certainly knew what monsters looked like. Back home in Germany, one of history's greatest monsters, Hitler, was slouching toward them, hell-bent on his own form of payback. Partially disguised by his own anti-capitalist obsessions, two strains of Socialist thought, national and international, were about to collide. In a prolonged discussion about Wagner's anti-Semitism in his introduction to the 2003 edition of his book, now retitled *Metapolitics: From Wagner and the German Romantics to Hitler*, Viereck observes: "To the end, Wagner retained some kind of socialist ideal-ism, and his was in part a left-wing, anti-banker anti-Semitism." (The anti-Semitism was obviously a deal-breaker for the Frankfurt School, and their antennae were up early.) "Already in the 1941 edition I quoted Hitler's statement that 'whoever wants to understand National Socialist Germany must know Wagner.' "

Stalin, too, was caught in Satan's bands of illusion when he forged the short-lived Nazi-Soviet pact; he couldn't believe that a man he admired, Hitler, would be capable of such treachery as Operation Barbarossa. "For the first days, Stalin refused to defend Russia against the invaders, believing it was somehow a British-plotted provocation to destroy his comradeship with Hitler, with whom he had divided Poland," writes Viereck. "Only recently Stalin had sent Hitler, via Ribbentrop, the reas-suring message that Stalin, too, was gradually purging the government of Jews. And through Molotov in Berlin, Stalin had promised Hitler to join the Rome-Berlin axis against the West, in return for territorial con-cessions in the Balkans." Hell hath no fury like a lover scorned, and the Russian revenge against their former allies—the exception to "no enemies to the left!"—was terrible.

Of course, to this day, the "premature anti-fascists" of the Left refuse to admit their ancestors' kinship with the National Socialists. They have a conveniently sliding definition of "socialism," which means whatever they say it means—as words did for Humpty Dumpty in *Through the Looking Glass*:

> "When I use a word," Humpty Dumpty said, in rather a scornful tone, "It means just what I choose it to mean—neither more nor less."
>
> "The question is," said Alice, "whether you can make words mean so many different things."
>
> "The question is," said Humpty Dumpty, "which is to be master—that is all."

One way to regard the Critical Theorists of the Frankfurt School—the correct way—is as Rousseau's Romantic bastards who inherited their sense of mission from the nineteenth century. They were essentially men of the fin-de-siècle, but at the same time they grew obsessed with the bogus "scientism" of the new age. Why were not the hearts and minds of men subject to the same "scientific" laws that governed the rest of the world? Had not Marx shown that the very "laws" of history must be scientific? Had not Freud proved that the human mind could be "cured" of mental illness, in the same way that bodily illnesses could be cured by the timely application of the proper medicine? Only remove man's antiquated moral code and the whole animal was yours.

Their followers took these wrongheaded principles and kept going. What, really, was the difference between men and monkeys? After all, did we not share the vast majority of our genes in common? Who could prove any scientific difference among the "races," a social construct? Further, what were, really, the differences between men and women? Who could say for certain, except for the naughty bits, that there were any? Against the evidence of their senses, they insisted on the egalitarian principle, embodied for Adorno in Schoenberg's method of composing with the twelve tones—a system that required all twelve notes of the chromatic scale to be sounded individually in a sequence called a "tone row" before any one of them could be repeated, thus affording all notes equal importance. For Critical Theorists, dodecaphonicism (also known as the "twelve-tone system") was the perfect metaphor for the egalitarian world they sought to create.

Except, of course, it wasn't; Shakespeare's Hamlet knew more about science than did Adorno, and a rational person can spot the flaw in Adorno's arguments at once. The greatest difference in the universe is not the distance from Earth to the farthest star, or between 96 percent (the common gene pool of chimps and humans) and 100 percent, but between 0.00000000000001 percent and zero percent. It is the difference between nothing and something, between an infinity of darkness and a single point of light. It is the difference between the Void and Genesis—and even a committed atheist has to believe that the universe started somewhere, or else admit that it is timeless. It is the difference between atheism and God.

So back we go to this word, "really," and to the concept of illusion. For reason can sleep just as soundly when it is overtaxed, exhausted, left staring at words or numbers on a page until the lines begin to wiggle and hallucinations set in. Faust was a creature of pure reason, and yet it was not enough; the Critical Theorists thought of themselves as creatures of reason, and yet they indulged themselves in a bacchanalia of cultural destruction. They beat both philosophy and the arts into the ground, stripped them bare of all meaning, twisted history to conform to the ravings of a nineteenth-century obsessive in the British Museum—a true child of his time, a man of no social use at all, a freeloader, a sponger and a parasite, a stranger in a strange land he could not and would not trouble himself to understand, except superficially. A man whose economic theories were so wide of the mark as to be laughable—yet Marx was, and continues to be, admired and emulated because he *sounds* serious.

For the Left, any "revolutionary" idea can be entertained because, after all, there are no consequences to entertaining it; it's like the fly inviting the spider into the parlor, with tea steeping in the pot. What's the worst that can happen? Raised in a country at the peak of its international wealth, power, and influence, leftists could not conceive of any diminution (even the "fundamental change" they demanded) that could possibly affect their own personal standard of living—or anything outside that (everything within the Standard of Living; nothing outside the Standard of Living). Nothing could disturb their long march through the institutions or affect their pensions derived from the fly-infested corpse of the social state they were, however unwittingly, savaging.

The question then arises, as we survey the results of leftist philosophical ascendancy since 1964, did they know what they were doing? No animals, besides humans, attack their own living quarters. None deliberately destroys his own nest or invites predators into his home. Granted, there is a human impulse toward suicide. (Does any other animal willingly kill itself?) People kill themselves over losses in finance, over love, in frustration or despair, after defeat in battle. But to deliberately set out upon a program that can only result in mass self-destruction—this is something relatively new. I do not refer to the mass suicide of the Jews at Masada in 74 A.D., as the Romans were about to breach the walls of their fortress; or the desperate members of Custer's Seventh Cavalry who, when surrounded and well aware of the unutterable fate they would face at the hands, clubs, and knives of the Indians, shot themselves rather than fall victim to the enraged warriors of the Sioux, Cheyenne, and Arapaho nations. These deaths were both understandable and noble—they were a last gesture of defiance in the face of an implacable and merciless enemy. Better to die by your own hand than like a dog at the hand of your mortal foe.

But when reason sleeps, monsters follow, even when reason doesn't know it has dozed off. In our darkest moments, the bats alight upon our shoulders, and the raven taps on the window while we muse over our lost loves. Poe, instinctively, had it right, introducing his narrator pondering, like Faust, "weak and weary / Over many a quaint and curious volume of forgotten lore." Compare his situation with Faust's, complaining of his ignorance, despite all his scholarship:

> *Da steh ich nun, ich armer Tor!*
> *Und bin so klug als wie zuvor…*
> *(Now here I stand, poor Fool I!*
> *Just as smart as before…)*

Weary Faust, searching for answers that only Heaven can provide, easily falls prey to Hell. Mephistopheles offers to free him from the jail cell of his private study and show him a world he never dreamed existed—the real Tree of Knowledge. That world promised love, sexual pleasure, and forbidden fruit, yet ended with the deaths of Gretchen, her brother, her mother, and her baby by Faust. In the same way, the modern world proposed by Critical Theory promised heaven but brought only hell to the millions of people who fell victim to both strains of totalitarian socialism—Nazism and Communism—and who continue to suffer under some form of it to this day.

Since the fall of the Soviet Union, a large Russian community has found a home in the United States, and almost to a man, and woman, they want no part of the socialists' vision for America, having just fled it. They have seen this movie already and know the outcome in a way that most Americans cannot grasp. They were mugged both by the beautiful theory *and* the brutal gang of facts, and they would rather deal with facts, thank you very much. Americans, hitherto a fact-based, empirical people, have in recent decades been exposed to the siren song of European theory, with its "scientific" calibrations, parsed nuances, and confident projections. That almost none of what these theoreticians say ever comes true is, for a time, beside the point. The elites of academia and government, accompanied by their trusty stenographers in the press, have spoken.

But an unrelenting record of failure eventually begins to tell. What at first seemed impressive—charts! graphs!—turns risible, then mockable. Finally, the people realize they are being had. They see that the entire revolving-door system of academe, government, and the media—bound together through myriad incestuous ties, along with their offshoots, such as the left-leaning think tanks and nonprofits that funnel hundreds of millions of dollars to "global warming" and other questionable causes—is one giant, taxpayer-funded racket designed to enrich the "clerisy" and impoverish the proletariat. The truth will out: The people are being governed by a criminal organization masquerading as a political party.

At root, and as with any criminal organization, the primary goal of the Frankfurt School, its acolytes, and its Critical Theory adherents—however camouflaged by the squid ink of altruism, ideology, and philosophical pretenses—was the attainment and retention of power in order to amass wealth. No one who lived or spent any time in the old Soviet Union could miss that salient fact about that country. The *nomenklatura* drove through the sparse traffic on the streets of Moscow in limousines, summered at their dachas, patronized state-run *beryozka* shops, where they used *valuta* (foreign currency) to purchase luxury Western goods unavailable in the regular stores where proles shopped. Everybody else stole caviar from the kitchens, hawked bootlegged cigarettes from the trunks of their cars, or simply sold themselves. Russia at the end of the Soviet period was a country of a wealthy few, all politically connected, and the subsisting masses. In the same way, the Democratic Party's base consists of, at one end of the spectrum, the well-connected and often obscenely wealthy rich, who profit from their personal and business relationships with government, and, at the other end, the very poor, who depend on that same government.

But then, in the eyes of the Left, a nation of free citizens, equal before the law and not necessarily equal in much of anything else save opportunity, does not much look like the America that "fundamental transformation" is intended to bring about. By their lights, they are patriots, just not "American" patriots. They are patriots of America of the Future. The country they hope to bring into being will be still be called "America," it just won't *be* America.

This is what happens in a country created by the Enlightenment when reason goes to sleep. The men of the Frankfurt School pretended they were bringing typically German ratiocination to bear on a host of challenges: destroying tonal music, in the case of Adorno and Schoenberg; destroying the family, in the case of Gramsci and Lukács; destroying conventional morality, in the case of Marcuse and Reich. But they were no more intellectual than Faust after his wager with Mephistopheles, although their particular bargain was with another devil. They had the illusion of reason, to be sure; yet in no other country on earth has this illusion done more damage than in Germany, the country that gave the world both Marx and Hitler. But that the country of deep philosophers, brilliant scientists, Romantic poets, and towering composers produced such monstrosity should not come as much of a surprise. The sadistic mix is in the blood. As Faust shows, the problem with accomplishment is not mastery; it is the devilish boredom that follows mastery.

Symbolically, Wagner destabilized conventional tonality with the now-famous "Tristan chord" in the opening phrase of his opera *Tristan und Isolde*. It announces, in the second bar, not only the emotional core of the work but the disintegration of European musical culture that would soon follow in the wake of the opera's debut in 1865. The four notes of the chord (F-B-D#-G#, a perfect fourth on top of a tritone) appear throughout musical history, from Machaut and Gesualdo to Mozart, Beethoven, and Chopin, although the chord's harmonic function differs widely. But the prelude to *Tristan* atomized harmonic expectations through the opening line's floating chromaticisms, setting the mood of sexual desire and sexual frustration that, to this day, disarms audiences during the great "*Liebesnacht*" love duet in the second act (coitus interruptus in music) only to be erotically released by death in the final "*Liebestod*," when the chord finally stabilizes into B major—in retrospect, not very far from where the opera began, but a world away.

But after such mastery, what? European composers after Wagner went in several directions, but all roads ultimately led back to the anarchy implicit in the *Tristan* chord, featuring its harmonically unstable tritone, the "devil's interval," in the bass. Debussy, trying to reject Wagner, fled straight into his arms, with *Pelléas et Mélisande*; Schoenberg, edging away from tonality as fast as he could, wrote *Verklärte Nacht*, helping himself not only to the Wagnerian idiom, but to one of the composer's favorite words and concepts, *Verklärung* (transfiguration). One of Richard Strauss's early tone poems, *Tod und Verklärung* (*Death and Transfiguration*), couldn't possibly be more Wagnerian if it tried.

Symphonically, Anton Bruckner took the huge Wagner orchestra and redirected it back toward the explicitly sacred, erecting gigantic "cathedrals in sound" with his symphonies, and dedicating his final, unfinished Ninth Symphony to God. There is probably no greater spiritually triumphant moment in symphonic music than the closing measures of Bruckner's Eighth Symphony, when the composer's mighty orchestra dispels the doubts and clouds of illusion in a giant, wheel-of-the-world brass fanfare that proclaims the work's essential thematic unity: St. Michael's victorious flaming sword, in music.

In the novel *Doctor Faustus*, Thomas Mann explicitly linked the twelve-tone system to the composer Leverkühn's daemonic inspiration, brought on by a syphilitic infection contracted from a prostitute. The great novelist sensed there was something unholy about the method's egalitarianism, that in seeming to be the product of pure reason, it was monstrous. Schoenberg had moved in a careful musical progression from Romanticism to atonality (no fixed central key, inevitable after *Tristan*), via *Pierrot Lunaire*, to outright dodecaphony, creating ever more "rational" music that became progressively uglier and unlovable. The system of ratiocination had come to outweigh the music's purpose; or, rather, the music's purpose had come to serve the system.

That Mann felt the need to address the issue is not surprising. A great Wagnerian musical streak runs throughout his work, from the short stories—whose number includes "Tristan" and "The Blood of the Wälsungs"—to the use of Wagnerian-style leitmotifs in *The Magic Mountain*.

The Magic Mountain, which takes place in a Swiss tuberculosis sanatorium, was conceived around the time of World War I and published in 1924. It is a novel of ideas, but also of disease. (*Doctor Faustus* is also about disease, this one venereal, the curse of the *Ewig-Weibliche,* or the Eternal Feminine.) Castorp, the novel's holy fool, comes to Davos intending to stay a magical seven weeks; instead, he stays an enchanted, crippling seven years. Among Leverkühn's compositions are *Apocalypse* and his magnum opus, *The Lamentations of Doctor Faustus*. On the cusp of performing it for the first time at the piano for a few selected friends, Leverkühn collapses into madness.

Mann's works, in short, embrace all the salient elements and events of Central European history from the Kaiser to the birth of postwar Germany; very little escaped his attention. The members of the Frankfurt School may have thought they were modernists, moving beyond the culture, but in fact they were little more than perfect Wagnerians, their reason clouded by Klingsor's bands of illusion. "*Kinder, schafft Neues!*" ("Children, make something new!") wrote Wagner in an 1852 letter to Franz Liszt (nineteen months older than he and not yet his father-in-law). That they could not do so speaks of the Faustian bargain they had made: Thanatos without Eros, death without life, a world without love, and nothing new to show for their labors in the caves of Nibelheim.

CHAPTER FIVE

THE DESCENT INTO HELL

In the Apostles' Creed, which dates from around 700 A.D., there is this astonishing passage: "Jesus Christ ... suffered under Pontius Pilate, was crucified, died, and was buried; *he descended into Hell.* On the third day he rose again from the dead; he ascended into Heaven."

> *"Jesum Christum ... passus sub Pontio Pilato, crucifixus, mortuus, es sepultus; descendit ad inferna; tertia die resurrexit a mortuis; ascendit ad coelos."*

What?

The phrase "descended into Hell" has become so controversial within Christianity that it is often now dropped from the prayer. It has been interpreted to mean that Christ did not literally descend into Hell on the Saturday after the Crucifixion, that is, into Satan's abode, but rather dwelled among the dead, those deprived of the Light, there to give witness to the Good News of the imminent Resurrection. Augustine taught that Christ actually went to Hell, but he expressed puzzlement over the implication of his belief; Aquinas wrote that Christ visited both Purgatory (the souls confined there would eventually be saved) and Hell itself, to shame unbelievers (which seems a bit of an un-Christ-like victory lap).

In more recent cultural history, we have a parallel in the most influential work of art of the nineteenth century: Wagner's *Der Ring des Nibelungen*, complete with the chief god's own descent into Hell, or in this case, Nibelheim, the realm of the dwarves. Wotan must journey there to steal the magic ring and the rest of the treasure that the evil dwarf, Alberich, has fashioned from the stolen gold of the Rhine. (This occurs in the tetralogy's prologue, *Das Rheingold*).

In the *Ring*—which employs Nordic saga as semi-Christian allegory; at the end of his life, Wagner embraced Christianity explicitly in *Parsifal* and apparently was bruiting an opera about Christ himself when he died in Venice in 1883—Wotan brings about his own God-crisis, first by his brazen theft of the Rhine Gold and then via his concupiscence. Like the priapic gods of Greek and Roman myth, he has gotten himself into trouble by heedlessly fathering the *Wälsung* twins, Siegmund and Sieglinde. When, in *Die Walküre,* the second opera of the cycle, Siegmund arrives one dark and stormy night at the home of Sieglinde and her brutish husband, Hunding, the siblings (who were separated at birth) instantly fall in love and into an incestuous relationship that produces the hero, Siegfried. And it is Siegfried, the innocent, who must expiate Wotan's original sin. Like Christ, he must restore the natural order, a project that is cut off by his death at the hands of the treacherous Hagen. It is thus left to the *Walküre*—the Valkyrie, Brünnhilde—and the three Rhine Maidens to fulfill Siegfried's mission, destroy Valhalla, and cleanse the world with the healing waters of the Rhine.

But Christ is a greater hero than Siegfried, and a greater God than Wotan; not only does he face the most horrible and agonizing of deaths, but he ventures into the lair of Death itself and (unlike Wotan) destroys it. Death's eradication might take a while—it might take from here to eternity—but it has been done, and one can only imagine the consternation of the demons as they watched the Principal Enemy enter their own kingdom and slay Death itself. "And he said unto them, I beheld Satan as lightning fall from heaven," says Jesus to the disciples in Luke 10:18–19. "Behold, I give unto you power to tread on serpents and scorpions, and over all the power of the enemy."

But the ur-Narrative goes beyond that; it also includes the figure of the Woman Clothed with the Sun, crushing the Serpent beneath her feet. It is not for Christ to defeat Satan; his job is to kill Satan's lot, Sin and

Death, and rescue humanity from the scourge unleashed even before the Fall. Instead, that task is given to a woman, *the* Woman: Mary, the Mother of Christ.

Interestingly, Blake's two famous paintings on this subject, both drawn from Revelation, show not the familiar figure of Mary crushing the serpent but the Great Red Dragon, Satan, attacking the pregnant Virgin just before she is to give birth to the Savior. This is Woman at her most vulnerable. In these two pictures ("The Great Red Dragon and the Woman Clothed in Sun" and "The Great Red Dragon and the Woman Clothed with the Sun"), the laboring Mary seems helpless in the face of the Beast's onslaught. Revelation 12:3–4 describes Satan: "And behold a great red dragon, having seven heads and ten horns, and seven crowns upon his heads. And his tail drew the third part of the stars of heaven, and did cast them to the earth."

Still, we know the outcome: that in the profoundly and essentially feminist Christian myth, it is Eve who falls, beguiled by the serpent's flattery (in *Paradise Lost,* Adam addresses Eve as "O fairest of Creation, last and best of all God's works"), but it is Mary who confronts the demon and, even in the midst of her confinement, vanquishes him.

Female empowerment is a theme that, despite what modern, anti-female "feminists" claim, long ago entered Western storytelling. At the end of *Fatal Attraction*, it is not the Michael Douglas character who finishes off Glenn Close's psycho stalker but his long-suffering wife, who shoots the monster as she tries to resurrect herself from a near drowning in the bathtub. Countless other stories—harkening back even to *Beowulf,* in which the truly formidable monster is not Grendel, but Grendel's irate mother—feature formidable females, thus giving the lie to one of Critical Theory's most persistent critiques of Western culture, that it demeans women or places them in secondary positions to men.

This brings us to the most pernicious of Critical Theory's unholy offspring, political correctness, a kind of Hell in itself, bringing to mind Satan's plaintive observation in *Paradise Lost*: "The mind is its own place, and in itself / Can make a Heav'n of Hell, a Hell of Heav'n." Political correctness turns our innermost thoughts hellish and bids fair to punish humanity for the crime of free thinking. What could be more satanic?

Let us recall that in Milton, Satan created his daughter, Sin, who sprang directly from him (grotesquely parodying the birth of Athena from the head of Zeus); then Satan begat his only son, Death, upon the half-woman/half-fish mermaid body of his daughter. But Sin is cursed to eternal childbirth labor (the opposite of sinless Mary's sole, transformative, virgin pregnancy), giving birth to an endless succession of canine-like creatures that hound humanity. Sin is thus almost a parody of contemporary "feminists," who fantasize about a world without men—who can complain more about men than Sin, constantly impregnated without recourse?—but fail to understand the practical consequences of just such a world.

Political correctness is not simply a pack of Hounds of Tindalos (although it is all of that) but the most brazen assault on Western culture that one can imagine: a ravenous, lupine force that can never be satisfied. In Frank Belknap Long's memorable addition to H.P. Lovecraft's Cthulhu mythos, the eponymous Hounds of Tindalos are clearly the offspring of Sin: " 'They are lean and athirst!' he shrieked. ... All the evil in the universe was concentrated in their lean, hungry bodies. Or had they bodies?" Best described as "foul," the terrifying, ichor-filled Hounds pursue their victims with unrelenting ferocity across dimensions, space and time. Such vividly described creatures recall Milton's poem and thus fall into the overall ur-Narrative scheme I have been describing: the recurrence (or emergence) of figures from the primal myths of human origins.

The term "political correctness" seems to have originated with Trotsky to describe the early Bolsheviks who were forced to adapt to constantly changing "correct" modes of Soviet political thought, and it was later picked up by Mao, among others. Today it is the Unholy Left's counter-narrative, a fascism of the mind meant to discourage independent thought and encourage lazy sloganeering; in other words, a political tool that has nothing to do with "morality," "tolerance," "diversity," or "the arc of history." It is simply evil. But to say it is a very great evil is to underestimate it. It goes against liberty in all her forms, which is precisely its object, although it cloaks itself in the folds of another bogus virtue, compassion.

"Without freedom of thought, there can be no such thing as wisdom; and no such thing as public liberty, without freedom of speech," wrote "Cato" (British essayists John Trenchard and Thomas Gordon) in 1720. "Whoever would overthrow the liberty of the nation, must begin by subduing the freedom of speech." There's a reason that revolutionaries target newspapers and radio stations first.

Subduing the freedom of speech is precisely the goal of the Jacobins of the Unholy Left, who cannot countenance any thought unmoored from policy prescriptions or social goals. Over the past few decades, they have waged a war, at first covert and now overt, on the First Amendment, trammeling it wherever they can: in campus "speech codes," for example, or in social ostracism should a hapless renegade wander off the reservation and accidentally speak his mind.

Political correctness, for all its notoriety, has not received the full scrutiny it deserves, in part because, like everything else the Marxists touch, it wears a *tarnhelm*, a magic helmet—in this case, of kindness, politesse, and sheer righteousness. Busily formulating new lists of what can and cannot be said (lest it offend somebody, somewhere, either now or at some future date), and always in light of the Critical Theory imperative to be perpetually on the attack, political correctness's commissars resemble no one more than Dickens's implacable Madame Defarge in *A Tale of Two Cities*, clicking her knitting needles as heads roll into baskets. Common words, common terms, even the names of venerable sports franchises come under fire as they march ever forward toward the sunny uplands of perfect totalitarian utopia.

All this has sprung from the ordure of Critical Theory, a miasmic gas that chokes the life out of free-ranging rational discourse. When in doubt, PC supplies its adherents with a ready supply of rubrics and bromides, most of which reinforce the central idea that there are some things that simply cannot be said or even thought.

Let us think of political correctness as Ugarte's famous "letters of transit" in *Casablanca*, which cannot be rescinded—or even questioned. The letters are the central McGuffin of the great film—the "buy-in," as people say in Hollywood, that the audience grants to the filmmakers in order to fully invest itself in the story. Without the letters, there is no story. Ugarte cannot give them to Rick Blaine for safekeeping; Ferrari can't try to buy them from Rick; Rick cannot provide them to Ilsa and Victor Laszlo to ensure their escape; nor can Ilsa and Victor escape at all. Everyone accepts them uncritically, even the Nazis, despite the fact that they are signed by General Weygand, a Vichy official, whose order could easily have been countermanded by Major Strasser, the German officer. (They are not signed by de Gaulle, as is sometimes misheard; Peter Lorre's Hungarian accent confuses things. And, in any case, that would make no sense at all.)

So, in political correctness, the Left has its "letters of transit," its trump card in the great game it endlessly wages against its enemies. But they are false, counterfeit; no one need pay any attention to them. But by simply declaring whole swatches of argumentation invalid, the Unholy Left seeks to erect a Devil's Pleasure Palace around itself, a world of illusion peopled with fake monsters and hallucinatory apparitions, an anti-fun-house of horrors whose only purpose, directly antithetical to the United States Constitution, is to stifle opposition and debate.

The thinkers most responsible for the rise of political correctness were Antonio Gramsci and Georg Lukács, who were among the first to grasp that while economic Marxism could not work, cultural Marxism could. If instead of seizing the means of the production to (someday) be turned over to the proletariat, they could instead occupy culture, wouldn't the revolution have a far better chance of succeeding? They had been let down by the grubby, unwashed workers of the world, who largely rejected the great gift they had been offered; now they would approach their equals in the intelligentsia, a far more receptive and persuadable audience. As any con man knows, the easiest mark is the one who wants to believe.

Gramsci therefore targeted mass media such as newspapers, magazines, radio, film (à la Hitler and Lenin), and education, in order to—as Brecht famously later suggested—dissolve the people and elect another. For Gramsci, the proletariat was blinded by its Faustian bands of illusion; what it needed was liberation from the Christian West, something the Left had long been itching for. Lukács, a Hungarian-Jewish aristocrat from a prominent banking family named Löwinger, went a step further, believing that the old order had to be eradicated before a new kind of citizen could sprout up.

Lukács dreamed of creating a void in the soul of humanity, in a world that supposedly had been abandoned by God, a collectivist world in which there would be no room for the individual—which is to say an ant farm that would admit of no heroic Siegfrieds or supermen. He wrote of the necessity of an *Aufhebung der Kultur*—an abolition of culture, specifically Judeo-Christian Western culture, although the word "*Aufhebung*" might be better translated in this instance as the "uprooting."

Writing in 1962, in the preface to his *Theory of the Novel*, and reflecting on his experience of World War I, Lukács underlined his anti-Western sentiments:

> *My own deeply personal attitude was one of vehement, global and, especially at the beginning, scarcely articulate rejection of the war and especially of enthusiasm for the war.... There was also some probability that the West would defeat Germany; if this led to the downfall of the Hohenzollerns and the Hapsburgs, I was once again in favour. But then the question arose: Who was to save us from Western civilisation?*

Who indeed? One unpleasant answer came quickly enough in the form of Hitler's National Socialist German Workers' Party, which emerged victorious from its pitched street battles with the other party of the Left, the Communists, and then quickly set about eliminating both Jews and Communists, whom it saw as essentially interchangeable. Hitler had little or no love for Western civilization, which he regarded as an anti-Aryan enterprise spearheaded, sequentially, by the Romans, the Church, and the Jews. He idealized the *Volk*, the German people uncorrupted by the world-manipulating International Jew, exemplified in his eyes by, among others, Lukács and the rest of the Frankfurt School. Still, Lukács lived long enough to have the last laugh. He rode out the war in his beloved Soviet Union and returned to Hungary to help form the postwar Communist government—which, to his death in 1971, he thought could compete with the West while maintaining its own socialist terms.

Today, in the wake of the fall of the Berlin Wall in 1989 and the dissolution of the U.S.S.R. in 1991, such fantasies seem absurd. To anyone who traveled extensively behind the Iron Curtain in the years before its collapse—the sight of the empty shops, the endless lines, the rigid conformity, the blaring loudspeakers summoning the populace to this or that Party occasion highlighted by a long-winded speech from a series of gray functionaries—the idea that anyone would willingly embrace such a soulless hell is laughable. Only those with no experience of Communism admire Communism. Seeking a victory for cultural Marxism in the Warsaw Pact countries, Lukács and his ilk signally failed; having experienced the dictatorship of the proletariat, the suddenly free peoples of what we used to call the "captive nations" opted for fresh bananas and porn, and were thrilled with the trade.

Why anyone would want to live in the world Lukács and his cohorts envisioned remains an open question. And yet, to an increasing extent, many do. I believe the attraction lies, in part at least, in its very impossibility. The generation that grew up in the United States and Western Europe after the dissolution of the Soviet Union has had a hard time imagining any adverse consequences that might arise from their seemingly noble, benevolent beliefs; they live "within the context of no context," to borrow the title of a 1980 *New Yorker* essay by George W.S. Trow. They are unaware of the consequences of fearing no consequences. In the world of Marxist fantasy, the blind man is king.

Nevertheless, many seem willing to trade liberty for some form of security; and in a bountiful society, there seems no end to the riches that can be squandered in the name of "compassion," "tolerance," or "diversity." It was said of Tammany Hall, the Democratic-gangster political machine that ran New York City for the better part of a century, that it was wise enough never to steal *all* the money flowing into the city's treasury. It left just enough for careful administration so the peasants would never realize they were being fleeced even as the sachems showed up at their weddings, funerals, and bar mitzvahs.

What saved the Frankfurt School was its transplantation under duress to America. The brutal efficiency of the Nazi regime opened their eyes to the consequences of what they had imagined would have no consequences. Had they proclaimed their destructive anti-American, anti-Western intentions openly—made those the most conspicuous feature of their teachings—they might rightly have been regarded as spies, sappers, and saboteurs, and hanged. But twinned with another Central European intellectual conceit, Freudian analysis (many of whose tenets synchronized happily with *Institut* theory), they appeared to be relatively harmless, nutty-professor refugees with funny foreign accents who were seeking shelter in America, pleading tolerance for lofty ideals. What went unnoticed was that the ideals for which they sought tolerance were themselves anything but tolerant. Indeed, they were fundamentally antithetical to the American ethos and experience. America would not have to descend into Hell; Hell had come to America—disguised, naturally, as Heaven, and now lying in wait for the unwary.

CHAPTER SIX

THE ETERNAL FEMININE

The assault on the citadels of Western culture had many fronts, but foremost among them was sex—the most powerful engine in human existence, the one that brings us closest to the Godhead, a force of such overwhelming power that it can change the courses of our lives, bringing death or transcendence in its wake. Children are its primary issue, but also transformative insight, bravery, courage, altruism, self-sacrifice; great works of art are born from the union, lives sacrificed and won, everything ventured, worlds gained.

So no wonder the relationship between the sexes and the hard-won morality attending such congress was one of the focal points of the attack by the Frankfurt School and their fellow travelers in politics, academe, and the media. The "transgressive" assault on Western culture had to start somewhere, and it started with the idea of the nuclear family.

The first step was to mock it (in the 1960s and '70s, the idealized "Father Knows Best" and "Leave It to Beaver" worlds of the pre-hippie era came in for particular scorn), then to accuse it of various crimes against humanity (particularly the newfound charge of "patriarchy"), then to illustrate that there were "really" other sorts of families, just as good, just as loving, just as valid as the traditional two-parent, opposite-sex nest. Finally, the nuclear family was simply dispensed with altogether, as behavior considered acceptable in the underclass, where sexual license had always just barely been suppressed, percolated into the higher culture. The morals of those with nothing to lose and everything to gain from a dysfunctional social-welfare system bubbled upward from the black and white underclasses into the middle classes, who had been induced to feel guilty on behalf of the "underprivileged." And those considered "marginal" or "disadvantaged" no longer bore any responsibility for their destructive personal choices and behavior. It is no accident that the new social acceptance of out-of-wedlock pregnancies coincided with the rise of both bastardy and the abortion culture, the growing demand for contraception, and, later on, gay rights. Once Pandora's Box was opened, all sort of things flew out, some of them at first seemingly contradictory, but all related by the very fact of their confinement in the box. The box had stayed closed for a reason, but under pressure from Critical Theory, it had to be opened.

Many have observed, the historian Arnold Toynbee prominently among them, that society begins to crumble when the morals of the underclass become mainstream. Toynbee noted that when self-expression begins to substitute for disciplined creativity, civilization has a problem. Critical Theory's obsessive compulsion with its genitals is not the sign of a mature culture but a childish one. Discussing the chapter "Schism in the Soul" from Toynbee's *Study of History*, Charles Murray wrote in the *Wall Street Journal*, in 2001:

> *He observes that one of the consistent symptoms of disintegration is that the elites—Toynbee's "dominant minority"—begin to imitate those at the bottom of society. His argument goes like this:*

> *The growth phase of a civilization is led by a creative minority with a strong, self-confident sense of style, virtue, and purpose. The uncreative majority follows along through mimesis, "a mechanical and superficial imitation of the great and inspired originals." In a disintegrating civilization, the creative minority has degenerated into elites that are no longer confident, no longer setting the example. Among other reactions are a "lapse into truancy" (a rejection, in effect, of the obligations of citizenship), and a "surrender to a sense of promiscuity" (vulgarizations of manners, the arts, and language) that "are apt to appear first in the ranks of the proletariat and to spread from there to the ranks of the dominant*

minority, which usually succumbs to the sickness of "proletarianization."
That sounds very much like what has been happening in the U.S. Truancy
and promiscuity, in Toynbee's sense, are not new in America. But until a
few decades ago they were publicly despised and largely confined to the bot-
tom layer of Toynbee's proletariat—the group we used to call "low-class" or
"trash," and which we now call the underclass. Today, those behaviors have
been transmuted into a code that the elites sometimes imitate, sometimes
placate, and fear to challenge. Meanwhile, they no longer have a code of
their own in which they have confidence.

In his 1964 opera *Der junge Lord*, the German composer Hans Werner Henze parodied—in this context, "aped" is apposite—precisely this phenomenon. A wealthy, eccentric English nobleman arrives in a small German town with an entourage of slaves and wild animals and succeeds in passing off an ape as his nephew, "Lord Barrett," whose simian behavior charms the impressionable townsfolk until his costume falls apart and everyone can see him for the glorified chimp that he is. (Interestingly, Henze was a committed Communist, although "limousine liberal" or "champagne Socialist" might be a more apt description of him. Having fled Germany—West Germany, not Nazi Germany—for its perceived conservatism and intolerance of homosexuality, he lived la dolce vita in Italy.)

In the end, however, the sexual behavior of ancient cultures (the Greeks) or other primates (bonobo chimps) is not relevant to the problems we face today. No culture until ours has so willingly abjured procreation, so enthusiastically practiced abortion, so demonized (an apt word) those who demurred, and so refused to understand the demographic "consequences of no consequences." If procreation is only an afterthought or an optional lifestyle choice, our Ponzi-schemed social-welfare programs, such as Social Security, which depends on future generations to make it function, will collapse. Indeed, we could be looking at the demolition of the entire "social safety net"—though one would think radicals would want to save this, if we are to believe them when they express grave concern for humanity.

"Who will save us from Western culture?" The good news for the Left is that they have been saved—by Western culture itself, which succored them in the breasts of academe and nurtured them in what the late Andrew Breitbart memorably described as the "Democrat-Media Complex." This is the tight, rotating network of college gigs, media jobs, and government "service" that rewards intellectual conformity to the leftist narrative, even as many of its adherents live their private lives according to conservative principles, raising small nuclear families within the two-parent structure and ensuring their children's safety by living in economically segregated, sometimes gated, communities.

Meanwhile, beyond the borders of Potomac, Maryland, Bel Air in Los Angeles, or the Upper West Side of Manhattan, the citizenry is subject to whatever laws its betters choose to make—and the more the laws, the better, so that, in the words of Harvey Silverglate, just about everyone unknowingly commits "three felonies a day" (the title of his 2009 book) while simply going about his daily business. And to prevent future generations from rising up against what they must eventually perceive as tyranny, anti-procreationists and abortion "providers" are busily erasing the next generation in the name of "women's rights." Few cultures, if any, have been as gleefully self-righteous about the moral righteousness, the transcendence, of their suicide as the West.

Thus, like Rosemary's baby in the iconic movie of that title, the culture of death was born in a country that had formerly welcomed babies and children. Up until the 1960s and '70s, and prior to *Roe v. Wade*, American culture had prized babies as a necessity in a muscular, growing, culturally confident republic. Fittingly, in Roman Polanski's 1968 horror film, Death, in the form of Rosemary's baby, arrived in the intellectual precincts of the nation's greatest city, New York. In order to make its anti-life, anti-procreation argument work, the Marxist squid had to exude great quantities of ink—most of which landed on the pages of the house organ of Leftism, the *New York Times*—to obscure its true purpose. The Malthusian myth of overpopulation was trotted out once more. Leftists love zero-sum games and "scientific" prophecies of certain doom: "climate change," "diminishing resources," "peak oil," etc. It would be a crime to bring a child into this terrifying world, they warned, and subject him to a shrunken future. Overpopulation was an omnipresent theme of the period. Even the movies got into the act—*Logan's Run, Soylent Green*. The world would soon be crawling with mewling, starving people, and the most merciful thing would be to kill them and maybe even eat them. Thus was the leftist suicide cult born.

It's crucial to remember how quickly this transformation was accomplished. The cultural revolution of the late '60s took place during a period marked by widespread dislocation. The Tet Offensive, LBJ's abdication, Martin Luther King Jr.'s assassination, Bobby Kennedy's murder—all occurred in the first six months of 1968. Still to come that year were the Soviet invasion of Czechoslovakia, the Chicago riots at the Democratic convention in August, and the launch of Apollo 8. By the mid 1970s, there was no going back. After *Deep Throat* (1972) and *The Devil in Miss Jones* (1973), porn shops and peep shows popped up across the land, Hugh Hefner's "Playboy philosophy" began its cultural ascendancy, and the sexual revolution got well and truly under way.

But what, precisely, was the problem that the Left sought so desperately to fix? What required the destruction of the preexisting system of cultural and social mores? The answer—despite the earlier battering by the Fabian Socialists in 1880s England, by the Bloomsbury Group of Virginia Woolf and her compatriots, by Margaret Sanger's "progressive" eugenics movement of the 1920s—was nothing.

When the businessman/villain Gordon Gekko is asked in the 1987 movie *Wall Street* why he wants to wreck a company that's his takeover target, he irritably replies: "Because it's wreckable, all right?" The hit movie was co-written and directed by another man of the Left, Oliver Stone, and Gekko's remark was meant to illustrate the mean-spirited avariciousness of the "greed is good" Reagan-era businessmen. And yet, looked at another way, it says more about the ethos of the eliminationist Left than it does about the Right's putative avarice.

Even earlier, in *The Wild One* (1953), the glamorous biker-gang leader Johnny Strabler (Marlon Brando) is asked by a local girl, "Hey, Johnny, what are you rebelling against?" His reply—"Whaddya got?"—is one of the most famous lines in film history and a perfect encapsulation of the sense that for the nihilist new Romantics, civilization *tout court* was worthless. Significantly, the first complete draft of the script was written by Ben Maddow, who was blacklisted in 1952, taking him off the project as well as stopping his work on the first draft of *High Noon*. Maddow was a Columbia-educated leftist who under the pseudonym David Wolff was a poet of considerable renown in bien-pensant circles. Allen Ginsberg even cited Wolff's "The City" (1940), a sprawling account of urban horror and alienation, as the inspiration for Ginsberg's own, better-known "Howl."

Like many artists who came of age in the inter-war years, Maddow—and the rest of the herd of independent minds—had come to believe that an apocalyptic broom would need to sweep clean the detritus of the broken world and remake it anew.

The system had to go because it was blocking the Marxist arc of history, that rainbow that would end somewhere, somehow, in a pot of gold in a humble proletarian field. And who better represented "the system" than the modern incarnation of Adam and Eve, a man and a woman, their bodies designed to act reciprocally in the matters of procreation and pleasure, the creatures that God himself had interposed between Heaven and Hell, free to be strong or weak as the mood took them, and thus a perfect target for the satanic impulse, whether literarily or literally?

The family was the first target, but even that was a feint, collateral damage from the principal target: the nature of the sexual relationship itself. And for that, we must once again turn to our evocation of man's primal dark side, Goethe's *Faust*.

When Faust first sees Gretchen (in a magic mirror, having been warmed up by a witch's potion), he is immediately smitten—and just as quickly mocked by the Devil, who remarks: "With this drink, you see Helen of Troy in every woman." (As it happens, Helen will play a large role in *Faust,* Part Two.) This is how Faust describes Gretchen to Mephistopheles, after first encountering her in person in the street and having had his advances rebuffed:

> *By Heaven, this child is beautiful!*
> *I've never seen anything like her.*
> *She's so rich in purity and virtue*
> *And just a little saucy, too.*
> *Her lips red, her cheek fair,*
> *'Til the end of days I shan't forget it!*
> *The way she cast down her eyes*
> *Deeply impressed itself into my heart;*
> *How curt she was with me,*
> *Now that's pure enchantment!*

Faust is thunderstruck, just as Mephisto had predicted he would be. But look at what he reacts to: his opposite, the "other." Faust is old;

Gretchen is young. Faust has seen everything in the course of his studies; Gretchen is a simple girl, but he has never seen anything like her, nor she him. Faust is stiff and cold; Gretchen is pert, with a telling hint of sexy mischief in her sparkling eyes. Faust is blunt; but with one shy downward glance, Gretchen binds his heart forever.

Faust, in short, has been bewitched, charmed, enraptured—in other words, he is going through the same thing he is currently experiencing with Mephistopheles, though in the physical realm. But the *Ewig-Weibliche*, the Eternal Feminine here instantiated by Faust's fantasy of the pure and innocent Gretchen (soon enough to be defiled) and ultimately the end point of the entire two-part poem, proves a far greater force than Mephistopheles's satanic temptations. Sex is, for Goethe and innumerable other artists, the greatest single force in creation—so powerful that in Milton, in Book Nine of *Paradise Lost*, the first thing Adam and Eve do after they both taste the forbidden fruit is to make love in what is one of Western literature's first sex scenes:

> *So said he, and forbore not glance or toy*
> *Of amorous intent, well understood*
> *Of Eve, whose eye darted contagious fire.*
> *Her hand he seized, and to a shady bank,*
> *Thick overhead with verdant roof embow'red*
> *He led her, nothing loath; flowers were the couch,*
> *Pansies, and violets, and asphodel,*
> *And hyacinth, Earth's freshest softest lap.*
> *There they their fill of love and love's disport*
> *Took largely, of their mutual guilt the seal,*
> *The solace of their sin, till dewy sleep*
> *Oppressed them, weary with their amorous play.*

After you disobey the only commandment God has given you, what else is there to do but have sex?

And so we have a twinning in the cultural mythos of forbidden fruit and Eros/Thanatos, for both Adam and Eve realize that now they must surely die, now that they have tasted both celestial knowledge and human love in its purest form, and have experienced for the first time *la petite mort* of orgasm. And the twinning is crucial to the formation of humanity—another unsuspected benefit of the Fall. The heterosexual human sex act is unlike that of most mammals in that it can happen at any time, not only when the human animal is rutting (our species is always rutting, for good or ill).

Animals respond to the power of the sexual urge; they flock to its smell and its call; they indulge in it with ferocious, sometimes lethal abandon. Humans (and not just in the female's fertile months) are always on the lookout for the entire panoply of human sexual experience: the main chance, the quick score, the illicit affair, the eternal love, the one-night stand, and the enduring relationship that survives even death. At once unspoken and yet the subject of countless works of literature, poetry, theater, film, and the musical arts both high and low, this salient feature of the Fall is continually celebrated by mankind even as its primal power causes us so much pain and heartache.

At the first sight of Gretchen, Faust's lust for knowledge is alchemized into his lust for her. The embodiment of the Eternal Feminine, she is what drives him from this point in the poem—onward but not necessarily upward. Seduced and impregnated, Gretchen (saucy but pure) is the innocent Eve turned murderess. Awaiting Faust's arrival in her virgin bedchamber, she inadvertently kills her mother by administering a fatal dose of sleeping potion; later, she drowns her bastard child and is condemned to death. Upon seeing Mephisto appear alongside Faust in her dungeon, she calls Satan the spawn of darkness: "*Was steigt aus dem Boden herauf?*" ("What climbs out of the earth?")

This is the elemental power of sex—that for all its complexity and difficulty, it nevertheless points the way to transcendence. Almost every religious cult is based around it (with the transient guru having unlimited access to the most nubile and desirable females). Those that aren't—say, the Shakers (the United Society of Believers in Christ's Second Appearing)—rejected it as too powerful but still throw themselves into transports of quasi-sexual religious ecstasy, sublimating the erotic impulse while paying it religious homage.

Critical Theory attacked all of this, principally the idea of transcendence. Not every sex act has larger meaning, of course, but the goal of Critical Theory was to reduce human beings to the level of animals ("If it feels good, do it") and to deny the transcendent component that had driven creative artists for centuries. Tellingly, the word "sex" came to mean the same thing as "gender," an impersonal grammatical term that includes masculine, feminine, and neuter. Primal notions of masculinity and femininity were redefined and "nuanced," which in practice meant shattered and rendered meaningless. Herbert Marcuse, the author of *Eros and Civilization,* celebrated "polymorphous perversity," advocating the liberating power of sex, but only in the narrowest sense: liberation from the (in his view) arbitrary and capricious strictures laid down by culture and civilization. By following the directive to "make love, not war," the gullible individual might well have felt that he was striking a blow at the hierarchy; in reality, though, perhaps he was simply expending his creative, sexual energy in useless and unproductive ways. But Marcuse knew that a populace engaged in pointless sexual intercourse was a populace uninterested in much of anything else; thus "polymorphous perversity" weakens the foundations of the society he sought to undermine.

Again, we must use the word "satanic," which, rightly defined, means the desire to tear down a longstanding, even elemental, order and replace it with … nothing. Critical Theory very effectively harnesses resentment, transmuting it into rage; it excuses solipsistic indolence, presenting it as "self-realization." The Frankfurt School rejected Jung's collective unconscious—the only truly collective thing about humanity—describing it as an "obscurantist pseudo-mythology," vastly preferring Freudianism. The psychoanalyst Erich Fromm, who founded "socialist humanism," in particular devoted a great deal of his attention to Freudian theory, and while he found "contradictions" within it, he described Freud as one of the "architects of the modern age," placing him in the pantheon alongside Marx and Einstein.

In his most important work, *Escape from Freedom* (1941), Fromm explicitly rejected Western notions of personal freedom, preferring instead the ordered society of—of all things—feudal Europe. (There is no Progressive like a Regressive.) "In having a distinct, unchangeable, and unquestionable place in the social world from the moment of birth, man was rooted in a structuralized whole, and thus life had a meaning which left no place, and no need for doubt." ("Structural" is a favorite word of the Marxists, believing as they do in a "scientific" basis for what is little more than a resentful nineteenth-century revenge fantasy.)

To take a step back from the Frankfurt School and its curious, culture-specific obsessions is to note what a stunningly self-referential and limited world these intellectuals inhabited. They were a group of tiresome, quarrelsome, pedantic, mostly German- or Austrian-born intellectuals endlessly rehashing the theories and merits of an earlier generation of tiresome, pedantic, mostly German- or Austrian-born intellectuals, with the added layer of their largely shared (or rejected) Jewishness in common.

One is reminded of the historian Paul Johnson's memorable chapter on Marx in *Intellectuals*, with a title that recalls Satan himself: "Howling Gigantic Curses." In it, Johnson describes the political devil of our narrative as he set about his war with God:

> *He never received any Jewish education or attempted to acquire any, or showed any interest in Jewish causes. But it must be said that he developed traits characteristic of a certain type of scholar, especially Talmudic ones: a tendency to accumulate immense masses of half-assimilated materials and to plan encyclopedic works which were never completed; a withering contempt for all non-scholars, and extreme assertiveness and irascibility in dealing with other scholars. Virtually all his work, indeed, has the hallmark of Talmudic study: It is essentially a commentary on, a critique of the work of others in the field.*

Perhaps that is ascribing too much to Marx's Jewish roots, which included prominent rabbis on both sides of the family; as Johnson notes, Marx's father was baptized in the wake of an 1816 Prussian edict that banned Jews from the legal and medical fields, and he had his six children baptized as well. Ascribing innate "racial" or cultural traits is a dangerous business in the aftermath of the Holocaust; still, the fact remains that the overwhelming majority of the members of the Frankfurt School were Jewish, as were many of the early Bolsheviks, including Trotsky, Sverdlov, and Zinoviev; like all Bolsheviks, they were fiercely anti-Jewish, banning teaching in Hebrew and religious instruction (not that it saved them from Stalin, whose own Georgian anti-Semitism rivaled Hitler's). Nevertheless, although Jews made up a high percentage of the German intellectuals of the period, well out of proportion to their small share of the population, the philosophical terms of the debate were German, not Jewish.

Another of Marx's traits was evident from his youth: his passion for destruction, expressed in the poetry he wrote as a young man, including "Savage Songs," one of whose verses ran: "We are chained, shattered, empty, frightened / Eternally chained to this marble block of being / ... We are the apes of a cold God." *Faust* was one of his favorite poems, of course, but he took the side of Mephistopheles, quoting the Devil's aphorism "Everything that exists deserves to perish" in his essay *The Eighteenth Brumaire of Louis Bonaparte.* Johnson concludes his study by remarking: "Marx is an eschatological writer from start to finish."

In other words, not to put too fine a point on it: a madman. For Marx resembles nothing more than those monomaniacs convinced of the righteousness of their cause (or, in this case, an anti-cause dressed up as a cause), desperately scribbling upon acres of foolscap and furiously buttonholing just about everyone they meet, with a lecture or harangue always ready to hand. How anyone could have fallen for this load of quasi-scientific, pseudo-intellectual, anti-human codswallop remains a mystery, and yet in a world where even Charles Manson can find love behind prison bars, anything is possible. A selfish, ravaging monster in his personal life, Marx is the archetype of the modern leftist, an apotheosis of hypocrisy who makes others suffer and die for his sins.

Again, note the Christian allegory. Marxism is often compared to a religious cult in its outward trappings and external rituals, but a closer look at its founder and practitioners reveals even greater similarities. Marx's own self-identification with Mephistopheles might well be proof enough, but let us go further. The sense of having been wronged—by fate? the universe?—runs throughout the Left's list of grievances against a God they profess not to believe in. Their own lives bear little scrutiny, as they are too often revealed as duplicitous, deceitful, and treacherous toward even those they claim to love. The media today shriek in glee whenever a putative conservative is caught with some part of his body in a honey pot, yet they consistently turn a blind eye to those on their side in the same predicaments. Their lame explanation is always the same: Conservative (or better yet, religious fundamentalist) hypocrisy is news. After all, it is a violation of Alinsky's Rule No. 4: "Make the enemy live up to their own book of rules." Whereas the Left has no rules, only objectives, and since "by any means necessary" is a perfectly acceptable moral code, there can be no hypocrisy among leftists, just as there can be no enemies.

Consider that much of leftists' enthusiasm for sexual freedom stems from their own, shall we say, irregular personal lives; for them, the love that dare not say its name instead shouts it from the rooftops. And, by extension, they have assumed that what works for people who are often engaged in creative and artistic pursuits (who tend to be highly sexed) ought to work for everybody else, even those whom they dismiss as plebeian. The Bloomsbury Circle was a hotbed of hot beds, both gay and straight; the rapaciously bisexual Simone de Beauvoir was an early advocate of women's adopting a masculine view of serial sexual conquest, passing along her often underage female conquests to her lifelong partner, Jean-Paul Sartre. Famously, the lascivious Nadezhda Krupskaya, Lenin's wife, became the butt of jokes in the Soviet Union, the most notorious of which goes like this:

A Soviet filmmaker makes a film called "Lenin in Warsaw." Everybody shows up for the premiere. The film opens—on Krupskaya, naked, having mad sex with another man. And then another. And another. And so on. The film goes on and on in the same vein for ninety minutes. Finally, the lights come up and the director takes questions from the audience. First question: "Very interesting movie, comrade, but—where was Lenin?" The director answers: "In Warsaw." (Marx's own sex life, like Rousseau's, also bears little scrutiny.)

And yet the Judeo-Christian example is always reproachfully before the "transgressive" leftists, the thing they cannot avoid even when they try. In 1898, Debussy tried to rebel against the musically puritanical Wagnerism outlined in Wagner's seminal 1849 essay, "*Das Kunstwerk der Zukunft*" ("The Artwork of the Future"), but that Wagner expressed most completely in *Das Rheingold* (with its lack of arias, choruses, etc.). As I mentioned in the previous chapter, the French master wound up writing the ineffable *Pelléas et Mélisande*, which conforms precisely—in a way that even *Rheingold* does not—to Wagner's theoretical strictures. Wagner's ideas themselves were a direct reaction to the "Franco-Jewishness" of the works of Giacomo Meyerbeer, then the darling of the Paris Opera and a man whose success Wagner fervently desired to emulate and, failing thereat, decided to resent.

One of Meyerbeer's greatest successes was the satanic opera *Robert le diable,* from whose themes Liszt fashioned one of his most popular concert showpieces. Wagner himself picked up the Meyerbeerian thread with his early opera *The Flying Dutchman* (1840), bringing the circle of resentment and imitation to completion. Art imitating life, or life imitating art? Or something even more elemental, the unity of the two?

Robert le diable, shockingly for the day, featured a chorus of dead nuns rising from the grave, casting off their habits, and writhing temptingly nude before the hero. In *Dutchman,* by contrast, the temptation is toward goodness and the light, as exemplified by Senta, the village girl who eventually frees the Dutchman from the power of his terrible curse, sending his doomed ship to the bottom and both him and her to Heaven through her *Selbstmord* (suicide). Both operas, though, feature the *Ewig-Weibliche* to drive home the elemental point: Eros and Thanatos, together again, with Eros triumphant.

Wagner's heroines are a panoply of redemptive femininity: Senta, Elisabeth (*Tannhäuser*), Elsa (*Lohengrin*), Isolde (*Tristan und Isolde*), Eva (*Die Meistersinger*), Brünnhilde—strong women who often outlive the men they love. They are the musical and dramatic idealizations of Gretchen, both temptress and redeemer, the spark of the divine made flesh that drives their poor, often weak heroes to their deeds of glory. All of them owe a debt of gratitude to the archetypal operatic feminist heroine, Beethoven's Leonore in *Fidelio,* who rescues her imprisoned husband, Florestan, by disguising herself as a boy and then holding the evil governor of the prison, Don Pizarro, at gunpoint until the cavalry finally arrives.

And yet this most elemental force in human life, the *Ewig-Weibliche,* is routinely scorned and denigrated by the offspring of the Unholy Left, the increasingly deracinated "feminist" harpies whose anti-male rhetoric bespeaks not so much impotent rage as sexual jealousy.

The attack on normative heterosexuality—led by male homosexuals and lesbians, and invariably disguised as a movement for "rights," piggybacking on the civil rights movement of the 1960s—is fundamental to the success of Critical Theory, which went straight at the hardest target (and yet, in many ways, the softest) first. The reason was simple: If a wedge could be driven between men and women, if the nuclear family could be cracked, if women could be convinced to fear and hate men, to see them as unnecessary for their happiness or survival—if men could be made biologically redundant—then that political party that had adopted Critical Theory could make single women one of their strongest voting blocs.

And so Eve was offered the apple: In exchange for rejecting a "traditional" sex role of supposed subservience and dependency (slavery, really), she would become more like a man in her sexual appetites and practices (this was called "freedom"), and she would be liberated from the burdens of motherhood via widespread contraception, abortion on demand, and the erasure of the "stigma" of single motherhood (should it come to that) or spinsterhood. Backed by the force of the government's fist, she would compete with men for jobs, high salaries, and social status, all the while retaining all her rights of womanhood. The only thing she had to do was help destroy the old order.

The result has been entirely predictable: masculinized women, feminized men, falling rates of childbirth in the Western world, and the creation of a technocratic political class that can type but do little real work in the traditional sense. Co-educational college campuses have quickly mutated from sexually segregated living quarters to co-ed dorms to the "hookup culture" depicted by novelist Tom Wolfe in *I Am Charlotte Simmons* to a newly puritanical and explicitly anti-male "rape culture" hysteria, in which sexual commissars promulgate step-by-step rules for sexual encounters and often dispense completely with due process when adjudicating complaints from female students.

Crucially, at every step of the way, "change" from the old norms was being offered as "improvement" or "liberation"—more fulfillment, more pleasure, more experience. And yet, with each step, things got worse—for women. Eve's bite of the apple sent humanity forth from the Garden, sadder but wiser. Today's transgressive Western woman is merely sadder and often ends her life completely alone, a truly satanic outcome. G.K. Chesterton's parable of the fence comes to mind, in "The Drift from Domesticity," in *The Thing* (1929):

> *In the manner of reforming things, as distinct from deforming them, there is one plain and simple principle; a principle which probably will be called a paradox. There exists in such a case a certain institution or law, let us*

say, for the sake of simplicity, a fence or gate erected across a road. The more modern type of reformer goes gaily up to it and says, "I don't see the use of this, let us clear it away." To which the more intelligent type of reformer will do well to answer: "If you don't see the use of it, I certainly won't let you clear it away. Go away and think. Then, when you can come back and tell me that you do see the use of it, I may allow you destroy it."

A splendid example of Chesterton's Fence was the Immigration and Nationality Act of 1965, championed by Senator Edward Kennedy of Massachusetts. "Contrary to the charges in some quarters, [the bill] will not inundate America with immigrants from any one country or area," said the Massachusetts senator. "In the final analysis, the ethnic pattern of immigration under the proposed measure is not expected to change as sharply as the critics seem to think. ... The bill will not flood our cities with immigrants. It will not relax the standards of admission. It will not cause American workers to lose their jobs." Half a century on, those predictions have proven dramatically wrong; the question is whether Kennedy and his fellow leftists knew quite well at the time that their forecasts were bogus—although (as someone or other famously said) what difference, at this point, does it make?

In the same way, much of contemporary "reform" is marked by impatience, ridicule, and haste, cloaked in "compassion" or bureaucratic "comprehensivity," disguised as "rights" prised out of the Constitution with a crowbar and an ice pick, and delivered with a cocksure snort of derision against any who would demur.

The last words of *Faust*, Part One, belong not to Faust or even Mephistopheles, but to Gretchen as her soul ascends to heaven, calling out to her lost lover: "Heinrich! Heinrich!" He has failed to rescue poor, mad Gretchen; now she must rescue him, if only beyond, in the next life. But the drama continues nonetheless.

English readers may not at first appreciate the familiarity and intimacy of this last line. Goethe does not use Faust's Christian name until Scene Sixteen, directly after the famous *"Gretchen am Spinnrad"* verses (also famously set to music by Schubert). Faust and Gretchen have exchanged their first kiss; her virgin world has been turned upside down; her body now aches for his, as suggested by her use of his Christian name, Heinrich, in the next scene. It's an extraordinarily intimate moment—Germans of that period and well into the twentieth century did not easily move from the formal terms of address to the more intimate "*duzen,*" using the second-person familiar "thou" with each other. Even close friends and married couples might wait years before using the intimate form of address, if they ever did at all. Faust's problem is that he can't see the light until it's too late for his love and almost too late for him.

What is to awaken *us* from the long slumber of reason that has marked American culture since the end of World War II? The Frankfurt School intellectuals found the perfect moment to attack their host country, not when it was weak but when it was strong. In times of trouble, societies often coalesce around their core values, but when times are flush, people are more inclined to a little social experimentation, especially if it contains a basket of forbidden fruit. Prior to the American victory in the Second World War, men like Adorno, Horkheimer, Gramsci, Lukács, Reich, and Marcuse would probably have been shunned, their philosophy rightly considered the ravings of bitter, dangerous malcontents. But the very fact that America emerged with a high moral standing after its defeat of Nazi Germany and Imperial Japan, whose crimes were inarguable, left the homeland open to the serpents who slithered in while nobody was looking and hissed, "Why not?"

Why not question authority? Why not overturn your moral code? Why not do it if it feels good? The secure children of the 1950s had become the spoiled college students of the 1960s and '70s; their natural inclination as youths was to regard their parents as fools and idiots. The civil unrest of the 1960s added racism to the mix; Vietnam contributed futility and, paradoxically (as things turned out), suspicion of government. (Can government save us from government?)

The United States may have crushed Fascism, but what had it done for us lately? In for the long haul—fashioning the long march through the institutions in the same way that one of their icons, Mao, had effected his Long March to escape the Kuomintang in China and ultimately win control of the country—the leftists set about their business. It would take time, but the game was worth the candle. Besides, as Mephistopheles observes to an angry Faust, "There's nothing more ridiculous in the whole world than a Devil who despairs." They radiated confidence in their morals and their mission of cultural "liberation."

Gretchen's cry of "Heinrich! Heinrich!" to Faust is a cry of despair, but it contains within it a seed of hope; he is her husband, and she the *Ewig-Weibliche,* his better half. Critical Theory's purpose was to remove any shred of such emotion; purposelessness became an end in itself. The slightest glimmer of hope (in this case, doubt about the correctness of the leftist cause) would be the candle in the darkness, illuminating the universe. That could not be.

When Gretchen, in extremis, calls out her lover's name, it is her final attempt to break through Mephisto's darkness and send a ray of Heaven's light stabbing down into the hollowness of Faust's soul. She has long been suspicious of his strange companion; Mephisto gives her the willies. His appearances never lead to anything good. As the dawn breaks on the day of her death, Gretchen alone forces Faust to see the Devil for what he is: a vampire, the spawn from deepest darkness. "What does he want in this holy place?" she cries to Faust. "He wants me!" Just as, one might observe, the Serpent wanted Eve in the Garden.

So, there it is. In the end, the Devil is interested not in Faust but in the woman, the Eternal Feminine, she who will eventually crush him under her feet. Faust's soul, Mephistopheles believes, he already possesses. But the innocent, corruptible Gretchen—she is the one he really wants. In a sense, the entire poem (like *Paradise Lost*) has been a gigantic misdirection, and Mephisto's (and the poet's) true intentions are revealed only at the end. But then Faust steps forward and tells Gretchen, "You shall live." She consigns her soul to God, confident in Eve's revenge upon the Red Dragon.

MEPHISTOPHELES
Sie ist gerichtet! (She is damned!)

A VOICE FROM ABOVE
Ist gerettet! (Is saved!)

Defeated, Mephisto claims the only prize left. He turns to Faust and, beckoning, says: "Here, to me!" And as they both vanish in brimstone, we hear the last lines of the first part of Goethe's masterpiece, spoken by the ascendant Gretchen: "Heinrich! Heinrich!" Hers is the voice of hope in the wilderness, the light in the darkness of what otherwise would be eternal night, and the promise that, no matter what our sins, if only we have faith, this, too, shall pass. Even in death, the Eternal Feminine draws us ever onward, into the Light. And so it is to the Light that we now must turn.

CHAPTER SEVEN

OF LIGHT AND DARKNESS

God's first words in Genesis are "Let there be light." They are, in a very real sense, the beginning of our ur-Narrative, both in story and in physical reality. Whether you accept the existence of God as an article of faith or see him as merely a character in the longest-running story ever told, even the most ardent atheist must agree that the universe had some sort of beginning. We know the universe is expanding (expanding *where*?). The commonly accepted Big Bang theory, when played in reverse, must have an origination point, the moment when light combusted out of darkness and sent fiery suns and planets whirling on their merry celestial journey to somewhere.

We use the word as metaphor—the "light" of knowledge, the "light" of reason, "seeing the light." Things dawn on us, become clear. We have moments of clarity. The discovery and taming of fire brought our cave ancestors heat, but it also brought light. Life is impossible without it. So why, then, the rush to return to darkness?

The struggle between light and darkness is, as the conservative commentator Bill Whittle has pointed out, unequal. For darkness—Satan's realm—to triumph, it must be complete and total, infinite blackness. And yet the light of a single candle, somewhere in the universe, defeats it; there is now light where formerly there was none. Either there is Light or there is not; there can be no synthesis. The most important element for our survival is ridiculously potent. No wonder Genesis begins with it, for God's creation of Heaven and Earth cannot truly exist until it can be seen.

It is therefore no accident that the path to destruction and darkness must be enforced by totalitarian means; and for the same reason, totalitarian states must inevitably fall, since it is impossible for them to maintain absolute control over 100 percent of their population all the time. As the collapse of the Soviet Union proved, the light of a single refusenik was enough to keep the flame of freedom burning until it eventually ignited the rotting structures of the corrupt government and brought it down.

The notion of Light and Darkness runs throughout man's storytelling, naturally. Light-Bringer, the gift of fire: The Titan, Prometheus, stole fire itself from Olympus to give it to humanity and was eternally punished by being chained to a rock and having his liver ripped out by an eagle daily. Similar stories appear across all cultures, including the Indian, Polynesian, and Amerindian. Fear of the darkness and the satanic creatures that might lurk within it is a staple of tales of terror and suspense, not to mention horror films. Indeed, the spooky attraction of the horror genre lies in its partial rejection of the light-defeating-darkness premise; a flick of a lighter can reveal eldritch horrors better left unseen, even at the cost of your life.

This is the underlying premise of the works of H.P. Lovecraft and his Cthulhu mythos. Once dismissed as the pulp-fiction nightmares of a New England eccentric, the dark world of the Great Old Ones (ancient gods now imprisoned in deathlike slumbers who must not be awakened) has found new resonance in the slumbering unconscious of the post-Christian West. "*Ph'nglui mglw'nafh Cthulhu R'lyeh wgah'nagl fhtagn*" ("In his house at R'lyeh, dead Cthulhu waits dreaming") is a phrase familiar to anyone who has a passing familiarity with this mythos. Lovecraft's works feature a panoply of monsters. They're not from the id, as are the creatures of *Forbidden Planet*, the 1956 science-fiction movie that introduced a wide audience not only to bits of Freudian psychiatry but also to Robbie the Robot, with an underlying plot inspired by Shakespeare's *Tempest*. Lovecraft's beasts are from beyond space and time itself (which, as Wagner posits in *Parsifal*, are one and the same thing).

"The most merciful thing in the world, I think, is the inability of the human mind to correlate all of its contents," reads the famous opening line of Lovecraft's 1926 short story "The Call of Cthulhu," first published two years later in the pages of *Weird Tales*. But better to quote the first paragraph in its entirety as it continues:

> *We live on a placid island of ignorance in the midst of black seas of infinity, and it was not meant that we should voyage far. The sciences, each straining in its own direction, have hitherto harmed us little, but some day the piecing together of dissociated knowledge will open up such terrifying vistas of reality, and of our frightful position therein, that we shall either go mad from the revelation or flee from the deadly light into the peace and safety of a new dark age.*

Thus speaks the voice of seductive nihilism. For Lovecraft's tormented three-named mini-Fausts (Francis Wayland Thurston, George Gammell Angell, Charles Dexter Ward, et al.), nihilism is the only possible reaction to the overwhelming terrors of an unholy Creation. In Lovecraft, who set many of his most famous tales in the haunted environs of Massachusetts (generally, the fictional town of Arkham, wherein is located the equally fictional Miskatonic University), the seekers after the light of knowledge come to bitterly regret their inquiries, begging for a merciful death as the madness of their discoveries—the forbidden knowledge—overwhelms and overtakes them. Their scientific inquiries, like Faust's, lead straight to Hell, this particular Hell consisting of the entire shell of the cosmos, save only poor pitiful Earth, where an insect-like humanity dwells in a fool's paradise, to be lost at any moment.

That such nihilism has a powerful hold on the human imagination is indisputable, especially among the young. For those for whom the very real physical and moral ailments of age lie off in a distant, unimaginable future, a flirtation with Sin and Death often proves irresistible. There is a certain frisson to be had from realizing, as in a Hercule Poirot mystery by Agatha Christie, that the murderer must be *one of us*, that guilt is collective, not personal. In the aftermath of the breakdown of the studio system in Hollywood in the late 1960s and early '70s, a parade of movies with a nihilistic bent emerged from the generation of hot young writers and directors, often ending with the hero unable to break through the veil of evil as the bad guys get away.

Foremost among these pictures is probably Robert Towne's *Chinatown* (1974), directed by Roman Polanski, whose wife, the actress Sharon Tate, had been the most prominent victim of the Manson family's butchery spree in 1969 Los Angeles. Set in the City of the Angels, *Chinatown* tackled L.A.'s very own creation myth, the bringing of the water of the Owens Valley to the nascent and very thirsty metropolis—here depicted as Tinseltown's original sin. Caught up in a plot whose machinations he cannot begin to suspect, private dick J.J. Gittes is no match for the monstrous Noah Cross who, in the end, gets away with not only the money and the girl but also, literally, murder. The script's famous last line ("Forget it, Jake—it's Chinatown," delivered in the noir darkness of a Los Angeles night) symbolizes man's inability to fully comprehend evil and his utter impotence in the face of its relentless, unsparing malevolence. Evil cannot be pleaded with or reasoned with, and sometimes it cannot even be defeated.

Nihilism, however, comes with its solution: the heroic impulse, action. Satan may be able to destroy, but he cannot create. Beyond a young man's fashionable flirtation with death, his testing of the boundaries, his sheer delight to be living on the edge, lies the desire to win, not lose. This is why soldiers are drawn from among the young; not only are they at their peak of physical fitness, but to them death is merely theoretical, even fascinating, and they have not yet had their idealism completely beaten out of them. The question for civilization is how to harness this bravery (for so, in war, does it appear) and make it useful. In the ongoing battle against the suicide warriors of Islam, the Western soldier might appear at first to be at a disadvantage. He desires to survive contact with the enemy. He does not dream of "martyrdom," a word whose principal meaning (a principled, selfless death at the hands of the enemy, illustrating the superior moral quality of his faith) has been hideously corrupted and unthinkingly passed along by a media unmoored from our culture's Christian roots. If the Western soldier does not wish to be a martyr to God, he has proven willing to sacrifice himself to save his comrades in arms, and this can inspire even greater feats of heroism. By contrast, the nihilistic fighters of Islam, as they constantly remind us, love death more than they love life.

As tastes and times change, so do story endings. In the *Chanson de Roland*, Roland dies, but not in vain—his death rouses Charlemagne's Christian Franks to victory against the invading Muslims. It would be easy to recast the victory as the triumph of nihilism, to conclude that

Roland, led into a trap and too proud to call for reinforcements in a timely manner, ultimately dies for nothing. Looking at the quickening pace of the current Muslim *Reconquista*—this time of the entire *Dar al-Harb* (non-Islamic world of war) that must be brought to submission so that the peace of Allah might reign, via the infiltration disguised as "immigration" of the Crusader homelands (Islam has a long memory)—one could easily envision such an ending, depending on the outcome of the current struggle. Will that be the West's fate? Or are there still enough Rolands to fight, both morally and physically, for what used to be considered a superior way of life?

One of the seeming paradoxes in modern American political life is the alliance between the Unholy Left and recrudescent militant Islam. It does not seem to matter that a worldwide Muslim caliphate under barbarous sharia law would mean the executions of homosexuals, the removal of women from the public sphere, the extinction of art and musical culture— all things the Left professes to care about passionately. And yet they were silent when the Taliban, after it seized power in Afghanistan in 2001, dynamited to smithereens the sixth-century Bamiyan Buddhas on the grounds of idolatry. Nor has the destruction of priceless Mesopotamian artifacts in Iraq or Roman ruins in Syria bothered "progressives" overmuch.

And yet there is no real mystery. As the fighting emperor, Marcus Aurelius, wrote in his collection of battlefield musings known as the *Meditations*: "Ask yourself, what is this thing in itself, by its own special constitution? What is it in substance, and in form, and in matter? What is its function in the world? For how long does it subsist? Thus must you examine all things that present themselves to you." What the Left and Islam have in common is the only thing that matters to either: a will to power and a desire for submission on the part of their enemies. Doctrinal differences (and there are many) between two innately totalitarian movements can be sorted out later. What matters is that the Principal Enemy first be defeated, since he—us—represents an immediate moral and mortal threat. The swiftest path to victory for both lies not in confrontation, but in our unilateral cultural disarmament.

The theoreticians of the Frankfurt School could offer aught but sweet utopian nothings in place of anything constructive; they preached freedom but brought only slavery ("freedom is slavery," as in *1984*); they promised the self-actualization of all men but instead reduced the populace of whole nations to the status of collaborators and clerks; they guaranteed peace but brought only the unending warfare that obtains when too much is never (and never can be) enough. The pursuit of earthly perfection, as Faust discovered, ends in misery, murder, and death. However tarted up in their often impenetrable German turns of phrase, at the root of their deceptive philosophy lie incitement and rage in the service of a quest for power over their fellow men. The Devil always wears the same mask, and yet each generation must penetrate the disguise for itself or perish.

But not until recently has cultural nihilism leapt the bounds of literature and, to a lesser extent, philosophy and found its expression as a full-rigged, democratically installed political system instead of merely savage tyranny, dispensed by conquering warlords. The injected poison of Critical Theory undermines at every step the kind of muscular cultural self-confidence that distinguished Western warriors and leaders through the end of World War II. A general such as George S. Patton Jr. would be nearly unthinkable today. Darkness descended upon Eastern Europe in the wake of the postwar political stalemate, and with no one to stop it, it was only partially dispersed by the fall of Communism in the East Bloc. The ethics of the Soviet Union were unhappily transplanted, like an airborne virus, to the child of the Enlightenment, the New World.

Not for nothing has the age of European artistic, scientific, philosophical, and geographic discovery been called the Enlightenment, which followed the Renaissance's rediscovery of Greco-Roman culture after a century of European feudalism (the period idealized by Erich Fromm, when the serfs and peasants knew their place). Scholars generally date the beginning of this extraordinary flowering of knowledge at around 1685, which just so happens to be the year of Johann Sebastian Bach's birth. Although a good deal of modern scholarship has been devoted to dispelling the notion of Europe's "Dark Ages" (a chauvinistic coinage of the Renaissance), there is no doubt that the liberating influence of the Italian Renaissance, paving the way to the breakthroughs of the Enlightenment, led Europeans into an age of unprecedented discovery.

Most of the commentary on the Enlightenment addresses the scientific and philosophical advances in Western European culture, but we should not overlook the role of music and opera, particularly one of Mozart's last works, the German *Singspiel* (sing-play) known as *The Magic Flute*. No clearer representation of the conflict between the forces of light and darkness exists in the operatic canon, and it is worth spending some time with it.

In Milton, light and darkness symbolize the opposing forces of God and Satan. The poet opens Book Three with this invocation:

> *... since God is light,*
> *And never but in unapproached light*
> *Dwelt from eternity, dwelt then in thee,*
> *Bright effluence of bright essence increate*
> *. . . . .*
> *... thou, celestial light*
> *Shine inward, and the mind through all her powers*
> *Irradiate, there plant eyes, all mist from thence*
> *Purge and disperse, that I may see and tell*
> *Of things invisible to mortal sight.*

Such imagery was and is particularly potent in northern Europe with its short winter days and long nights. There, the return of the light at Christmas, both literally and symbolically, is visible in a way that it is not in the more southerly climes of the United States. The sun's daily ascendancy can be measured in minutes, not seconds, and the solar orb's progression across the southwestern and western skies offers a daily reminder of the march of the seasons that is wholly absent at the equator.

Light and darkness figure prominently in many works of art, both visual and on the stage, but Mozart's *The Magic Flute* is paradigmatic. The composer's penultimate or even last opera, depending on how you count (*La Clemenza di Tito* was mostly written after the bulk of *The Magic Flute* but beat it to the stage by a few weeks), was composed for Emanuel Schikaneder's Theater auf der Wieden in Vienna, to a Masonic libretto by the impresario himself. Schikaneder also appeared as Papageno in the first performances in the fall of 1791, just a few months before Mozart's death in December of that year.

Conducted by the ailing composer, and sung in German with spoken dialogue in the same language, it was more akin to what we might regard as musical comedy, as opposed to the more "operatic" *Tito*, sung throughout in Italian. It was instantly popular, combining folk elements (the "bird man" Papageno and his mate, Papagena) with the more ethereal main story of Prince Tamino's love for Pamina, the daughter of the Queen of the Night, and the trials the lovers must endure to earn their happiness at the opera's end.

So far, so conventional. But what distinguishes *The Magic Flute* as the opera par excellence of the Enlightenment is the very moral issue we have been discussing throughout: the masking of evil as good, the shrouds of illusion that the forces of darkness cast upon the innocent and the unwary. As the opera opens, Tamino (a "Japanese Prince") is lost in a strange land, pursued by a giant serpent, which causes him to faint in fear. The unconscious man is rescued by Three Ladies. They show him a picture of the beautiful Pamina, telling him she has been kidnapped by the evil sorcerer, Sarastro. Tamino immediately vows to rescue her, both in gratitude for his deliverance and because, like Faust with Gretchen, he has instantly fallen in love with her image.

The reality turns out to be quite the opposite. Before the three temples of Wisdom, Reason, and Nature, Tamino encounters Papageno and the lovely Pamina, but he is quickly separated from her by Sarastro and his cult of high priests, who are actually servants of the Light. (In storytelling parlance, this is known as "the reversal.") He learns that Pamina's mother, the high-flying (both dramatically and musically) Queen of the Night, and her attendants are creatures of Darkness, and that he and Pamina must undergo biblical trials of fire and water, to be purified and made worthy of each other before they may unite.

The trials symbolize the path to Enlightenment that only the strongest and most worthy may undertake. Though he fainted dead away in the face of adversity at the story's beginning, Tamino finally becomes a man, while Pamina is cleansed of whatever sins she may have inherited from her mother, who is vanquished and cast down by the power of the Sun: "*Die Strahlen der Sonne vertreiben die Nacht,*" proclaims Sarastro near the end of the opera as he defeats the Queen of the Night. "*Zernichten der Heuchler erschlichende Macht.*" ("The streaming rays of the sun drive away the night / Destroying the hypocrites' conniving power.") As the Queen and her Ladies sink into the earth, they exclaim, "We are all fallen into Eternal Night!" And this from the character who sings, in one of opera's most challenging coloratura arias, "The vengeance of Hell boils in my heart."

Remember, *The Magic Flute* was popular entertainment. Perhaps it was popular because of, not in spite of, its elemental nature. *Tito*, written nearly simultaneously, was a throwback to the *opera seria*, or "serious opera," of Mozart's youth, tales often set in ancient Greece or Rome. *Tito* contains some marvelous music but is less often performed than *The Magic Flute* today. The Mozart operas that form the cornerstone of the contemporary operatic repertory all deal with human beings and human emotions; beside them, Handel's gods-and-monsters *opera seria* are excruciatingly dated and (thanks to the dreaded *da capo* arias) very long sits. We can practically date the full flowering of the Enlightenment from Mozart's *Marriage of Figaro, Così fan tutte, Don Giovanni,* and *The Magic Flute.*

Still, were *The Magic Flute* merely didactic or some form of special pleading for the Masonic values that informed the lives of Mozart and Schickaneder (and several other figures involved with the composition and production of the opera), we would probably see it today as a curiosity, an artifact of a vanished civilization. Naturally, it has come under attack from politically correct leftists, who view the depiction of the lonely, treacherous Moor, Monostatos, as "racist," mostly because of the libretto's now-often-censored lines: "*Weil ein Schwarzer haesslich ist ... Weiss ist schön, ich muss sie küssen / Mond, verstecke dich dazu.*" ("Because a black man is ugly ... White is beautiful! I must kiss her / Moon, hide yourself so I can.") As early as the 1970s, opera houses were already altering these lines to protect delicate sensibilities. I saw a production in that era that made Monostatos fat rather than black—which of course would be equally un-PC today.

Such "sensitivity" is just another hallmark of the attack on Western culture, and in particular that aspect of the attack that employs the wormwood of guilt as a weapon. Never mind that the figure of the Moor in the late eighteenth century was well recognized as a villain, the embodiment of a literally existential threat to Christendom. One of Mozart's earlier operas, *The Abduction from the Seraglio* (1782), dealt with the then-topical problem of Turkish Muslims employing captured European women as harem concubines. (The opera ends with a notable act of mercy from Pasha Selim, no doubt confounding modern expectations.) But in a world that filters everything through the lens of Critical Theory, no sin of the past may go unnoticed or unpunished.

If you can attack Mozart, one of Western Europe's greatest geniuses, then you can attack anybody. But that is precisely the point of Critical Theory. There is no need to consider the sum total of the artist's life and works; instead, all that is necessary is to find a single politically incorrect remark, attitude, or letter with which to discredit him, and the task is complete. The totalitarian Left (and its impulse is and must always be toward totalitarianism in the name of "compassion") cannot brook the slightest deviation from its self-proclaimed norms. As with satanic darkness, there cannot be a single point of light to disturb the suffocating blanket of orthodoxy, lest someone somewhere see the light.

Our forefathers knew that the Darkness was always out there, just beyond the reach of the candle, the torch, the floodlight, that the night held terrors we feared even to dream about. When the Irish writer, Bram Stoker, set about to pen his speculative epistolary novel, drawing on Middle European folklore and the nickname of Vlad the Impaler of Wallachia (1431–1476), he tapped into one of Central Europe's most primal fears. (In Bulgaria, a 7,000-year-old grave with skeletons staked through the heart was discovered in 2014.) The novel was *Dracula*, whose gloomy resonance we continue to feel to this day. Indeed, as shown by the *Twilight* movie saga and the *True Blood* books and TV series, vampires are more popular than ever. Personified in the 1931 film by Béla Lugosi in one of the earliest talkie horror movies, the vampire is suave, seductive, and sexy (well-dressed, too). He promises eternal life in exchange for eternal death; he is often irresistible, especially to women. Having consigned his soul to Satan, he wanders the eternal darkness, searching for fresh souls, in no need of light. He is, in fact, deathly allergic to light. Folklore has it that the rays of the sun—"*die Strahlen der Sonne*"—will destroy him, just as surely as they destroyed the Queen of the Night and her attendants in *The Magic Flute*.

Often in vampire myth, it is the woman, the monster's main target, who confounds and defeats him. In F.W. Murnau's sleek, seminal, Expressionist *Nosferatu* (1922), starring the aptly named Max Schreck as (for copyright reasons) Count Orlok, the heroine Ellen willingly sacrifices herself to the Count, opening her bedroom to him and keeping him occupied with her blood until, distracted by lust, he is turned to dust by the morning sun as the cock crows. (The sexual and religious imagery in the film comes thick and fast, up to and including an eroticized Agony in the Garden.)

At first, this might seem contradictory: Woman (except Pamina, freed from her mother's sin) is evil in *The Magic Flute*, while she is the victor over the vampire in *Dracula*. But it is all of a piece. Woman is closer to bloody, chthonic Darkness than is Man; she knows Evil more intimately. Made from Adam's hewn rib, she is the last and best thing in God's creation, the end point. Although the first to fall, she is also the *Redemptoris Mater*, the Mother of the Redeemer, the Woman Clothed in Sun whose final, transcendently vengeful victory over the Great Red Dragon—the Serpent who brought both her sex and mankind low—forms the climax to the great ur-Narrative implanted within our hearts and on the lips of our bards and storytellers.

How the most heroic tale in human history came to be transformed into an anti-myth of female enslavement is a wonder for the ages. But unless the Left can extinguish the Light of Woman and her godlike powers of human creation, it cannot hope to win. And so it hopes to convince Woman she is nothing more than an inferior man, to plant the seed of resentment, nourish it with bile, and hope it gives birth to reason's sleep—a monster.

The dark side is an essential aspect of the human character and psyche; no one denies that. Religion acknowledges this primal fact; so does storytelling. There can be no drama, no conflict, without good and evil, light and darkness, protagonist and antagonist. But storytelling also reminds us that while the darkness may win from time to time (as it does in *Chinatown*), it is a temporary victory. Everyone has a chance to see the light.

In 2007, the late novelist Doris Lessing published an essay in the *New York Times* upon winning the Nobel Prize in literature. Born in Iran to British subjects and educated in Rhodesia, Lessing embraced Communism as a young woman (her second husband, Gottfried Lessing, became the East German ambassador to Uganda, where he was murdered in 1979). She eventually settled in London, finally breaking with Communism after the 1956 Soviet invasion of Hungary, when the true nature of the Communist beast could no longer be disguised behind its humanitarian façade. In the essay, an adaptation of a *New York Times*

op-ed she originally published in 1992, she describes her disenchantment
with Communism:

> *The phrase "political correctness" was born as Communism was collaps-*
> *ing. I do not think this was by chance. I am not suggesting that the torch*
> *of Communism has been handed on to the political correctors. I am sug-*
> *gesting that habits of mind have been absorbed, often without knowing*
> *it. There is obviously something very attractive about telling other people*
> *what to do. ... It troubles me that political correctness does not seem to*
> *know what its exemplars and predecessors are; it troubles me more that*
> *it may know and does not care. ... I am sure that millions of people, the*
> *rug of Communism pulled out from under them, are searching frantically,*
> *and perhaps not even knowing it, for another dogma.*

The search for "another dogma" to replace the Judeo-Christian message of darkness and light, of sin and salvation, is as old as religion itself.
And yet, even in the folk tales that emerged long after Jesus of Nazareth,
the same elements remain in play. And it is remarkable, upon reading
the *Meditations* of Marcus Aurelius, how closely they foreshadow various
Christian tenets, which were not to come for more than a hundred years
after the emperor's death. The moral consistency contained in the world's
collected folk wisdom bespeaks some primal source that no amount of
mid-nineteenth-century Viennese pseudoscience can explain away.

In 1988, Joseph Campbell sat down with PBS's Bill Moyers, the former
White House press secretary under President Lyndon Johnson, to discuss
his book *The Hero with a Thousand Faces.* The topic was the power of
myth and legend, and their continued importance in our modern lives.
Referring to Prometheus and Jesus, the prototypical Light-Bringers who
delivered the world from darkness, Moyers offered a solipsistic analysis:
"In this sense, unlike heroes such as Prometheus or Jesus, we're not going
on our journey to save the world but to save ourselves."

To which Campbell replied:

> *But in doing that, you save the world. The influence of a vital person vital-*
> *izes, there's no doubt about it. The world without spirit is a wasteland.*
> *People have the notion of saving the world by shifting things around,*
> *changing the rules. ... No, no! Any world is a valid world if it's alive. The*

thing to do is to bring life to it, and the only way to do that is to find in your own case where the life is and become alive yourself.

As we have seen, Life is Light. Darkness is Death and the world of the undead: Stoker's vampires; Meyerbeer's nude nuns; the "willies" of Puccini's early opera *Le Villi* (set, fittingly, in the Black Forest of Germany during the Middle Ages), vengeful, wronged female spirits who force the opera's hapless hero to dance himself to death to atone for his infidelity with a seductive siren and for abandoning his lover, who died of a broken heart in his absence. Darkness envelops the Devil's Pleasure Palace, is home to Weber's Black Huntsman and Wagner's Flying Dutchman, stalks London in the unholy form of Dracula, and dates your daughter in *Twilight*. He can only be defeated by the Light, which is Love.

The word "vitality" means full of life, and it is the heroic spirit that infuses both Love and Light into the world and gives it renewed Life. You don't have to be a Christian to understand the impact Jesus had on the world, creating through a schism with Judaism (which awaits the *Moshiach*, the Redeemer, the Messiah) the world's largest religion, Christianity. Roughly a third of the world's seven billion people are professed or baptized Christians, far outnumbering Muslims (which are about 23 percent) and all other faiths.

So, naturally, Christians have become the target, not only of a renewed and aggressive Islam but of the non-Christians and the anti-Christians in the West, who regard the faith as something akin to Chesterton's Fence—something to be rashly torn down for its perceived uselessness (or actual malignance), instead of something to be studied and appreciated for what it has accomplished. The baleful Alinsky's Rule No. 4—"Make the enemy live up to their own book of rules"—has been unleashed with brute force upon the Christian sects. For leftists, the good-enough must always be the enemy of the perfect. "Good enough" mean imperfection, and that is their weapon.

They believe that a single failure renders an entire system false, and they have convinced a guilty and gullible, largely irreligious media to join them in this belief. No allowance is made for mere mortals, much less (in C.S. Lewis's phrase) "mere Christianity." They, who celebrate human weakness and moral deformity in all its guises, can find no tolerance—otherwise, one of their favorite words and most important "moral" principles—for fallibility when it comes to the West and Christianity. Zero tolerance is the order of the day, but only for things the Unholy Left cannot tolerate.

In battle, the high ground is always preferable to the low. The Charge of the Light Brigade in 1854 and the attack at Gallipoli in 1915 failed precisely because the attackers (always at a disadvantage against a well-entrenched enemy) rushed pell-mell into the teeth of withering fire, needlessly sacrificing their young men for no strategic advantage. And yet there was heroism in these risky advances, heroism that echoed down the ages to the Allied landing on the beaches at Normandy during Operation Overlord. Without the earlier examples, would the American, British, and Canadian soldiers who hit the beaches on June 6, 1944, have otherwise rushed toward what was sure to be, for many of them, certain death? And yet, in the face of murderous machine-gun fire from Wehrmacht units atop the cliffs, they established a beachhead and kept on moving, crossing the Rhine and finishing whatever hopes the shrinking Third Reich had of staving off the advancing Russians and striking a separate peace with the Allies.

It is telling that, since that June day in 1944, the United States has failed to win a single military campaign. The battles of the Korean War etched a series of memorable moments for the United States Marine Corps—at Pusan, Inchon, Seoul, and the Chosin Reservoir—but no clear-cut American victory. Vietnam ended ignominiously with the American abandonment of its erstwhile allies in South Vietnam and the humiliating spectacle of American helicopters fleeing from the advancing North Vietnamese. The campaigns in Iraq (a foolish war waged by a failed-president son of another failed president) and the embarrassment of Afghanistan (a war easily won and then, with great difficulty, lost under a Democratic president) point not to a failure of American military prowess or tactics, but to a lack of political will to finish the job. In the aftermath of the clear-cut, unconditional victory in World War II, that will has been poisoned, soured in part by the ethos of the Frankfurt School, which whined "Why not?" when the question should always be "Why?"

Speaking at the funeral of his assassinated brother, Robert, the late Massachusetts senator Edward Kennedy quoted his fallen sibling: "Some men see things as they are and say why? I dream things that never were and say why not?" Telling words, which reveal which side of Chesterton's

Fence these two Kennedys were on, and how much cultural mischief they have caused. Conservatives believe there is a reason—a very good reason—*why* things that never were, never were.

And where did that line, uncredited, come from? From this passage in George Bernard Shaw's 1921 play *Back to Methuselah*: "I hear you say 'Why?' Always 'Why?' You see things; and you say 'Why?' But I dream things that never were; and I say 'Why not?' "

The speaker is the Serpent.

Once safely in the United States, the Frankfurt School sappers had one philosophical objective: to remove the moral high ground of the American Way and replace it with self-doubt. Having lost Germany to an equally murderous leftist ideology, Nazism, the Communists of the Frankfurt School were perfectly content to sit out the war for ideas in the safety of Morningside Heights. There, they unabashedly continued the undermining of Western civilization that they had begun at the Goethe University in Frankfurt. Puny avatars of Mephistopheles, they determined, for reasons large and small, to turn Siegfried into Faust, cut him down to size and send him to Hell.

Near the end of *Götterdämmerung* (*Twilight of the Gods*), the final opera of Wagner's *Ring* cycle, Siegfried has a flash of clarity in which, freed from his magic-potion spell, he fondly recalls the moment he walked through flames on the mountaintop to free Brünnhilde from her magic-fire-induced slumber. At that moment, two ravens fly squawking out of a bush, circling Siegfried and then disappearing into the air. Hagen, the vengeful son of the dwarf Alberich, asks the hero, "Can you understand those ravens' cry?" Siegfried is following the ravens' flight, and he can understand their speech. Before he can reply, Hagen cries, "*Rache rieten sie mir!*" ("Revenge, they cried to me!") and plunges his spear into the hero's back. Game to the end, Siegfried turns on Hagen and attempts to crush him with his now-useless shield, but his great strength fails him as his life ebbs away, and he topples backward upon his shield, dead.

The key word in this passage is "rache," revenge. The word has given its name to an entire genre of Hollywood films (think *Taken*, along with numerous Clint Eastwood Westerns, including, most memorably, *Unforgiven*). "Rache" is also the clue scrawled in blood upon the walls in the London flat of the very dead Enoch Drebber in Sir Arthur Conan Doyle's first Sherlock Holmes novella, *A Study in Scarlet*. (Scotland Yard's bumbling Inspector Lestrade immediately mistakes the word for an incomplete attempt at the name Rachel.)

Revenge is one of the most primal human emotions—after sexual desire, perhaps the most elemental—at once both destabilizing and stabilizing, restoring a temporary balance to wrongs committed by force. It is the fulcrum of the seesaw of human battles, of the endless tide of war between two roughly equal adversaries. It spurred the attacks of 9/11 on New York City and Washington, D.C., and the quick rout of the Taliban in Afghanistan and the crushing of Saddam Hussein's Baathist Iraq (although in the latter case the revenge was on behalf of the Bush family, rather than the United States of America). And it will be the wellspring of many other atrocities and retaliations in the future.

But what, precisely, was the target of the Frankfurt School's revenge? Their war with God is well documented, as is their war on Western institutions. Antonio Gramsci, an Italian Protestant who died in 1937 after a decade-long stint in a Fascist prison ("we must stop this brain from functioning," said the prosecutor), advocated a boring-out of the system from within—the successful "long march through the institutions"—in order to achieve "cultural hegemony."

For Gramsci, always playing the long game, incrementalism was a byword. Like Satan, the Marxists of the Frankfurt School realized they could not storm and conquer the West from the outside, either militarily or economically. Rather, the hollowing-out had to begin from within and do its work over the course of decades. The slowly boiling frog comes to mind.

And so if the moral high ground was occupied by the still-Christian West after its spectacular victory over neo-pagan "Aryan" National Socialist Germany and the cultish, tribal emperor worship of Imperial Japan, the task was not to frontally overcome the West but to imprison its citizens with the bands of illusion, to make them think that, "really," war was peace, freedom was slavery, and ignorance was strength.

In other words, the mission was to make reality negotiable: subject to analysis, reinterpretation, nuance, parsing. Otherwise rational people could be brought to doubt the empirical evidence of their own senses; they would stare at the evidence so long that it turned upside down and sideways. Everyone has had such an experience: Merely contemplate a single word long enough, and soon you will doubt the correctness of the spelling, the pronunciation, even the meaning.

Even after a half-century and more, the Kennedy assassination in Dallas is proof of this theory. It was a simple Texas murder: Lee Harvey Oswald, a Marine sharpshooter and self-described Marxist and Castro sympathizer with all the motive in the world to attack an anti-Castro president, saw the route of Kennedy's motorcade published in the newspapers that day, brought his rifle to work (concealed in a curtain-rod tube), went up to the sixth floor of the Texas School Book Depository, and shot John F. Kennedy at relatively short range with a scoped rifle in a classic United States Marine Corps shot pattern: Miss, hit, kill.

Still, JFK conspiracy buffs peer into the fine grain of old photographs, search endlessly for clues, seeing things that drive them, literally, crazy. (James Pierson's 2013 book on the assassination, *Camelot and the Cultural Revolution: How the Assassination of John F. Kennedy Shattered Liberalism,* is indispensable on the topic. For a more literary treatment of the assassination, please see my novel *Exchange Alley,* based in large part on the CIA and FBI files in the National Archives.) It is, for many, inconceivable that the president of the United States could have been killed by a *pisher* like Oswald, except that most assassins are nobodies with a chip on their shoulder and a grudge that can be settled only by what they see as revenge. Stephen Sondheim wrote an entire musical on the subject, *Assassins* (1990). The Left tends to believe in the Great Man theory of history only when the Great Men are on their side; otherwise, the impersonal forces of dialectical materialism go on about their grinding, impersonal millstone work.

If we can make the JFK assassination negotiable—despite its being one of the most photographed events in American history—then anything is negotiable. Once you begin as a matter of course to call into question the evidence of your own senses—in other words, once you become a lifelong graduate student, a junior-league Faust perpetually engaged in the study of everything, and therefore nothing—nothing is off-limits. Nothing is so ridiculous that you might not some day come to believe it. As Pontius Pilate said before condemning Jesus to death: *Quid est veritas?* What is truth? For one possible answer, let's go to the Christian world's foundational text, John 18:37–38, from the King James Bible:

Pilate therefore said unto him, Art thou a king then? Jesus answered, Thou sayest that I am a king. To this I was born, and for this cause came I into the world, that I should bear witness unto the truth. Everyone that is of the truth heareth my voice. Pilate saith unto him, What is truth? And when he had said this, he went out again unto the Jews, and saith unto them, I find in him no fault at all.

And as the Austrian conductor Herbert von Karajan added centuries later, perhaps mindful of his own membership in the Nazi party when it stood him in good stead with the German authorities: "The truth is nowhere."

But everything should not be negotiable. The Unholy Left would like it to be so, since negotiability is crucial to Critical Theory: What is truth? The truth is nowhere, answer the National Socialists. And yet, for leftists, their own philosophy is very much *not* debatable. Along the one-way street that is Marxism-Leninism, whether of the political or cultural variety, what's mine is mine, and what's yours is negotiable. It's a Three Stooges routine that's lasted long enough to achieve some sort of authenticity. As Noah Cross says to Jake Gittes in *Chinatown*: "Politicians, ugly buildings, and whores all get respectable if they last long enough."

On the high ground, there is no negotiating. Only those on the low ground seek an advantage through palaver, temporary truces, and false flags. The Germans, faked out by Allied disinformation, were not entirely prepared for the D-Day onslaught. Other assaults on impregnable redoubts have been repelled, unless a siege finally starved out the defenders. The Germans besieged Leningrad for almost 900 days and still failed to take the city.

The classic ratio for attackers to defenders is three to one; and if the defenders have the odds on their side and open supply lines, they can last indefinitely. Vastly outnumbered by the forces of the Mahdi, General Gordon held out in Khartoum for ten months in 1884 and 1885, waiting for Prime Minister Gladstone to send a relief column, which arrived two days late; Gordon's head was cut off by the Mahdi's dervishes and stuck up in a tree, and his body was thrown into the Nile as food for the crocodiles. In an act of then-characteristic Western vengeance, shortly after the Mahdi's death (probably from smallpox), General Kitchener annihilated the Muslim forces at Omdurman, outside Khartoum, destroyed the Mahdi's tomb, severed the corpse's head, threw the bones in the river, and either retained the skull or, by some accounts, sent it to Queen Victoria as a souvenir.

Today, the West takes the news of the latest Islamic beheading video in stride—that's just what those Muslims do, people seem to think—but would never think of reciprocating in kind should the need arise. Indeed, the American way of warfare is to do nothing to "insult" the enemy except, perhaps, under exigent circumstances, kill him. Wars are no longer run by generals in the field but by lawyers; in Afghanistan, the decision to kill even a midlevel Taliban commander had to go through layers of sign-offs before a drone or sniper could take a shot. One wonders what Kitchener, who mowed down the Mahdi's men without compunction, would have made of this moral cowardice disguised as morality. As Hilaire Belloc's famous couplet has it: "Whatever happens, we have got / the Maxim gun and they have not." But now we won't use it, lest it be deemed "disproportionate," "unmeasured," or simply "unfair."

The loss of cultural confidence was precisely what the Frankfurt School and its descendants sought and still seek to engender. It is their only path to victory, which is why—even as they have seized the high ground of the academy and the media—they continue to roll over and expose their bellies like whipped curs whenever they are directly confronted. Pleas for "tolerance," a weakness masquerading as a virtue, still serve them well. It is long past time to give them a taste of their own "repressive tolerance," à la Marcuse, to mark the boundary clearly between dissent and sedition, between advocacy and treason. By consistently claiming that some solutions are "off-limits" to "civilized" peoples, they undermine the very principles of civilization they pretend to advocate—the first of which is the right to civilizational and personal self-defense. They are a suicide cult enticing the rest of us to join them.

But the moral high ground is not yet theirs, as much as they would wish it so. Constantly forced into a strategy of subterfuge, dissimulation, misdirection, and open deception—I have dubbed it "American *taqiyya*," a counterpart to the Muslim concept of religiously acceptable dissimulation—there is no lie the Left will not tell in the furtherance of its sociopolitical goals. To maintain the martial metaphor, they are essentially double agents, operating behind the lines of Western civilization. That they are not called out and dealt with aggressively in the court of public onion and, when necessary, in courts of law, is one of the shames of our age. The only weapon they have is words—but we can hear the music behind them.

CHAPTER EIGHT

OF WORDS AND MUSIC

A free society is one marked by what you *can* say, which is and should be just about everything. We thought we had enshrined this principle in the First Amendment, which applies primarily to government censorship of speech, both at the federal and, latterly via the doctrine of incorporation, among the several states. In a free society of free citizens, speech is the medium and proof of freedom itself.

An unfree society, on the other hand, is noteworthy for what you *cannot* say, which is just about anything that might disturb the overall leftist narrative or that might be at variance with an ever-changing series of politically expedient norms. In an unfree society, people keep their heads down and their mouths shut, fearful of exposing themselves in any way to such treatments as one might find in Room 101 of Orwell's Ministry of Love.

This is the central conundrum of our time. We live in a free society that cannot speak its mind, and we have created an unfree society that cannot admit that fact to itself. Talk about cognitive dissonance. And yet, as in an opera, what is *said* and what is *sung* may often be very different things.

To approach an opera as if it were a play is wrong, because there is an additional and very important level of meaning going on beneath the surface of the words, one that can either reinforce it or completely contradict it. We give creative primacy to the composer in opera and not to the librettist, because it is just this layer of added meaning that distinguishes opera from nearly every other art form except perhaps the cinema at its highest levels. Wagner's leitmotifs in the *Ring*—short phrases that stand for particular things (Siegfried's sword, Wotan's spear) or concepts (the redemption-by-love motif)—are perhaps the most evident example, and yet composers going back to Mozart employ similar techniques in different ways.

At the end of the Stone Guest scene in Mozart's *Don Giovanni*, in which the rakehell is finally dragged down to perdition, the orchestra triumphantly thunders out the final chords in the "light" key of D major— not the spooky "dark" of D minor that has attended the Don throughout the opera, from the Overture on. Thus, musically, the triumph is society's, not the anti-hero's. For the later Romantics, *Don Giovanni* was the most important opera of the eighteenth century and the starting point for their efforts in the otherworldly genre. Similarly, Mozart's Symphony No. 40 in G Minor was highly prized as a passionate excursion into the dark side of tonality.

In an early scene from the relatively sunnier *Così fan tutte*, the two men, Ferrando and Guglielmo, declare their love for their fair lady friends, and the orchestration positively vibrates with sexual passion— making their later betrayal of the sisters Fiordiligi and Dorabella that much more painful and ironic. Lorenzo da Ponte's perfectly crafted libretto exudes the rakish cynicism about love we expect from the late eighteenth century, but Mozart's music transforms it with the warm humanity of the Enlightenment. *Così*, conceived as a harmless game by its librettist, is transformed by the composer's music into something deeply, affectingly human—so much so that to this day, stage directors debate whether to return the initial pairs of lovers to each other, or let them stay with the person we've watched them falling in love with throughout the show.

Sometimes no words are needed at all, as in the famous intermezzo from *Cavalleria rusticana*, by Mascagni—a very strong candidate for the greatest three minutes of dramatic instrumental music ever written—the calm before the fatal storm of passion that will take Turridu's life in a fight over a woman. The music is so potent that it has been used to great dramatic effect by filmmakers: Martin Scorsese chose it to accompany the opening titles of *Raging Bull*, and Francis Ford Coppola used it to under-score the lonely death of Michael Corleone at the end of *The Godfather* trilogy. It is music that guides the doomed hero of each of these sagas to an end that he not only knows is coming, but that he also in some sense has willed for himself as the only possible outcome.

In other words, what is unsaid is nonetheless communicated in music and is far more important than what is said. The context and subtext contain the real message. This is true on both sides of today's political battles. On the one side, we have the remnants—scratched and bleed-ing, but still partially cohesive—of the old American Christian culture, largely Protestant but with a strong admixture of Catholics; on the other is the far less numerous but culturally potent Unholy Left, adhering to its own secular religion, although it professes atheism. As with the battle between radical Islam and the West, one side has explicitly avowed war on the other, while the other, more powerful, refuses to acknowledge it or even conceive of it. Which side, under these circumstances, is more likely to be successful?

In retrospect, it is instructive, upon reviewing the works of the Frankfurt School scholars, to see how poorly they argue, even in the areas of their putative specialties. Rhetoric directed against their enemies can just as fittingly be applied to them. When Adorno denounces "a humanity to whom death has become as indifferent as its members," he thinks he is talking about Nazi Germany, but he could just as easily and accurately be talking about Soviet Russia, ruled for nearly a century by the extremely dead hands of Karl Marx and the Devil's disciple, Lenin. Or, alternatively, he could be speaking of the culture of abortion today in the United States, with its horrific death toll and a population inured against equating "choice" with death.

Theodor Adorno (born Theodor Ludwig Wiesengrund; he later adopted the surname of his Corsican Catholic mother) presents an especially interesting case. They say of newspapers that a reader tends to believe most of what he reads until he comes to a story that concerns his own area of professional or personal experience, and then he laughs and tosses the paper in the trash. I spent a quarter-century as a music critic for three American publications, the *Rochester Democrat & Chronicle*, the *San Francisco Examiner*, and *Time* magazine, and to say that my own work was never in the slightest influenced by Adorno would be an understatement. Nor did he influence any of my colleagues, as far as I could tell. Who could possibly be impressed by such a pedestrian, quotidian observation as this parade of clichés and banal wordplay, from Adorno's essay "Music and Language: A Fragment" (1992):

> *Music resembles a language. Expressions such as musical idiom, musical intonation are not simply metaphors. But music is not identical with language. The resemblance points to something essential, but vague. Anyone who takes it literally will be seriously misled.*

In the world of practical, as opposed to theoretical, music criticism, Adorno is a non-entity, a far lesser figure than, say, Wagner's nemesis, Eduard Hanslick; the erudite Americans James Huneker, Harold C. Schonberg, and Joseph Kerman; and one of the earliest and best music critics, the great composer Robert Schumann. Like every other member of the Frankfurt School, Adorno lies in his grave largely unread.

My own mentor, Schonberg—for many years the chief music critic of the *New York Times*—used to say that critics ought to be remembered for their hits, not their misses, the talents they discovered, not the talents they overrated. In my case, I am proud to have championed the works of Steve Reich, Philip Glass, and John Adams at a time when they were scorned by others as "needle-stuck-in-groove" minimalists. Schumann's famous hailing of the young Chopin—"hats off, gentlemen, a genius!"—remains the classic of the genre, written in Schumann's very first published review:

> *It seems to me, moreover, that every composer has his own particular way of arranging the notes on paper; Beethoven looks different to the eye than Mozart, just as the prose of Jean Paul differs from that of Goethe. But now I felt as I were being watched by strange, wondering eyes, the eyes of flowers, of basilisks, peacock-eyes, young girls' eyes. In a few places the light became clearer—I thought I could discern Mozart's* Là ci darem la mano *wrapped in a hundred chords. I saw Leporello blinking at me and Don Giovanni flying past in a white cloak.*

The piece in question, Chopin's Op. 2, was the Variations on "*Là ci darem la mano*" from *Don Giovanni*, for piano and orchestra, with which the young French-Polish composer announced his arrival on the

European musical scene in 1831. Chopin and Schumann were both born in 1810, a few months apart, with Schumann the younger. And yet, as the music critic of the *Allgemeine Musikalische Zeitung* and a budding composer himself, he was keenly sensitive to, and appreciative of, contemporary musical trends. Schumann and Chopin had little stylistically in common, especially pianistically, but Schumann knew genius when he heard it, perhaps because he was one himself.

Contrast Schumann's poetic description of Chopin's gloss on Mozart with these plodding and flatly wrong observations from Adorno (one of Alban Berg's composition pupils and an Arnold Schoenberg devotee, one should remember) when discussing the contemporary music of his time. Apologies in advance for the mind-numbing prose (ably translated by Robert Hullot-Kentor) of Adorno's *Philosophy of New Music* (1949):

> *The best works of Béla Bartók, who in many respects sought to reconcile Schoenberg and Stravinsky, are probably superior to Stravinsky's in density and ampleness. And the second neoclassical generation—names such as Paul Hindemith and Darius Milhaud—has adjusted to the general tendency of the age with less scruple and thus, at least to all appearances, reflects it with greater fidelity than does the movement's own leader, with his cloaked and therefore absurdly exaggerated conformism. This is not, however, because historical priority is their due and the others are derivative of them but because they alone, by virtue of their uncompromising rigor, drove the impulses that inhere in their works so far that these works become legible as ideas of the thing itself.*

It is difficult to take this gibberish (like the meaningless but emphatically Marxist phrase "false musical consciousness") seriously, either as musical criticism or philosophy, despite the whiff of Kant. Bartók has little or nothing to do either with Schoenberg or Stravinsky, the two great rival expatriates in Southern California when Adorno also was living in Los Angeles. The German Schoenberg, the father of the twelve-tone system (and the unhappy model for the mad, syphilitic serialist composer Adrian Leverkühn in Mann's last novel, *Doctor Faustus*), and the Russian Stravinsky were rival leaders of two camps: one adhering to the new "comprehensive" system of egalitarian twelve-tone composition, and the other representing an older wing of the avant-garde, now tamed and transmogrified into neoclassicism. Stravinsky would later turn to the twelve-tone system himself in such later works as *Agon,* signaling a surrender to the "arc of history."

Bartók, by contrast, was a stubbornly Hungarian composer and musicological researcher, making liberal use of Magyar—not Romany—folk elements in his compositions. Outside of Hungary, he established no "school of" and left few acolytes. Neither was he as formally innovative as either Schoenberg or Stravinsky, although his music is every bit the equal of theirs technically and a good deal superior to Schoenberg's, expressively. About the only relationship between Bartók and Stravinsky might be their shared interest in folk music (much greater on Bartók's part) and that both wrote early ballets. It's also hard to see how either Milhaud or Hindemith figures into the argument, since those two composers have little or nothing do with each other.

But then Adorno wasn't very much interested in the *musical* side of music criticism; rather, it was the larger philosophical issues that obsessed him. Music just happened to be the vehicle for his musings, "new music" in particular (specifically the so-called Second Viennese School of Schoenberg, Berg, and Webern). Proving to a largely uninterested world the value of the dodecaphonic (twelve-tone) method of composition became Adorno's particular axe to grind, and he concludes his essay on "Schoenberg and Progress" in this way:

> *The world is the Sphinx and the artist is the blinded Oedipus, and the artworks resemble his wise answer, which topples the Sphinx into the abyss. Thus, all art stands opposed to mythology. Its natural "material" contains the "answer," the one possible and correct answer, always already contained, though indistinctly. . . . New music sacrifices itself to this. It has taken all the darkness and the guilt of the world on itself. All its happiness is in the knowledge of unhappiness; all its beauty is in denial of the semblance of the beautiful. No one, neither individuals nor groups, wants to have anything to do with it. It dies away unheard, without an echo. Around music as it is heard, time springs together in a radiant crystal, while unheard it tumbles perniciously through empty time. Toward this latter experience, which mechanical music undergoes hour by hour, new music is spontaneously aimed: toward absolute oblivion. It is the true message in the bottle.*

And "absolute oblivion" is about where the "new music" has ended up. Theoretically dominant in my student days at the Eastman School of Music, in Rochester, New York, the works of the Second Viennese School are rarely played in concert today. Berg, Adorno's teacher, remains in the repertory, especially via his operas *Wozzeck* (not twelve-tone, except in one section) and *Lulu*, but Schoenberg's influence as a teacher has waned almost to the vanishing point, his "comprehensive" method of composing with all twelve tones now all but abandoned by twenty-first-century composers.

From a distance, one hears the echoes of a degenerate Wagnerism in Adorno's simultaneously overwrought and stultifying writings—a Wagnerism evident in the only major work of Schoenberg still performed with any regularity today, the early tone poem *Verklärte Nacht* (Transfigured Night). "Absolute oblivion" is nothing if not Wagnerian; the desire for death is never very far from the same Central European ethos that gave us both the Frankfurt School and Hitler's Reich, however much they might appear to otherwise oppose each other. The modern suicide cult of the Left owes a great deal to these leftist movements: a desire to sink slowly, lifeless, to the ground in the manner of a Wagnerian heroine.

But when you look closely at Adorno's writing, as in these all-too-representative excerpts, you see a hollowness at the core: fire from ice, amounting to nothing. Adorno's effect on the musical life of his time was negligible: special pleading for a "system" that had found only theoretical favor and that has now lost even that. Its pretensions to "comprehensitivity" destroyed, we can now see this "system" as a form of intellectual charlatanism, a studied fascination with process and minutiae that bespeaks the true soul of the born bureaucrat—the man who does nothing in particular, and to no societal good, but who by his own lights does it very well.

In Adorno's music criticism, there is plenty of criticism but precious little about music, all Faust and no Heinrich. It is as if the art existed purely for his exegetical pleasure, an opportunity to torment the "awful German language" (in Mark Twain's famous phrase) the way Mephisto tormented poor Faust. (Mr. Morgan, in Twain's *A Connecticut Yankee in King Arthur's Court*: "Whenever the literary German dives into a sentence, that is the last you are going to see of him till he emerges on the other side of his Atlantic with his verb in his mouth.")

Complexity comes with the language, the territory, and the mind-set. Germany is a land in which a pianist cannot properly probe the depths of the late Beethoven piano sonatas until he is a decade or so past the age that Beethoven was when he died (fifty-seven); Liszt, somehow, managed to play the thorniest of them all, the "*Hammerklavier*," in Paris in 1836, when he was about twenty-five, and he ran through most of the rest of the cycle in the 1840s. Today, an eighty-year-old conductor might barely, just barely, be able to plumb the depths of *The Magic Flute*, written when Mozart was thirty-five.

Adorno is very much a child of his time and of his native language, his sentences crossing and re-crossing the Atlantic like a steamship line with no home port. The facile twist, which he learned from Marx, is one of his stocks-in-trade, as if he were a cheeky *New York Times* op-ed columnist: "All satire is blind to the forces liberated by decay. Which is why total decay has absorbed the forces of satire" (*Minima Moralia*). Defending his beloved new music, he is so caught up in the majesty of his own analysis that he inadvertently makes the case for the opposition: "Among the reproaches that they obstinately repeat, the most prevalent is the charge of intellectualism, the claim that new music springs from the head, not from the heart or the ear; or likewise, that the music is not sonorously imagined but only worked out on paper. The poverty of these clichés is manifest." This is a near-perfect description of the bulk of Schoenberg's output and most of what followed him: music worked out on paper.

Adorno seems to have learned nothing from his teacher, Berg, who showed in works such as his *Lyric Suite* and Violin Concerto to what magnificent use some of Schoenberg's theories and methods could be put in the hands of a proper musician. "They are put forward as if the tonal idiom of the past 350 years were itself given by nature," Adorno complained in *Philosophy of New Music*, "and as if it were an attack on nature to go beyond what has been habitually ground in, whereas, on the contrary, what has been ground in bears witness to social pressure." On the contrary!

Black is white, up is down, war is peace. What is, isn't; and what isn't, is. Who are you going to believe? Adorno, or your lying ears? Like Faust, we have rejected the familiar for the unknown and then, belatedly, found out we didn't much care for it after all. But, just as it was when I was a music student, what was *good for us* had to be plainly better than not only what we liked but also what we *felt in our hearts*. A System had arrived, express delivery from Darmstadt (one of the postwar centers of "new music" after the war). Like all systems, it purported to solve all the problems of the earlier systems, to supersede them. Like Islam, it would be the seal of revelation, after which nothing further would be necessary. Thereafter, it would just be a matter of study and mastery, with an infinite world of expressivity lying just beyond the horizon, once everyone had completely rejected the old way of thinking and composing and adopted the new.

The irony was, as many of us noticed at the time, that there was little difference aurally between rigorously serialized music (in which no note could be repeated before the other eleven in the "tone row" had been heard) and what was called aleatoric, or "chance," music (in which many of the musical lines were simply improvised in an often random and haphazard fashion). That is to say, complete control of the material and a near-complete lack of control curiously produced more or less the same aural results. Audiences couldn't really tell the difference, so why bother?

The answer from the serialists was: because. Because a great deal of intellectual work had gone into the structure of the dodecaphonic piece, worked out on paper; it could not be compared with chance music, even if there was a resemblance in performance. One was "deep," the other was not. And both were superior to the tonal idiom of the past 350 years because ... they were new.

This circular reasoning is, I believe, one of the attractions of Critical Theory and progressivism in general. It appears to require thought, but in fact all it requires is faith—faith in the ritual and the dogma and in the trappings of thought, but always in the service of novelty for its own sake, masquerading as "dissent" or "revolution." As Orwell predicted in *1984,* sloganeering eventually must replace free inquiry if the System is to survive and prosper; there can be not even a single ray of light in the darkness, lest the people glimpse the truth.

CHAPTER NINE

THE VENUSBERG OF DEATH

It is the thesis of this book that the heroic narrative is not simply our way of telling ourselves comforting fairy tales about the ultimate triumph of Good over Evil, but an implanted moral compass that guides even the least religious among us. Note here that the Left constantly invokes morality—indeed, often quotes from scripture—while refusing to identify the source of its morality. If "social justice" morally demands equality of outcome, obtained by stealing property and selling it to someone else in exchange for his vote, then what is to stop "social justice" proponents from arbitrarily announcing at a future date that it also morally demands the death of its opponents? What, after all, is the material difference between "thou shalt not steal" and "thou shalt not kill?"

To the Left, there is no material difference; for them, effectively, both Commandments have been repealed, one by the legislative process (the welfare state) and the other by judicial fiat (*Roe v. Wade*).

No issue motivates them more than the demographic self-destruction known as abortion; as has often been noted, "a woman's right to choose" (their favored euphemism) is for them a secular sacrament, and the more babies killed in the womb, the better. Never mind that a rational person would think that a woman's right to choose might be better and less lethally exercised at the moment when she considers whether to have unprotected sex with any given man; if you are going to stop conception, why not start at the beginning? It's not as if condoms and other prophy-lactics are not readily available. But there is no logic to their malevolence. It is not enough, in the leftist scheme of things, to be able to have as much sex as one wants; no, it must be *consequence-free* sex. The wages of libertinism might be death, but death only for the unwanted by-product of libertinism itself. According to their lights, no female participant in the sex act should ever be held responsible for anything. She should have absolute right to the Pill, to an abortifacient, to an abortion, even a partial-birth abortion. Or—should she finally invoke her "right to choose" upon childbirth, and choose life, she should have the unquestioned right to financial support from the father, whoever he may be. The chant of Thanatos as the prescription for Eros is never very far from their lips.

In a larger sense, however, that would be death for thee but not for me. Despite their cultish fascination with the deaths of others—whether babies in utero or the millions who have died under National Socialism and international Communism—leftists generally try to live as long as possible themselves; cowards to a man, there is literally nothing they would die for, not even their own alleged principles. Largely deficient in the self-sacrifice gene, and with the word "altruism" essentially foreign to them, they are obsessed with their health, with medical care and coer-cive government schemes to "provide" such services at someone else's expense. Always cloaking their demand for larger, more intrusive, and more punitive government in the guise of "compassion," the only thing they are willing to fight for (other than "the Fight" itself) is their own survival, even as they declare it to be utterly meaningless.

And yet Death fascinates them. Whether it is the death of society (think of Lukács's constant invocations of "destruction" and "annihila-tion") or the deaths of millions of innocents in the purges and atrocities of National Socialism and Soviet-style Communism (can't make an omelet without breaking some eggs), death is a constant feature both of their philosophy and their political prescriptions, which include not only abortion but, increasingly, euthanasia. Wearing their customary mask of solicitous compassion, they can't wait for you to die to steal your stuff.

There's a remarkable passage in the second act of Wagner's *Siegfried* in which Mime—the brother of the evil master dwarf Alberich, who has raised the orphan foundling Siegfried to young manhood—tries to tell Siegfried how much he cares for him and loves him. But Siegfried has just slain the dragon Fafner and tasted its blood, which has given him the power to understand the speech of animals and penetrate human lies and illusions. So he understands all too well that Mime simply wants to kill him and take the hoard of gold—as well as the magic *Tarnhelm* and the powerful Ring—for himself. After hearing his stepfather out, Siegfried dispatches him with a snickersnack of his vorpal blade, *Nothung* (his father Siegmund's sword, handed down from Siegmund's father, Wotan). Then he tosses Mime's corpse on the golden hoard and blocks the entrance to Fafner's lair with the dragon's own dead body.

It is a powerful and lesser-remarked moment of symbolism in the *Ring*, which has otherwise been exhaustively analyzed. Siegfried has come to Fafner's cave not to seek treasure but to learn the meaning of fear. But he fails to find it in the former Giant (and one of the builders of Valhalla) who has transformed himself into the dragon, a *Wurm* who, though terrifying, spends most of his days napping as he guards the Rhine Gold that Alberich stole from the Rhine Maidens—the original sin that sets the entire cycle in motion.

Although the opera is called "Siegfried," for the first two acts it might as well be called "Fafner," since it is the dragon's suffocating presence that suffuses the musical language from the opening of the first act: low strings and low brass color the orchestration, and we sense that Siegfried's confrontation with the monster approaches with every beat and bar. It is only in the third act that the hero finally encounters the only thing he will ever fear: Woman, in the form of the enchanted Brünnhilde, leading to the cycle's most inadvertently comical line, *"Das ist kein Mann!"* ("That is no man!"), which Siegfied exclaims as he removes the sleeping Valkyrie's breastplate to suddenly confront what lies beneath.

And yet it's not really funny, now matter how buxom the soprano portraying Brünnhilde might be. Siegfried has met everything in his short life—dwarves, monsters, even his own grandfather, Wotan, disguised as The Wanderer, whom he defeats in combat by shattering the Spear (the visible and aural symbol of Wotan's authority), thus sealing his fate, Brünnhilde's, and the fate of all the gods—but he has not yet met The Other, the *Ewig-Weibliche*, the Eternal Feminine. Only Brünnhilde can strike fear into his fearless breast; only she can bewitch him. It takes that favorite Wagnerian device, a magic potion, to make him betray her. Only she can redeem him and consummate his quest to return the Ring to its rightful owners, the Rhine Maidens (who, with their voluptuous bodies, try in vain to seduce him) and bring about the end of the gods, a doom that, by the end of the tetralogy, is something the defeated Wotan, hoist upon his own petard, himself devoutly wishes.

Wagner began as a man of the Left: a firebrand during the Continent-wide republican, anti-monarchical Revolutions of 1848, a fugitive for years thereafter, and a vicious anti-Semite (except musically; Wagner's first major opera, *Rienzi*, consciously aped Meyerbeer, and when it came time for the premiere of his Christian epic, *Parsifal*, he chose a Jew, Hermann Levi, to conduct it). He was also a relentless seducer of other men's wives and taker of other men's money, including most famously that of King Ludwig II of Bavaria, who partly built Bayreuth for him. Most notoriously, Wagner was an idol of Adolf Hitler's. Born six years after Wagner's death, Hitler, as *Reichskanzler*, attempted to stage *Die Meistersinger von Nürnberg* with all Germany as the set and wound up producing *Götterdämmerung* instead.

(It is an oddity of history that Wagner privately feared he was part Jewish, as did the high-ranking Nazi Reinhard Heydrich—the principal architect of the Final Solution—and as did even Hitler himself. Wagner's uncertainty about his paternity—his stepfather, the actor Ludwig Geyer, who may or may not have been Jewish, may also have been Wagner's biological father—was a source of deep concern to him.)

But musically and dramatically, it is another story. In this arena, Wagner was no scapegrace. Without question, he is the dominant fig-ure of nineteenth-century music, perhaps of any art of the Romantic period. Yes, "Wagner has his great moments and long half hours," as the possibly apocryphal saying goes. (This has been attributed variously to, among others, Mark Twain and Rossini, who died in 1868, shortly before the premiere of *Das Rheingold*, the first of the *Ring* operas, and well before most of Wagner's mature works.) And yet Wagner's influence has been so profound that, almost from the start, he created a cult of personality around himself (as "the Master") that has lasted well over a century and counting.

True, some acolytes—Friedrich Nietzsche, in *Nietzsche contra Wagner* and in *Der Fall Wagner: Ein Musikanten-Problem* (*The Case of Wagner: A Musician's Problem*)—broke with him, criticizing him both personally and musically. Freed of Mephisto's "bands of illusion," or, in Wagner's case, Klingsor's (how ironic that in Goethe's poem, Faust's pupil is named Wagner), these acolytes came to see him as a cheap trickster, a manipulator of conventional musical tropes—new wine in old bottles—and purveyor of half-baked philosophical ideas derived from his betters, such as Fichte and Hegel. Nietzsche wrote of Wagner's musical technique:

> *If we wish to admire him, we should observe him at work: how he separates and distinguishes, how he arrives at small unities, and how he galvanizes them, accentuates them, and brings them into preeminence. But in this way he exhausts his strength; the rest is worthless. How paltry, awkward, and amateurish is his manner of "developing," his attempt at combining incompatible parts.*

There is much truth in this statement. Wagner's control of inherited musical forms was shaky at best. His early piano sonatas are forgettable, and the "Centennial March," written for the American birthday of 1876, feels mercenary, knocked out for the money. (As it was: Wagner had lifelong financial problems, and 1876 was the year of the first performance of the *Ring* cycle at Bayreuth, a particularly desperate time.) The fake counterpoint in the *Meistersinger* overture is perhaps the low point of Wagner's mature technique; it's really just ornamentation, made to feel structural, but we fall for it anyway. Aside from the music dramas, Wagner has little else to offer, and were it not for them and his overwhelming drive to succeed across all cultural fronts, he would probably be a minor or even forgotten figure today.

David Goldman (who often writes as "Spengler") takes on *Der Fall Wagner* with characteristic perspicacity and eloquence in a long essay written for the magazine *First Things* in December 2010. He sees Wagner as a false Redeemer—the quintessential leftist—a magician who loses his luster once you catch on to his tricks. Goldman places Wagner squarely in a Faustian context:

> *Wagner had a gift, as well as an ideological purpose, for the intensification of the moment. If Goethe's Faust bets the Devil that he can resist the impulse to hold on to the passing moment [Werd' ich zum Augenblicke sagen: / Verweile doch! Du bist so schön! / Dann magst du mich in Fesseln schlagen / Dann will ich gern zugrunde gehn! (Were I to say*

to the moment: / "Abide with me! You are so beautiful!" / Then you may
clap me in irons, / Then may I wish to go to perdition!)], Wagner dives
headfirst into its black well. And if Faust argues that life itself depends
on transcending the moment, Wagner's sensuous embrace of the musical
moment conjures a dramatic trajectory toward death....

Wagner was more than a musician. He was the prophet of a new artistic
cult, a self-styled poet and dramatist who believed that his "totalizing work
of art" (Gesamtkunstwerk) would replace Europe's enervated religion. His
new temporal aesthetic served a larger goal: the liberation of impulse from
the bonds of convention.

In other words, a classic leftist: anti-religious, anti-Semitic, and
obsessed with death. Nearly all of Wagner's heroines meet their demise;
as Goldman quips: "The opera's not over 'til the fat lady dies." The heroes
fare little better. Wagner even provides us with his own version of the
Devil's Pleasure Palace, the seductive erotic prison of the Venusberg in
Tannhäuser.

So is there a contradiction in praising Wagner within the context of
our ur-Narrative? I think not. The solution lies in separating the man
from his work. Most among us would find Wagner the man reprehensible;
we would not want him for a friend or an ally or a son-in-law. However,
he had what I term the "necessary selfishness of the artist," the drive that
pushes everything else before it, subsuming all life's tragedies, triumphs,
and experience into fuel for the larger mission—the creation of art, which
is what brings us closer to God.

It is perfectly possible to think that Wagner was, "like the Nazis, a
neo-pagan," as Goldman puts it, adding: "Wagner provided much of the
Third Reich's background music, and not without an underlying affinity.
... Very little distinguishes Siegfried, who is too impulsive to pay atten-
tion to rules, from Parsifal—the protagonist of Wagner's last opera—
who is too innocent to understand them. ... If the Germans, in Franz
Rosenzweig's bon mot, could not tell Christ from Siegfried, it is because
Wagner deliberately conflated the two."

But Siegfried never feels Christlike; his sacrifice is pathetic but
unmoving. He dies because he has made a cardinal error; fearing nothing but Brünnhilde's sexual allure, he turns his back on the Nibelung's

bastard, a mortal enemy he cannot not recognize. Whereas Christ, in his sacrifice on the Cross, consciously picks up Satan's gauntlet and accepts the mortal challenge posed by the Battle in Heaven, after the spawning of Sin and Death. On his visit to Hell, Christ not only defeats Satan but vanquishes Sin and Death as well, for all those who (in the Christian theology) believe.

Let us contrast for the moment, Wagner's heroic Romanticism —like Beethoven, he shook his fists at the heavens—with that of a true believer, J.S. Bach, and specifically Bach's *Goldberg Variations* (1741). At first glance, no two works could be more unlike than this set of variations, which, according to legend, were written to cure the insomnia of one Count Kaiserling, the Russian ambassador to the Saxon court, who brought along his attendant, Goldberg, to play the harpsichord for him during his sleepless hours and requested a piece from the great court composer.

Nothing could have prepared Kaiserling or Goldberg or posterity for what followed. At a single stroke, Bach established the variations form, daring all subsequent composers (including Beethoven, who tried with *"Diabelli"* *Variations*, and Brahms in the *"Handel"* *Variations*). But more: Putting the little theme through its paces in what is essentially an extended chaconne, Bach colors a canvas of unearthly proportions, each variation moving inevitably to the next, until the great "Thirtieth Variation," which finally reveals the true harmonic and melodic possibilities inherent in the melody. The last variation is a magic trick worthy of Klingsor himself, a revelation of the immanence in all God's works. At once sacred and profane, a combination of the harmonic structure of the initial theme and several German folk songs, it stunningly proclaims Bach's musical command—"Look at what I have wrought!"—and then immediately self-effaces with a quiet recapitulation of the melody, which just might be the greatest humblebrag of all time.

(The playwright Peter Shaffer may well have had this effect in mind when he wrote the scene in *Amadeus* in which Mozart takes Antonio Salieri's simple "March of Welcome" and turns it into the "Non più andrai" march from the end of Act One of *The Marriage of Figaro*, humiliating his rival in front of the emperor and earning his undying enmity.)

Both Bach and Wagner champion man's unique nature; both reach for the stars, although it may be Wagner who lies in the gutter while Bach tidies up the Thomaskirche in Leipzig. Still, their unpoliticized mission (for we must see music and art as separate and apart from politics, no matter the quotidian circumstances that give them birth) is the same: to make man transcend himself and become closer to God. (Wagner's musical genius overrode his crude politics, fortunately.) To reject the transcendence of art is to reject God. Art that is cheap and vulgar no more approaches the Godhead, or taps into that inner ur-Narrative, than cotton candy approaches the state of either cotton or candy.

And this is the distinction we must make when assaying the Western cultural canon. Like Marcus Aurelius in his *Meditations*, we must ask: "What is this thing in itself? What is its function in the world?" The answer is the same as Milton's in *Paradise Lost:* to justify the ways of God to men.

The question of text, therefore, becomes subordinate to the question of meaning. The text of the *Goldberg Variations*, the "aria" that opens and closes the great keyboard work, is trivial, as is, for that matter, the theme of the "*Diabelli*" *Variations*. The poems of the four *Ring* cycle operas could not stand alone as poetry, although Wagner might have supposed they could. In fact, he wrote them in reverse order as he hammered out his massive masterpiece, waiting for his musical expertise to catch up to the demands of *Siegfried*'s third act and *Götterdämmerung*. (In between, on a break that lasted more than a decade, he wrote *Tristan* and *Meistersinger*.)

The error comes in putting text before subtext, which is to say misreading the purpose of both dramatic music and "absolute" music (music without a text or programmatic subject). Music was part of the medieval *quadrivium*, the four subjects, derived from the Greeks, along with arithmetic, geometry and astronomy, which is to say that it was deemed to have its own independent meaning. Combined with the *trivium* (grammar, logic, and rhetoric), it was one of the foundations of a young man's education.

Both Salieri and Richard Strauss wrote operas that examine the relation of words and music, Salieri in his *Prima la musica, e poi le parole* ("First the music, then the words"), and Strauss in his last opera, *Capriccio*, in which his heroine, the Countess, must chose between two suitors: the poet Olivier and the composer Flamand. "Is there any ending that isn't trivial?" she wonders to herself at the end, leaving us hanging. It's a joke by Strauss: To the man who made himself the hero of his own tone poem, *Ein Heldenleben*, the question was never seriously in doubt. It's a joke as well to every other composer who has ever composed an opera; the pride of place always goes to the music, a tradition maintained today in the accreditation of pop songs, which list the composer's name first and the lyricist's second—such as "Rodgers and Hart." Opera can be sung in translation, which does not change its essential meaning, but *Carmen* cannot be tricked out with a new score and remain the same. The words put us into the dramatic situation and outline its overall progression, but the music is the heart of the work.

What Critical Theory and political correctness seek to do is remove the music from our lives, to strip it, Soviet-style, of all secondary meaning, of all its layers, its poetry and (surprisingly, for this is one of the Unholy Left's favorite words) nuance. Nothing means more than what we can take at face value, except empirical evidence, which must be subjected to ceaseless analysis in an attempt to change plain meaning into something unknowable. For the Left, music functions didactically, its capacity to incite and inspire channeled into the service of the state, not the human heart. Thankfully, a losing proposition.

The Left's pleasure palaces are all around us, in their promised utopias of social justice, egalitarianism, sexual liberation, reflexive distrust of authority, and general nihilism. What they've brought about instead—as all pleasure palaces must—is death, destruction, and despair.

In 1966, Michelangelo Antonioni dropped a bombshell of a motion picture called "Blow-Up" upon an unsuspecting public. The Production Code was in hasty retreat, and *Blow-Up* titillated American audiences with its nude models writhing on purple paper with an anomic photographer played by David Hemmings. It was at once a documentary of Swinging London, a product of the Italian cinema at the top of its form, and an examination of the unknowability of knowledge. Coming just three years after the Kennedy assassination, it also played on the country's darkest obsessions—is that Black Dog Man I see in the grainy blow-ups of the grassy knoll? But most of all, it expressed precisely what was about to drive the United States of America crazy: self-doubt.

It is fitting that the screenplay was based on a short story, "Las babas del Diablo" ("The Droolings of the Devil"), for it opened the door to the daemonic that would soon flood into American movie theaters—most prominently, the quintessential alienation of Walter Penn's *Bonnie and Clyde* (1967) and Polanski's psycho-sexual horror show *Rosemary's Baby*

(1968), which made Satan one of the protagonists and the father of the eponymous baby.

The nudity in *Blow-Up* of Jane Birkin and Gillian Hills attracted a good deal of critical and prurient attention, as did a brief topless scene by Vanessa Redgrave, but the central appeal of the movie lay in Hemmings's mesmerizing performance (fittingly, in later life, he became a magician) as Thomas, the seen-it-all fashion photographer whose pointless life, illustrated by his even more pointless sex life, suddenly comes into focus when, on a whim, he snaps some shots of Redgrave and a mysterious man in Greenwich's Maryon Park. Grainy blow-ups later reveal what might be a man with a gun. Upon a return to the park, he finds a dead body but has forgotten his camera. In a timely snapshot of the zeitgeist, Thomas stops in at a nightclub where Jeff Beck, Jimmy Page, and the Yardbirds are playing; infuriated by a problem with his amp, Beck smashes his guitar on stage (à la The Who's Pete Townshend at the time), then tosses the broken guitar neck into the crowd, where Thomas scuffles for it. Out on the sidewalk, Thomas throws it away: pointless.

The daemonic, the diabolical, even a touch of "Listzomania" (the title of an over-the-top 1975 film by Ken Russell, starring The Who's lead singer, Roger Daltrey, in the title role)—*Blow-Up* had it all. But it was the haunting pantomime tennis game at the end, spontaneously played by a passing group of mimes in an open Jeep, that summed up the then-fashionable nihilistic futility of Thomas's search for the truth. When even the dead body that he thought he'd found disappears, Thomas is reduced to retrieving an imaginary tennis ball and tossing it back onto the court as everything but the grass vanishes.

Judged politically, *Blow-Up* might seem a dated piece of postwar cultural ennui. What is truth? What does it matter? Let's get laid! But that's not the way it plays. Hemmings's dispassionate photographer comes fully to life only in the presence of Death, when, in developing his pictures, he realizes that he may inadvertently have witnessed and recorded a crime, set up by Redgrave's femme fatale. The actress's haunting, aristocratic beauty was never better used, and her moment of attempted seduction—sex in exchange for the possibly incriminating photographs—remains in the mind long after other films of the period have faded. In the final scene, Hemmings casts off the bands of illusions—what he took for reality was really just a series of futile gestures, like screwing the young models or callously discarding Beck's broken guitar neck after fighting furiously for it. Only when—transformed by a woman—he accepts the reality of the pantomime tennis game does he finally become a recognizable human being; in short, redeemed.

In the end, all art conforms to the same principles, whether it is created by the Left or the Right. Nearly every Disney movie ever made tracks the hero's journey Joseph Campbell laid out, even when the hero is a heroine. The most "conservative" movie ever made is probably *High Noon* (1952), which was written by a blacklisted Communist, Carl Foreman, from a partial draft by another blacklistee, Ben Maddow. While some see a subtextual evocation of McCarthyism, the text is the story of brave marshal Will Kane (Gary Cooper) who, abandoned by the wimpy townsfolk of Hadleyville and even for a time by his pacifist Quaker wife, is forced to stand alone and face the vengeful badbellies arriving on the noon train. In the end, he's saved by his new bride, played by Grace Kelly, who shoots one of the criminals herself and tackles the head bad guy to provide her husband a clear shot at the man who has vowed to kill him.

Hollywood "formula" storytelling is often derided by those with no experience in filmmaking, or with little understanding of just what exactly that "formula" entails. But the ur-Narrative dwells deep within us, from Finn MacCool to Roland to Will Kane, and its stories are always the same—even when, on the surface, they aren't. Art has its own tricks to play on the Devil.

Illustration to Goethe's "Erlkönig," Moritz von Schwind, 1917.
A dying child and a desperate father fleeing seductive Death.

Satan Cast Out of the Hill of Heaven, Gustave Doré, 1866. The Paradise that has been irrevocably lost is not ours but Satan's. No wonder those who advocate the satanic position fight for it so fiercely.

Mephistopheles in Flight,
Eugène Delacroix, 1828.
The fallen angel, his wings still intact,
flying impudently naked above the
symbols of the Principal Enemy.

*Fantasy abandoned by
reason produces impossible
monsters: United with her,
she is the mother of the
arts and the origin
of their marvels,*
Francisco Goya, 1799.

The Great Red Dragon and the
Woman Clothed in Sun,
William Blake, 1805.
It is not for Christ to defeat Satan.
Instead, that task is given to a
woman, the Woman: Mary, the
Mother of Christ.

Gretchen im Kerker (Gretchen in
Prison), Peter Cornelius, 1815.
Sie ist gerichtet! (She is damned!)
Ist gerettet! (Is saved!)

In the Venusberg, John Collier, 1901. Wagner provides us with his own version of the Devil's Pleasure Palace, the seductive erotic prison of the Venusberg in *Tannhäuser*.

Lilith, John Collier, 1892. "She most, and in her looks sums all Delight / . Such Pleasure took the Serpent to behold… / fawning, and licked the ground whereon she trod."

CHAPTER TEN

WORLD WITHOUT GOD, AMEN

In his final book, *The Fatal Conceit*, the economic philosopher Friedrich Hayek wrote that "an atavistic longing after the life of the noble savage is the main source of the collectivist tradition." While his criticism aptly applies to all leftist critics of Western social organization, Hayek's primary target was Rousseau, the harbinger of postmodernism and the man perhaps most responsible, even more so than Marx or Gramsci or Alinsky, for the state of the modern world. If the pen is mightier than the sword, then Rousseau is Exhibit A, influencing the French Revolution, the upheavals of 1848 (in which Wagner took part) and its encore, the student "revolutions" in both Europe and America in 1968.

That year, 1968, remains one of the most significant in modern American history; it was the year things came apart and the center could not hold. During the student riots in France in May that caused de Gaulle to dissolve the National Assembly and call for new elections (which he won), my college French teacher turned to us and said, in a remark I did not fully understand at the time, "You are all just the children of Rousseau." To this day, given the passions of the moment, I am not sure whether he meant it as criticism or compliment.

For the historian Paul Johnson, the Swiss-born Rousseau is "the first of the modern intellectuals, their archetype and in many ways the most influential of them all," as he writes in his 1988 book, *Intellectuals*. He continues:

Rousseau was the first to combine all the salient characteristics of the modern Promethean: the assertion of his right to reject the existing order in its entirety; confidence in his capacity to refashion it from the bottom in accordance with principles of his own devising; belief that this could be achieved by the political process; and, not least, recognition of the huge part instinct, intuition, and impulse play in human conduct. He believed he had a unique love for humanity and had been endowed with unprecedented gifts and insights to increase its felicity. An astonishing number of people, in his own day and since, have taken him at his own valuation.

In other words, Rousseau might as well be the Second Coming of Christ. Or, failing that, the Second Coming of God himself. For what is the power to remake humanity except godlike? The more militant the atheist, it seems, the more godlike he wishes to become. His "atheism" stands revealed not as disbelief in a higher power but as an affirmative belief in *himself* as that higher power. It's often remarked that atheism is simply religion by another name (as the officially atheist, now deceased Soviet Union demonstrated). Else why would atheists be so adamant and aggressive about their beliefs? Not only do they choose not to believe in God, or even a god, but they demand that their fellow citizens submit—there is that word again—to their ideology and purge all evidence of the (Christian) religion from the public square. Never mind that the Founders were Christians (even if some of them only nominally) and fully expected their faith to undergird their new country. While the First Amendment forbids Congress from establishing a national religion, there was no such proscription against the states, and both Massachusetts and Connecticut had established churches—Congregationalism—well into the nineteenth century.

An established Church of Atheism now seems the likely fate for a country whose official motto, "In God We Trust," was codified into law as recently as 1956; the phrase "under God" had been added to the Pledge of Allegiance only two years earlier, both events during the Eisenhower administration. As usual, leftists are employing the shields of their enemy as swords against them, waging "lawfare" against American institutions with audacity and near-total impunity. Thus, in their zeal, they demonstrate the need for some sort of faith, even it is anti-faith; there is, after all, a hierarchy in Hell.

Rousseau, a man of the Enlightenment, is identified with the cult of the "noble savage," but the scope of his indictment of civilization is much wider. Rejecting nascent materialism, he espoused a view of nature that took the Romantics by storm (where would nineteenth-century Germany have been without Rousseau?) and created a new version of the Fall of Man, this time brought low not by the Serpent in the Garden but by the material advancement of the Industrial Revolution. Mankind had become divorced from the state of nature and seduced by the acquisition of property, Rousseau argued. Humanity, in his view, had become competitive, preening, boastful, and vain—in short, alienated. Born a Genevan Calvinist, and later becoming a "convert of convenience" to Catholicism in Italy, Rousseau was the archetype of the modern, dissatisfied leftist, an insolent failure at just about every trade he plied, relying for sustenance upon the kindness of strangers, especially women. Finally finding his métier, he hit upon his true calling: telling others what to do via the medium of essay and autobiography, with himself as his own hero.

As with Wagner, a cult of personality formed around the constantly querulous, paranoiac, hypochondriacal Rousseau ("one of the greatest grumblers in history," notes Johnson). He preached truth and virtue, although he had little of either—indeed, of the latter, almost none. He regularly deposited his bastard offspring by his lifelong mistress, Thérèse Levasseur (of whom he wrote, "the sensual needs I satisfied with her were purely sexual and were nothing to do with her as an individual"), on the steps of the nearest foundling hospital—five in all—and never even bothered to give them names. Like so many after him, Rousseau was one of those liberals who loved humanity but couldn't stand people.

Often contradictory in his views on atheism and religion, Rousseau nevertheless was certain of one thing: that the State should be the final arbiter of the human condition, in the name of something he called the General Will. Only the State, he thought, could make postlapsarian man well again. One can practically smell the fascism coming off his pages, all in the name of compassion, of course. No wonder his more perceptive contemporaries, including Voltaire, considered him a monster.

Many others, however, were greatly influenced by him, including most of the great monsters of the twentieth century. Without Rousseau, Marx is unthinkable; without Marx, Lenin is unthinkable; without Lenin, Stalin is unthinkable; without Stalin, Mao is unthinkable; without Mao,

Ho Chi Minh and Pol Pot are unthinkable. In *The Communist Manifesto*, Marx and Engels claimed of their Principal Enemy, the bourgeoisie: "It has left remaining no other nexus between man and man than naked self-interest, than callous 'cash payment.' It has drowned the most heavenly ecstasies of religious fervor, of chivalrous enthusiasm, of philistine sentimentalism, in the icy water of egotistical calculation."

And so on. The bit about "religious fervor," as if either of them cared a whit for it, is a nice touch, although the crack about "philistine sentimentalism" rings truer to their real ethos. La Rochefoucauld defined hypocrisy as the tribute vice pays to virtue, but what if the virtue itself is counterfeit? What if it is all a sham, a satanic illusion—the mouse emerging from the comely witch's mouth in the *Walpurgisnacht* scene from *Faust*?

In this famous scene, Faust and Mephistopheles have magically flown to the Brocken, atop the Harz Mountains, Germany's most haunted spot, to partake of the Witches' Sabbath. Mephisto is feeling old, and he identifies his own weakness with the end of the world:

MEPHISTOPHELES
I feel the people drawn to Judgment Day
For I scale this mountain for the last time
Because my keg runs turbid.
The World, too, is down to the dregs.

Then the revelries begin. Faust tells the Young Witch about a dream he's had, a dream of apples, as it happens: "I had the most wonderful dream / In which I saw an apple tree / Two beautiful apples gleamed thereupon / They lured me, and I climbed up." To which the Young Witch replies: "The little apples please you very much / Because they came from Paradise. / I feel myself moved by joy / Because they grow in my Garden as well."

This little exchange—the sacred—is immediately followed by the profane utterings of Mephistopheles, who is dancing with the Old Witch and makes a crude remark about a "cloven tree" with a hole in the middle of it: "*So—es war, gefiel mir's doch.*" ("So … it was, I liked it though.") To which this Old Witch lewdly counters with a challenge to Mephisto to provide something large enough to fill the hole.

Fruit forbidden and fruit readily available—we have seen from *Paradise Lost* that the eating of the one led to the taking of the other. From tasting of the Tree of Knowledge to history's first poetically interpolated recorded sex act—not exclusively, it should be noted, an act of love but an act of suddenly realized humanity, at once passionate, fearful, desperate, and defiant—was but the work of a moment. Which is to say, from Original Sin to the birth of the first child, Cain, history's first murderer. Condemned from the start? Or free to choose? Were Eros and Thanatos inseparable from the beginning? And which came first?

It should be here noted that there is a double sexual subtext to Milton's recounting of what took place in the Garden during that fateful encounter: Eve's desire for the apple is palpably sexual, but then so is the Serpent's desire for Eve. ("She most, and in her looks sums all Delight / Such Pleasure took the Serpent to behold ... / Fawning, and licked the ground whereon she trod.") He gazes at her naked body in highly eroticized awe and, appealing to her vanity, tells her that she is too beautiful not to be admired by all.

His temptation to her, remember, is to remove God from Paradise by becoming like a god herself. So, practically from Creation, the notion of a world without God was formed. And yet, as history shows, man has signally failed at replacing God. Rousseau's life and works are proof that vice and virtue may be, when combined in the same man, not hypocrisy but evil. That Rousseau's life, like Marx's, was devoted entirely to self-aggrandizement masquerading as empathy for his fellow man is beyond dispute. (Rousseau conflated himself and his own needs, wants, desires, and hopes with those of all humanity, something entirely characteristic of many a leftist.) So is the fact that so many fell (and fall to this day) for his professions of benevolence.

Earlier we have noted, in the case of Wagner for example, that one must separate the man from his art to get a clearer picture of each and make a true assessment of the art. It is easy, in this age of political correctness, to trump up a series of latter-day charges against almost any dead individual, exhume his corpse, and, like a Cadaver Synod run by a grad-school Nuremberg court, like Cromwell or the Mahdi (the two have much in common besides the manner of their posthumous desecration), cut off his head, mount it on a pike, and chuck the body into a ditch.

So let us look, then, at the art: What we see in the works of Rousseau is something archetypically inimical to Western civilization, the godless worm at the core of Eve's apple. Rousseau was the viper in the breast, "the whisperer in darkness" (the title of another memorable Lovecraft short story), the tempter hissing in the bulrushes.

There are few more arresting images in all of literature than the opening of *Paradise Lost*, which finds Satan and his cohort chained to the Lake of Fire and wondering how the hell they got there. The bard dares open his long poem in medias res; the Battle in Heaven has already played out before curtain rise. What is Satan's first desire? Revenge. Helpless to restorm Heaven, the fallen archangel who once attended the very throne of Heaven can now only plot against God's new toy, humanity. In the poem's second book, during the infernal conference among Satan and his henchmen, Moloch makes the argument:

> *Or if our substance be indeed divine,*
> *And cannot cease to be, we are at worst*
> *On this side nothing; and by proof we feel*
> *Our power sufficient to disturb his heaven,*
> *And with perpetual inroads to alarm,*
> *Though inaccessible, his fatal throne:*
> *Which if not victory is yet revenge.*

Satan and his minions have one small advantage. God has given mankind pride of place over the angels, because unlike them, Man has free will. (Which raises the question: Why was Lucifer suddenly afflicted with the very human sins of pride and jealousy, which occasioned the rebellion in Heaven in the first place? Was that not a human characteristic?) But the angels cannot protect Man against Satan's blandishments; mankind is, to mix a metaphor, a sitting duck.

Sin and Death come before human love. The sexual act—the thing that brings humans closest to God—is only possible after the Fall. The first human child, Cain, kills his brother, Abel, and then receives the Mark of Cain from God in return—not as a sign that he is cursed but that he is protected, and that God and God alone may be allowed vengeance upon Cain for his transgression.

So the innate nature of Man is not divine, but wild: his hand against every man's, and every man's hand against his. (As the voluptuous Toon occasion of sin, Jessica Rabbit, says to the human detective, Eddie Valiant, in *Who Framed Roger Rabbit*: "I'm not bad, I'm just drawn that way.") This would seem to be evidence that the myth of the noble savage is not foundational, since the story of the Fall well precedes Rousseau; Adam and Eve did not begin as savages, but their children became them, and they were hardly noble.

For "savage" is the operative word, not "noble." The Unholy Left has little use for nobility, except in the service of its moral fantasies. But the savage … oh, him they admire. The child of nature, needless of religious superstition and heedless of civilization. Running free, living off the land, a tomahawk or spear in his hand, killing as he goes. The very thought shivers their knickers.

Destruction fascinates them; they find satisfaction and even con-summation in the tearing-down, not the building-up. Creation is a bore; annihilation is a joy. They take a childish pleasure in extermination, and the most extreme eliminationist rhetoric (meant purely rhetorically, of course!) is never very far from their lips. So much of leftist art of the past century and more is the tiresome mud-splatterings of those whose mantra is *épater le bourgeois*, while they finger their imaginary daggers and wish they had the courage to plunge them into their patrons' breasts. Not believing in Heaven, they not only wish their own heaven here on earth, but its earthly revenge as well.

But that is what the atheist State is for. That would be the *armed* atheist State, whose agents are legally equipped with lethal means to force compliance with its wishes and diktats. In the State's precincts, one is free only insofar as one's actions and predilections and even thoughts conform with those of the State—Rousseau's General Will.

Anyone who lives in a major American city controlled by leftists is familiar with a notice posted in front of many of the best houses in the poshest (and usually therefore the most racially segregated) neighbor-hoods: ARMED RESPONSE. This does not mean that the inhabitants of such a dwelling are in favor of the Second Amendment, which guarantees the individual's right—the *right*, not the State's optional dispensation— "to keep and bear arms." Far from it. Rather, it signifies that the owner reserves the right to have a secondary, contracted employee arrive at his premises in response to an electronic alarm and possibly employ deadly force against whichever miscreant may be in the process of violating the laws against burglary, especially if that violation occurs when the owner—who in fact does not believe in the Second Amendment and on moral grounds would never have a gun in his house—is at home.

This is the essence of La Rochefoucauld's dictum that hypocrisy is the tribute vice (anti-Constitutionalism) plays to virtue (self-defense). It is also the sign of a degenerate culture posing as a virtuous one; it is as if Gary Cooper's Will Kane, faced with his own imminent demise, had tossed away his six-shooter, embraced his wife's Quaker passivity, and gone willingly to his death at the hands of the varmints coming to kill him—but with the foreknowledge that his own hired band of gunslingers would show up at the station just in time to save him from the consequences of his unmanly rectitude. Where is the heroism in that?

There's the rub. I have been discussing the inherent, innate ur-Narrative that is implanted in every human's breast, but I've failed to note that there are two different versions of heroism, and of the hero's archetypal journey. I've thus far failed to note it because one version is anti-heroism aping heroism, the heroism of the suicide cult, which decrees it is better to die "nobly"—that is, passively, "like a dog!" as Joseph K. exclaims right before he is executed at the end of Franz Kafka's *Der Prozess* (*The Trial*)—than to fight back. This is not heroism; it is the behavior of a goldfish being flushed down a toilet, and with as much moral resonance and suasion.

Kafka, the greatest Jewish writer of the fin-de-siècle, and one of the greatest writers of the modern age, is an especially persuasive witness on this point. The poet of Prague and its discontents could not have been more prophetic about our rancid past century had he tried. A more anti-savage intellectual—the anti-Rousseau in almost every particular—could hardly be imagined. Here was a man who foresaw the horrors to come, looked at them unflinchingly, and recorded his nightmares in lucid, beautiful German.

"Someone must have slandered Josef K., for one morning, without having done anything truly wrong, he was arrested," begins *The Trial*, and there is probably not a more arresting opening sentence in modern literature. Like Gregor Samsa in *Die Verwandlung* (*The Metamorphosis*), Josef K. awakens from what must have been uneasy dreams to find his life transformed, and not in a good way. An "investigation of a citizen above suspicion" (to quote the title of the 1970 Italian film directed by Elio Petri) then ensues, and Josef K. becomes ever more deeply drawn into the insane workings of a "justice" system that bears no resemblance to any justice he can conceive of. What is his crime? What has he done? What is the truth? Who knows? Who cares? The State, like God, has its reasons, and they are not for mortals to know. "The proper understanding of any matter and the misunderstanding of the same matter do not wholly exclude one another," the priest instructs Josef K. Three felonies a day, etc.

Josef K. has entered the Devil's Pleasure Palace—a topsy-turvy, not-so-fun house in which "up is down, black is white," as the line in the Coen brothers' masterpiece, *Miller's Crossing,* goes. In that film, Tom Reagan (Gabriel Byrne) takes Bernie Bernbaum (John Turturro) out to Miller's Crossing to whack him. Bernie exclaims: "I can't die here out here in the woods, like a dumb animal," echoing Josef K.'s last words. And Tom (like Upham in *Saving Private Ryan*) lets him go, to his eternal regret. What's done may not be undone—"What's done is past! What's past is done!" exclaims Mephistopheles during the *Walpurgisnacht*—but what's not done in the past surely must be undone in the present for the future to have any meaning. Thus, eventually, Upham must kill Steamboat Willie; Tom must kill Bernie. Even though both killings are done in cold blood, and both are most certainly a crime, neither feels wrong. Rather, the universe has been put right, at whatever the cost to the killer's immortal soul.

Kafka himself died in 1924, six months before Adolf Hitler was released from Landsberg Prison. And yet Kafka had foreseen it all before it even happened: the blunt force of the State, in *The Trial* and *The Castle*; the savagery of the Soviet occupation of Germany, in "*Ein Altes Blatt*" ("An Old Manuscript"); even Henze's talking trained ape, in "*Ein Bericht für eine Akademie*" (A Report to an Academy"). Not to mention the adumbrations of the horrors of the Nazi concentration camps and their grisly "medical" experiments, and the Soviet Gulag, in "*In der Strafkolonie*" ("In the Penal Colony"), with its graphic depiction of a machine that tattoos the sentence on the condemned prisoner as he dies.

In Kafka's world, a world in which God is conspicuously absent, man is a plaything; he can be turned into an ape or a giant bug in the blink of an eye, condemned and executed for nothing. Even the Greeks had more of a chance than this. There is nothing of the noble savage about Kafka; on the contrary, Man is what stands between the State and utter anarchy, not the other way around. (One thinks of Terry Gilliam's best film, *Brazil*, in this context, which also takes *1984* as an inspiration.)

Were there in fact such as thing as a really Noble Savage—not as envisioned by Rousseau, but an authentic hero—what would he look like? Expressed in a modern context, he might be Winston Smith in *1984*; he would be any one of scores of Hollywood heroes who fight the power in service of individual freedom. He is Will Kane in *High Noon*, Hawkeye in *The Last of the Mohicans*, Neo in *The Matrix,* battling an endless army of Mr. Smiths. He is Man against the Machine.

In short, he's us. He has no need for the State. He has only a need for like-minded fellows to support him in his quest and carry on the work after he is gone. He is Jesus, the crisis in the life of God. The story, infinitely refracted, infinitely recursive, goes on. We keep telling it because we need to, to keep the forces of Hell at bay. Hell has no need for heroes; God does. That we keep providing them is one of the surest proofs of his existence.

CHAPTER ELEVEN

OF EROS AND THANATOS

In 1931, two strains of twentieth-century thought combined forces at the *Institut für Sozialforschung*: Freudian psychiatry and social Marxism. Among the shrinks was Wilhelm Reich, who later fled the Nazis and settled in America, where he (to quote the website Marxists.org) "developed his own doctrine of sexual liberalism as an antidote to political conformism and social psychosis." After Marcuse, no other member of the Frankfurt School had such a negative impact on the culture.

Too crazy even for the Freudians and the social Marxists, all of Reich's work after 1932 (he died in 1957) was initially self-published. Sex-mad in a way that embarrassed his Freudian cronies and amoral Marxist colleagues alike (he coined the term "the sexual revolution"), Reich believed that the problems of economic Marxism were caused by sexual frustration, which hindered the political consciousness of the proletariat. He stripped his patients nude, the better to break down their "muscular armor," and pursued "vegetotherapy" while chasing the perfect orgasm. *The Function of the Orgasm* is his most famous work. Reich also invented something he called "orgone," a kind of sexual "cosmic energy," and built "orgone accumulators" in which to contain it. The U.S. Food and Drug Administration called him "a fraud of the first magnitude." He died, intermittently psychotic, in the federal penitentiary in Lewisburg, Pennsylvania, a prison that had once held Al Capone.

"In the ideological confusion of the postwar period, when the world was trying to understand the Holocaust, and intellectuals disillusioned with Communism fled the security of their earlier political positions, Reich's ideas landed on fertile ground," wrote Christopher Turner in a 2011 essay in the *Guardian*. Assessing Reich's influence, he continued:

> *After the Hitler-Stalin pact and the Moscow trials, Reich's theory of sexual repression seemed to offer the disenchanted Left a convincing explanation both for large numbers of people having submitted to fascism and for communism's failure to be a viable alternative to it. Reich, capturing the mood of this convulsive moment, presented guilty ex-Stalinists and former Trotskyites with an alternative programme of sexual freedom with which to combat those totalitarian threats. ... In creating a morality out of pleasure, Reich allowed postwar radicals to view their promiscuity as political activism and justify their retreat from traditional politics. Reich made them feel part of the sexual elite, superior to the "frozen," grey, corporate consensus.*

Reich defended the scientific legitimacy of his crackpot ideas (Woody Allen parodied the "orgone energy accumulator" as the "orgasmatron" in *Sleeper*) in the preface to the second edition of *The Function of the Orgasm* with this classic example of Teutonic bafflegab:

> *Sex-economy is a natural-scientific discipline. It is not ashamed of the subject of sexuality, and it rejects as its representative everyone who has not overcome the inculcated social fear of sexual defamation. The term "vegetotherapy," used to describe the sex-economic therapeutic technique, is actually a concession to the squeamishness of the world in sexual matters. "Orgasmotherapy" would have been a much better, indeed more correct term, for this medical technique: That is precisely what vegetotherapy basically is. It had to be taken into consideration, however, that this term would have entailed too great a strain on the young sex-economists in their practice. Well, it can't be helped. Speak of the core of their natural longings and religious feelings and people will either laugh derisively or snicker sordidly.*

Summarizing something every teenage boy knows after his first encounter with porn, Reich goes on to illustrate the "scientific" principles behind his revolutionary new theory: "The orgasm formula which directs sex-economic research is as follows: MECHANICAL TENSION → BIOELECTRIC CHARGE → BIOELECTRIC DISCHARGE → MECHANICAL RELAXATION.... The immediate cause of many devastating diseases can be traced to the fact that man is the sole species which does not fulfill the natural law of sexuality."

If it feels good, do it. Many artists and intellectuals, and not all of them teenage boys, found Reich's theories compelling. Among Reich's mature enthusiasts were Saul Bellow, Norman Mailer, Arthur Koestler, and William S. Burroughs. As Christopher Hitchens wrote in his *New York Times* review of *Adventures in the Orgasmatron*, the book that the above-mentioned Christopher Turner wrote about Reich, "Is it too easy to simply speculate that men will make fools of themselves for the sake of sex?"

Hitchens characteristically ends his review of Turner's book with this arresting, contemptuous image:

Adventures in the Orgasmatron *has many fine and engaging passages, but I think my favorite must be this one, in which Alfred Kazin describes the pathetic trust in Reich shown by the writer Isaac Rosenfeld. Has there ever been a better description of the baffled naïveté of so many "New York intellectuals"?:*

"Isaac's orgone box stood up in the midst of an enormous confusion of bedclothes, review copies, manuscripts, children, and the many people who went in and out of the room as if it were the bathroom. Belligerently sitting inside his orgone box, daring philistines to laugh, Isaac nevertheless looked lost, as if he were waiting in his telephone booth for a call that was not coming through."

On the Unholy Left, there is no idea too stupid to try, no institution unworthy of attack, no theory not worth implementing without care for its results, no matter what the practical cost. Intentions are everything, results are nothing. Results are an illusion; theory is what counts, because theory can be debated endlessly within the safe harbors of academe. The key is to examine what those intentions really are. The answer lies in the Left's own sense of narrative or, rather, anti-Narrative.

The works of the Frankfurt School make up a contrarian manifesto, expressed as a political program. Individual words no longer have specific meanings but stand as categorical imperatives. Women, blacks, gays, the environment, "choice," and big government are all Good Things; their opposites are not. To use the word is to evoke the emotion associated with it, not the noun. ("Rape" has recently undergone a similar linguistic transformation, mutating from forcible sexual intercourse into acts of verbal aggression or "microagression," or whatever the "victim" dislikes.) Thus language is used to silence discussion and criticism; it is "anti," with "anti" now treated as an absolute good. To be "anti" almost anything is to be on the Right Side of History, surfing the Arc as it bends toward Justice. It requires no thought, only emotions. It requires no reflection upon the conundrum of Chesterton's Fence, only reflexes. It should be an embarrassment to anyone who cannot defend it intellectually, and yet it is not—because it is dogma.

Dogma creates its own reality. You do not have to think about it; it provides all the answers. It is easy to mock evangelical Protestants or Orthodox Jews who cite the book of Leviticus as the source of wisdom and instruction about food, health, or sexual morality; simply making an assertion from authority by citing scripture is no argument at all. So it is with the leftist catechism as it has evolved in the wake of Critical Theory and political correctness, which has the added advantages of being of recent vintage and widely disseminated by an enthusiastic media. It deserves to be questioned and mocked with every bit as much jollity as the atheists attack Southern Baptist preachers.

What, after all, did "sexual liberation" accomplish? What positive good did it achieve? Other than providing men with greater, easier access to women, how did it improve anyone's life? It promised us liberation from "sexual repression" (what teenaged boys used to call, sniggeringly, DSB), freedom from an old and tired sexual morality. It promised to tear down the Chesterton's Fence that stood between our libidos and our responsibilities. It is easy to see why it was popular, since it partly leveled the sexual playing field for beta males, whose chances of sexual "conquest" vastly improved once "conquest" was taken out of the equation and a woman's natural resistance to indiscriminate sex (or less discriminating sex) was broken down. In the guise of cooperative pleasure, it erected a new egalitarianism between the sexes, told women that their sex drives and their sexual responsibilities were exactly the same as a man's. (It's a mystery why no feminist of the time complained that, in effect, the new doctrine still portrayed women as lesser creatures who needed to raise—or lower—their sexual sights to the level of a man's.) The newfound "liberation" led to a rapid increase in abortion, HIV and AIDS, and illegitimate children. Finally, wearing the masque of "progress," it returned Westerners to primitive levels of sexuality, kicking out the moral underpinnings of the culture (even if the morals were often observed more in the breach than in practice). Who knew that the slogan "Every man a stud, every woman a slut" could be a winner? It is not for humanity to defeat Sin, but to be wary and canny in our interaction with it. And, in any case, the *Ewig-Weibliche* will never stoop to whoredom.

Whoever thought turning women into men was a good idea needs his head examined. And turning men into women (the necessary corollary, as it turned out, although that bit was less advertised) was even worse. Hence the very real consequences of "no consequences." Above all, the sheer charlatanism of it astounds, nearly a century on. What the hell were we thinking? How was it possible for the intelligentsia of the United States, having just participated in the great American victory in the Second World War, to embrace such an obviously cockamamie philosophy? The Greco-Roman medical theory of bodily humors, the selling of indulgences in the Middle Ages, and phrenology had more scientific bases than Reich's twaddle.

And what has been the effect? The "war between the sexes" has rarely been more hostile. The incidence of sexually transmitted diseases has soared; viruses once contracted only in a bordello can be found at the corner bar. What began as unconstrained sexual license—orgies, multiple sex partners, etc.—has turned into "yes means yes" affirmative consent for even a one-night stand. On campuses, young men and women now eye one another with suspicion: That attractive person you see might be not only a potential sex partner but also a future plaintiff in a lawsuit. The more sex, it seems, the more heartbreak; the less "repression," the less romance. Public billboards in Los Angeles promote the use of condoms and AIDS hotlines. The promised Venusberg has turned venereal.

Interestingly, it was right around the same time that the sexual-liberation movement got fully under way—the 1970s—that the thanatopic side of it arose in popular culture, in the movies. For this was also the heyday of horror and slasher films, movies about enraged, often immortal serial killers (*Halloween, Friday the 13th, The Texas Chainsaw Massacre,*

A Nightmare on Elm Street) who preyed upon nubile, often naked teens in various acts of sexual intercourse. Nearly every one of our perky protagonists wound up on the wrong side of the slasher's weapon of choice, save one: a young woman known in the trade as the Final Girl.

It's as if Newton's Third Law of Motion applied, setting off an equal and opposite reaction to Reich's prescriptions and nostrums: The more sex we have, the less satisfying it is, and the more culturally destructive. In Japan, more and more young men are forgoing marriage and even dating in favor of staying home, watching porn, and playing video games; as a result, the country is now in a population death-spiral, with adult diapers outselling baby nappies. Elsewhere, nudity abounds as an example of female "empowerment," and yet rabid feminists see rapists not only behind every bush but standing at the podium. A kind of insanity has gripped the West, a sexual hysteria far worse than anything Reich conveniently diagnosed in his attempt to get laid as often as possible.

Get laid young men most certainly have, but what has been the upshot? The sexual proclivities of a pasha in his harem or a gangsta with his "ho's," however, have exactly the same deleterious effect on Western culture as they have had on the Mohammedans or the black underclass. What Reich and the other Frankfurters forgot was that "repression" (to use their word) is a *good* thing when it is called by its proper name: "tradition."

But for them to accept tradition—the very thing they battle—would be the end of them. Then they would finally have to face the worst kind of death—the Thanatos of their philosophy, which is the only possession, besides rage, that they ever really had. Their Pleasure Palace, like Schubert's, would crumble into dust, and they, along with it, would be blown away.

CHAPTER TWELVE

THE CONSOLATION OF PHILOSOPHY

Faced with his imminent execution for having offended the emperor, the sixth-century Roman philosopher Boethius wrote *The Consolation of Philosophy*, an imaginary dialogue between a condemned man and a beautiful woman representing the spirit of Philosophy, who suddenly appears to him in prison:

> *"Could I desert thee, child," said she, "and not lighten the burden that thou hast taken upon thee through the hatred of my name, by sharing this trouble? ... Thinkest thou that now, for the first time in an evil age, Wisdom hath been assailed by peril? ...*

> *So there is nothing thou shouldst wonder at if, on the seas of this life, we are tossed by storm-blasts ... And if at times and seasons they set in array against us, and fall on in overwhelming strength, our leader draws off her forces into the citadel while they are busy plundering the useless baggage. But we from our vantage ground, safe from all this wild work, laugh to see them making prize of the most valueless of things, protected by a bulwark which aggressive folly may not aspire to reach."*

To put her most important lines in plain English: "Do you think that only now, in an evil age, Wisdom is under attack for the first time? And if at times evil-doers fall upon us with overwhelming strength, we take refuge in our citadel while they are plundering useless baggage. And we laugh at them."

Although it did not spare the Roman nobleman the chop at the hands of the Ostrogothic emperor, Theodoric the Great, *The Consolation of Philosophy* turned out to be one of the great best-sellers of the medieval period, widely copied and distributed, a constant source of solace for those afflicted with the unfairness of the world. Profoundly Christian without being explicitly so, *The Consolation of Philosophy* comforted readers for nearly a millennium before the arrival of movable type made it even more available. Essentially, the *Consolation* grapples with the age-old question of the role evil plays in the world and what our proper response to it should be: not abolition (for that is impossible) but acceptance of evil as both instructive and as an occasion of grace caused by suffering.

Boethius's spirit of Philosophy adds one more crucial element: mockery. As Martin Luther said: "The best way to drive out the devil, if he will not yield to texts of Scripture, is to jeer and flout him, for he cannot bear scorn." The most potent weapon the Right has against the Left—mockery of its sheer pretentious ridiculousness—is the one it most seldom employs.

There is no consolation in the leftist philosophy, only anger and hatred. It is the expression of impotence, and not only of the intellectual variety; recall that "intellectuals" from Rousseau to Marx to Brecht to Sartre to the aptly named Lillian Hellman were beasts in their private lives, and most of them, on some level, knew it. Perhaps their antisocial, amoral, and even immoral behavior was a reflection of their hateful ideology; trying to save humanity while despising people is the very essence of cognitive dissonance. So their philosophies, naturally, had to trump their personalities.

But to call them on it, to point out that the emperor is as naked as one of the doomed teens about to get sliced and diced by Michael Myers, Jason Voorhees, Leatherface, or Freddy Krueger—and, furthermore, that he is a singularly unimpressive specimen of manhood—is to set their hair aflame. In retaliation, as proof of their superior intellects, they will hurl their academic credentials at you, the fruits of their long march through the institutions—degrees that prove, more than anything else, the worthlessness of much of our higher education today.

Scorn drives the Unholy Left insane. They cannot bear to have their theories questioned, or the failed results of those theories laughed at. Dignity is one of the imaginary virtues—one of the last virtues, period—they possess, and to have that attacked along with their entire "belief system" (the jeering term they use for organized religion) is too much to bear. Mockery is the thing that brings them quickest to frothing, garment-rending rage, so wedded are they to the notion of their own goodness and infallibility when it comes to matters of impiety and immorals.

The goal of Critical Theory was to make dissent from Marxist orthodoxy impossible. By establishing that there could be nothing beyond criticism except Critical Theory itself, the Frankfurt School rendered a guilty verdict against society before there had even been a trial. But this is simply crazy. "Sentence first, verdict afterwards," as the Queen of Hearts says to Alice near the end of *Alice's Adventures in Wonderland*:

> *"Let the jury consider their verdict," the King said, for about the twentieth time that day.*
> *"No, no!" said the Queen. "Sentence first—verdict afterwards."*
> *"Stuff and nonsense!" said Alice loudly. "The idea of having the sentence first!"*
> *"Hold your tongue!" said the Queen, turning purple.*
> *"I won't!" said Alice.*
> *"Off with her head!" the Queen shouted at the top of her voice.*

What once was satire is now conventional wisdom, as is the Queen's choleric reaction to Alice's impudence. The stifling of debate and the outlawing of basic concepts of right and wrong, of social propriety, is the purpose of political correctness; and dissent, once the highest form of patriotism, is no longer to be tolerated. Like "tolerance," "dissent" was only a virtue when it was useful to the Left.

Let us examine that phrase, "the highest form of patriotism." Dissent doesn't mean demurral, even passionate objection. Here, it means a fundamental, radical, irreconcilable objection to all time-honored verities, which is then followed by a frontal assault: Critical Theory in action.

Tolerance, as we have seen from Marcuse's redefinition of it as "repressive tolerance," means *intolerance*. One suspects, for example, that "diversity" will no longer be deemed necessary once the white man has been knocked off his perch of "privilege" and effectively disinherited from his own cultural patrimony. Only "non-white" whites, the champions of the "diverse" masses, will be allowed to have power; and they will be selected by a nakedly political criterion, much like that the Viennese mayor Karl Lueger expressed when asked to justify his friendship with many Jews despite the anti-Semitic ideology he peddled for votes: "*Wer a Jud ist, bestimm' i.*" ("I decide who is a Jew.") At the real Ministry of Truth under the next Progressive regime, the words carved into the façade will read: DISSENT—TOLERANCE—DIVERSITY.

As for "the highest form of patriotism," all that ever meant was that the Left did not wish to have its patriotism questioned while it was busily going about the process of undermining the existing order (in order to create a better one, of course). Not only was its patriotism questionable, it was nonexistent. The patriotism the '60s radicals praised was not the patriotism of the past (now dismissed as "jingoism") but the patriotism of the America of the Future, the new State that would come into being once the old one had been destroyed and replaced with the Brave New World they were cooking up in poly-sci test tubes on campuses across the country.

Any leftist will tell you, usually indirectly as he may not admit it to himself, that he does not admire the world as it is but esteems the world as he wishes it to be. That few agree with leftists when this proposition is so bluntly stated simply means they must conceal it for the time being, until it can be forced on an unwilling but sullen public. They see themselves as inheritors of a noble tradition, perhaps best summed up by the composer Gustav Mahler when he declared, "My time will yet come." They look to the judgment of posterity, not history. The very fact of being *against* something—it doesn't much matter what—contributes to their sense of moral superiority, without which they are nothing.

This last is crucial to the understanding of the Unholy Left: that they consider themselves, like the Puritans they otherwise execrate, the party of the Elect, the Blessed. Likewise, they consider resistant conservatives— those who like things more or less they way they are, who trust the judgments of their ancestors and honor their wisdom and experience—to be the Damned who must be brought into the Light—that is to say, into the Darkness. (The resemblance to Mozart's Queen of the Night is obvious.)

The problem with their ideology, however, is that, after a few victories (the civil rights movement, for example, although even that was fiercely opposed by many of their fellow Democrats), it has nowhere to go. Once the perceived wrongs are righted, the revolution turns on itself, aiming its scorpion's tail at ever-smaller targets and stinging them ever more viciously until it is thrashing at phantoms. A good example is the strange obsession with "white privilege" (racism always lurks just beneath the surface of the leftist project; it is their eternal bugbear) and the terrible whiteness of being, which has now pushed past slavery as America's Original Sin. Overly fond of conspiracy theories as they are, "white privilege" affords the Unholy Left its best conspiracy yet, a conspiracy so vast that it took the combined efforts of multiple European countries to sail the Atlantic, discover America for themselves, found colonies, and populate the New World, all in an effort to deny People of Color what should have rightfully been theirs, had they only been able to cross the Atlantic from Africa or Asia and get there first. The United States, in other words, was not founded, somewhat haphazardly, in an attempt to flee the religious and economic strictures of the then-developed world, Europe (we can blame the Enlightenment for those strictures), but to deliberately offend "indigenous peoples" by effectively creating a political entity without them. Never mind that there were few People of Color in Europe at the time, and that the context in which the Voyages of Discovery were made was purely "white." It must have been a plot. Or at least unfair, for daring to assume European technological "superiority."

The following sentiment is, alas, typical: "I am as white as white gets in this country." So wrote Robert Jensen, a journalism professor at the University of Texas, in the *Baltimore Sun* in 1998. The confession continues:

> *I am of northern European heritage, and I was raised in North Dakota, one of the whitest states in the country. I grew up in a virtually all-white world surrounded by racism, both personal and institutional. Because I didn't live near a reservation, I didn't even have exposure to the state's only numerically significant population, American Indians.*

I have struggled to resist that racist training and the ongoing racism of my culture. I like to think I have changed, even though I routinely trip over the lingering effects of that internalized racism and the institutional racism around me. But no matter how much I "fix" myself, one thing never changes—I walk through the world with white privilege. There is not space here to list all the ways in which white privilege plays out, but it is clear that I will carry this privilege with me until the day white supremacy is erased from this society.

Substitute "sin" for the various racial buzzwords, and it's clear that what Jensen is after is redemption. He's giving testimony in a tent revival of that New Time Religion, Progressivism.

One thing the Left has on its side in its war on American "whiteness" is demographics. At some point around midcentury, whites (however defined, as the Left uses a conveniently sliding scale) will decline to less than half the total population, and the U.S. will be a minority-majority country; Ted Kennedy's Immigration Act of 1965 has seen to that. (When I was a boy growing up in San Diego, near the Mexican border, exactly nobody considered Mexicans "non-whites," and the words "Latino" and "Hispanic" were hardly ever heard. Mexicans were, well, Mexicans, distinguished not by the color of their skin, but by the fact that they spoke Spanish and came from Mexico, that foreign country twenty miles to the south.)

Between the last great waves of European immigration in the first two decades of the twentieth century and 1965, the nation took a long pause, absorbing the often fractious Irish, Italians, and Jews and smelting them into Americans. It wasn't easy. For many Americans of the period, the newcomers were little more than criminals fleeing misery. (The Marxist historian Noel Ignatiev, the son of Russian-Jewish immigrants, even wrote a book on the often painful transformative process, *How the Irish Became White.*) It took decades or longer. In the case of the Catholic Famine Irish, it was a full century before they were accepted so fully into American society that one of them, John F. Kennedy, was elected president. That he came from the criminal family of Joseph P. Kennedy was politely ignored, especially by the Irish themselves. Not until some years after JFK's election did the Irish begin to vote as anything other than a monolithic, alienated, immigrant bloc.

No such caesura has yet occurred with the new waves of immigration from Latin America, Africa, the Indian subcontinent, and East Asia—and this is by design. The Democrats, now almost explicitly the "anti-American" party (meaning "American" as the term was formerly understood), need to keep immigrants balkanized, dependent, and voting the straight Democratic ticket for as long as possible, alienated not from the lock-jawed, shrimp-forked WASP bogeyman of old but from the new global Devil, the White Man. "White privilege" is today's Original Sin, a meme gleefully transmitted by the Left's housebroken, pet media outlets. (The murderer is *one of us!* But crucially, not *us*-us. Them-us. White-boy us.) The meme will last just as long as its usefulness as a cudgel does, and not one second longer. Besides, who among us—with the example of the Soviet *nomenklatura* fresh in our minds—supposes that some sort of "white privilege" won't survive even "fundamental transformation?" The transformation is intended for the voting public, not the leftist ruling class. They'll just dub themselves non-white. *Wer a Jud' ist, bestimm' i'* and all that.

The key to understanding political correctness is its constant redefinition of what is acceptable regarding the use of language; it's Sisyphus on the euphemism treadmill. The way to fight it is to refuse to accept it. They have their Critical Theory; we have the Consolation of our Philosophy. They have the hammer; we have the anvil. They seek to forge a new *Nothung* from Western civilization's industrial shards; we aim to prevent them from wielding something unholy and obscene against us. They are weak, but strengthening; we are strong, but weakening. They brim with self-confidence; we cower in self-doubt.

But, as philosophy consoles the doomed Boethius, there really is nothing to fear; the only weapon they have is our own weakness. Without that, as the Frankfurt School readily understood, they are helpless. A spy, surrounded by armed soldiers, is a dead spy, soon shot or hanged. It is our wish to be seen as reasonable, as proportional, as judicious, as measured (all leftist terms) that hinders us from taking decisive action against them. Casting our weaknesses as the direct results of our sins, instead of our mistaken reactions to their charges and provocations, they have activated Alinsky's Rule No. 12: "Pick the target, personalize it, and polarize it."

A polarized target—for the Unholy Left, that would be Judeo-Christianity—is a frozen target, and a frozen target is a sitting duck. Ever on the attack, the Left faces great difficulty in playing defense. Their usual retort is simply a crude personal insult, not so much of a counter-argument but a "how-dare-you?" accusation. Their stocks-in-trade are in fact the two lowest forms of argumentation, the tu quoque assertion ("Oh, yeah? You are too!") and the ad hominem offensive ("Your mother was a hamster, and your father smelled of elderberries," to quote a choice insult from *Monty Python and the Holy Grail*). Of rational arguments they have none, since their philosophy is based exclusively on emotion and appeals to what "ought" or "ought not" be done; they argue from authority, minus the authority.

As conservatives know only too well, most arguments with true believers of the Left end in insults, comparisons to Nazis, tears, and the leftists' hasty retreat, leaving the conservatives frustrated and angry at their opponents' inability or refusal to engage. But, as leftists see it, they live to fight, and soul-sap, another day, which is precisely why they do not engage; to engage would be to give the whole game away and reveal the Potemkin village behind their confident assertions.

At its bluntest, the Marxist worldview is based on a demonstrable lie (or, to put it more politely and in Hollywood terms, a buy-in): that the forces of history are scientific, as predictable as the motions of the sun, moon, and stars. But this is nothing more than a very grim fairy tale, translated from the opaque, pseudoscientific German and given, like the Scarecrow in *The Wizard of Oz*, a fancy diploma from the Goethe University of Frankfurt. The truth is, as everyone from the ancient Greeks on has known, Fortune is a fickle mistress, lavishing her attention first here and then there, with no regard for the consequences of her actions. There is nothing at all scientific about fate, as Boethius writes:

FORTUNE'S MALICE
Mad Fortune sweeps along in wanton pride,
Uncertain as Euripus' surging tide;
Now tramples mighty kings beneath her feet,
Now sets the conquered in the victor's seat.
She heedeth not the wail of hapless woe,
But mocks the griefs that from her mischief flow.

Such is her sport; so proveth she her power;
And great the marvel, when in one brief hour
She shows her darling lifted high in bliss,
Then headlong plunged in misery's abyss

To the Left, there is something wrong with this state of affairs. It *ought* not to be. It is not fair that sometimes you're the windshield and sometimes you're the bug. That it is so is indisputable; therefore, what is *ought* to be outlawed or in some manner compensated for. (It is curious how often leftist solutions come down to simple financial extortion meant to ameliorate the perceived problem.) Such thinking is part of the Left's war on God and its war on the universe, which, when you stop to think about it, are completely contradictory. If there is no God, then the universe must be irrational and arbitrary, which is what leftists preach in metaphysics but rage against in society. If there is a God, and yet this is still the result, then what is the problem? That God is not as arbitrary as a random universe? That the Universe is too rational, too godlike?

The Occam-like simplicity of Right thought is, then, its greatest attribute. It requires no particular leap of faith beyond the initial buy-in (which Pascal's Wager also makes the rational buy-in). It presumes a belief in, but not necessarily a knowledge or proof of, a power greater than ourselves. It allows each individual to listen to his heart and follow the implanted heroic story he finds deep within himself. It frees Everyman to be a Hero, the leading character in his own movie, complete with dialogue and soundtrack. It unites all men into the ur-Narrative of stasis, sin, loss, change, conflict, redemption, and ultimate victory, even beyond death. It is the song of everyone. Why anyone should want to reject it is an enduring mystery.

By contrast, the philosophy of the Unholy Left, while ostensibly simple—Critical Theory, i.e., *Us v. Them*—requires repeated mental contortions, which might be why they constantly congratulate themselves on how smart they are, how appreciative of complexity, compared with crude, simplistic, reductionist conservatives. As the White Queen brags to Alice in *Through the Looking-Glass*, "Why, sometimes I've believed as many as six impossible things before breakfast." In the next chapter of this *Wonderland* sequel, Alice also encounters Humpty Dumpty, who imperiously informs her how he operates: "When *I* use a word, it means just what I choose it to mean—neither more nor less." The White Queen and Humpty must be two of the Left's favorite literary characters. They certainly are role models.

Easy for them to stay on the other side of the Looking-Glass, the fun-house mirror through which they see, confidently, the shape of things to come, while the Right continues to peer as best it can through faith's glass, darkly. When you can manipulate the language and convince an otherwise sane world that your mad version of events is the truth, you have a formidable, satanic weapon.

Which brings us back to the Garden, and to Milton. Stepping back for a moment from the particulars of the poems, it is sobering and refreshing to realize, especially at first reading, how optimistic Milton is about the future of humanity—which, having fallen, nevertheless is bathed in the light of God's love. And the gates of Hell shall not prevail against us. Even as we open the book, we know what's coming, that the apparently defeated Satan will break away from his chained bed on the Lake of Fire, slip the bonds of Hell, glimpse the now-lost Kingdom of Heaven, and set his basilisk gaze on God's newest playthings, Adam and Eve. We know that Eve will fail the test—not out of any innate female weakness, but from her sympathetic heart and insatiable curiosity, both quintessentially human traits; she is truly humanity's Mother. We know that Adam, her devoted spouse, will join his wife in the first biblical act of self-sacrifice (he cannot contemplate a life without her), immediately followed by the first biblical act of physical love, thus creating humanity itself. We know that Eve will suffer in childbirth for her transgression. We know that the firstborn of Eve's children will murder his brother and that God will mark him with a sign of divine protection. We know that humanity will start its long, slow, torturous journey back to the Light. We know that we, too, are part of that journey. We know, above all, that it is our story.

And we know that, ultimately, we will win. That God's sacrifice of his Son—the remarkable act of the Deity deigning to take on, and suffer from, the worst ills to which the flesh is heir, thus experiencing what it means to be fully human—brought us closer to him. We know there is a perfect circle out there: from Lucifer to Satan to Sin to Death to the Temptation in the Garden to the Fall of Man and Original Sin; from the instant in which humanity was truly born, and the long struggle to return not to Eden but to Heaven, this time as fully human creatures who have surpassed the angels and who return home as living examples of the fallibility of an infallible God. We have a thing or two to teach God, and he'd better get used to the idea once we all get home. It is the uniting of opposites, the end result of Boy Meets Girl. It is completion.

Thus runs the ur-Narrative, in which all our stories point to one, and only one, conclusion. Theologians sometimes portray God as an innocent bystander, the guy who starts the chariot races but neither wagers nor determines their outcome. C.S. Lewis departs from the conventional view of God's omniscience, and the problem of predestination, by picturing God as a Presence, not on a closed circle but on an infinite straight line of Time, where he exists at every plottable point, thus negating time as a concept. ("Here time and space are one.") Therefore, there can be no foreknowledge as God says to Moses, when asked his name, "I am who am." There is only the present tense, no future, no past. There's a reason that the verb "to be" is the cornerstone of all human language, for without it, we are, literally, nothing. It's not that God doesn't care: It's that, in a sense, he *can't* care.

He is a God of opposites, not a being but Being itself—"I am who am"—which may explain the images and likenesses that lie at the heart of our ur-Narrative. Omniscient yet clueless. Omnipotent yet powerless. Omnipresent yet eternally absent from us, who dwell in a temporal dimension.

In Michael Mann's epic remake of *The Last of the Mohicans* with Daniel Day-Lewis as Hawkeye (aka Natty Bumppo), a sneering British officer (who wishes to "make the world England") upbraids the colonial sharpshooter for not joining the King's militia: "You call yourself a patriot and loyal subject of the Crown?" To which Hawkeye replies: "I do not call myself subject to much at all." This is the voice of the true patriot, the difference between the Central European authoritarian and the American.

The goal of the Frankfurt School was, at root, to turn Americans into Central Europeans, to undermine the core self-perception of America—free individuals before God—and replace it with a Central European dependence on and worship of the God-State as an embodiment of the General Will, History, Social Justice, Diversity, or whatever divinized chimera represents Utopia at the moment. For a man who never used to call himself subject to much at all to transform himself into a ward of the state—to become, in other words, less of a man—should be a leap too far. To abandon the idea of heroism, of his own personal quest, and instead accept his newfound status as—if he's lucky—a clerk would be an enormity.

Hawkeye or a clerk? Sharpshooter or pencil-pusher? To which narrative do you wish to belong? Hero or schmuck? Good guy or a functionary in the Ministry of Love? Despite what both the Calvinists and the atheist Left say, we all are free to choose. There is no predestination. There is only free will—the essence of humanity. At the end, when all seems lost and the world is at its darkest, the hero is alone. As he must be, that we must also be.

Each of us must make the choice. Our inner narrative drives us one way; what we witness daily on television and in other media drives us another way. To dare or not to dare? To chase freedom or (in the odious phrase) to shelter in place for security? What did the Sirens whisper and sing to Ulysses, strapped to the mast of his ship (as curious as Eve) so he could hear the forbidden melodies? Just this, in the translation by Samuel Butler:

> *"Come here," they sang, "renowned Ulysses, honor to the Achaean name, and listen to our two voices. No one ever sailed past us without staying to hear the enchanting sweetness of our song—and he who listens will go on his way not only charmed, but wiser, for we know all the ills that the gods laid upon the Argives and Trojans before Troy, and can tell you everything that is going to happen over the whole world."*

The knowledge of the future. That—what Eve foresaw after tasting the fruit of the Tree of Knowledge—is what Ulysses gave up for his brief aural taste of the Sirens' delicious musical apples. Was it worth it? For him, to get home to Penelope, of course it was. And yet what might have been, had he stayed and survived. The motto of Britain's fabled Special Air Service (SAS) is "Who dares, wins." Not to dare is, by definition, the philosophy of a loser; as the saying goes, you can't win if you don't play.

But *"Don't* play" is the modern motto; better safe than sorry. Better dependent than independent. Better red than dead. To say this is an unmanly ethos is to state what was once obvious, but it's less so in an age when a cocoa-sipping metrosexual in a onesie is held up as a masculine ideal by the government of the United States. But this is what we should expect from an "elite" culture that prizes unmoored mental agility and snarky glibness over principle and purpose. The smart remark, the "transgressive" observation, the verbal poke in the eye—these are what occasion applause from the trained-seal class latterly. Above all, above everything, we must have peace. But a world without conflict ... is stasis ... is tyranny ... is Death.

For centuries, cowards, deserters, malingerers, and shirkers have been mocked, scorned, and shot. There is something greater, nobler, than the preservation of one's own skin: That is the consolation of our philosophy. Critical Theory, however, will have none of that.

The Frankfurt School's pernicious philosophy has corrupted an elite, educated segment of America; that is the bad news. The good news is that, given a stark choice between its wheedling defeatism, tricked out with scholarly pretension (the rise of the eternal graduate student followed closely in the Frankfurt School's Faustian wake) and nearly unreadable neo-Hegelian doublespeak, it has little popular appeal unless cloaked in deceitful appeals to the "better angels of our nature," in Lincoln's words. What is does have, however, is modern sympathizers, who feed like dung beetles off its cultural resentment and overweening sense of entitlement. Indeed, the sympathizers elected a president, twice, based entirely on resentment disguised as progress.

Disguise is the key; that we sometimes fall for it speaks well of us, not ill. In the Garden, the Serpent preyed on Eve's curiosity, her *goodness*, and her vanity in order to bring her low, down to his level, and he did so in the guise of an animal that Adam had named, with no stigma yet attached to it. Had the fallen Lucifer come to her in full Devil regalia, snorting fire and farting brimstone, she would rightly have fled; but then Satan would have been not God's enemy but his reinforcement, discouraging Eve from sin. Evil can succeed only by mimicking good; in Milton, the Serpent goes down to crawl on his belly like a reptile only after his transgression, not before; priapically, a walking erection, he approaches Eve upright. Had she laughed at his inadequacy, how different history might have been.

CHAPTER THIRTEEN

MEPHISTO AT THE MINISTRY OF LOVE

Speaking of the Devil, in his influential book *Rules for Radicals,* critical theorist Saul Alinsky famously invoked Satan—not as a dedicatee, as conservatives often mistakenly assert, but as someone to be admired and emulated:

> *Lest we forget at least an over-the-shoulder acknowledgement to the very first radical: from all our legends, mythology, and history (and who is to know where mythology leaves off and history begins—or which is which), the first radical known to man who rebelled against the establishment and did it so effectively that he at least won his own kingdom—Lucifer.*

Big deal. Pace Alinsky, Hell was not the kingdom Lucifer sought: It was Heaven itself. Nor could he bear to spend a minute longer there than God decreed.

The reason Alinsky has been so influential, and so dangerous, is that, in some respects at least, he is largely correct. He is right to acknowledge the relationship between mythos and history, and is he right again when he states that Lucifer is the first radical. What he does not mention, naturally, is that the "establishment" the proto-rebel rebelled against was God.

(A permanent Revolutionary Party always targets "the establishment," with the aim of becoming "the establishment," but never suffering any of its own consequences.) And unless you define "God" as "Evil"—a stretch even for the most dedicated atheist—you are stuck with the possibility that the first rebellion may not have been Lucifer's own idea, but God's.

This is how we first meet Satan early in Book One of Milton's poem:

> *So stretched out huge in length the Arch-fiend lay*
> *Chained on the burning Lake, nor ever thence*
> *Had risen or heaved his head, but that the will*
> *And high permission of all-ruling Heaven*
> *Left him at large to his own dark designs,*
> *That with reiterated crimes he might*
> *Heap on himself damnation, while he sought*
> *Evil to others . . .*

Some successful rebel, he who cannot even move his head without God's permission. But not only does God give the fallen angel liberty to move and speak, he even frees him from his chains on the Lake of Fire, allows him to pass through the Gates of Hell and make mischief on Earth. What kind of a kingdom, then, does Satan have, except at the sufferance of God? Only a fool can howl at the moon and then, as the sun rises, congratulate himself on his fearsome prowess that can affect the heavens.

Still, to give both devils their due, there is something in our earthly imaginings of Satan that is heroic; it is what makes him at once so attractive to some and such a compelling dramatic figure to others. Satan, or his surrogate, not only appears in two of the greatest poems in the Western canon, *Paradise Lost* and *Faust*, but in a host of other works as well, both as himself and in various disguises. Devils pop up in the works of the Russians, including Dostoyevsky, Tolstoy, and Bulgakov; the satanic figure of Naptha materializes to tempt the nubile soul of Hans Castorp in Mann's *Magic Mountain*. (Naptha, the Jewish Jesuit turned Hegelian Marxist, was based on Lukács, as Mann himself admitted, and the role of the Wagnerian "pure fool," Parsifal, is here taken by the novel's weak protagonist, Hans Castorp, with the Kirghiz-eyed Clawdia Chauchat, the hot kitten, as his Kundry.)

Operatically, the Faust legend has been brought to the stage in multiple incarnations, including by Gounod in *Faust* (which the Germans sometimes dismissively perform as *Margarete*), Arrigo Boito's *Mefistofele*, and Ferrucio Busoni's *Doktor Faust*; for many years, Gounod's was the single most-performed opera in the history of New York's Metropolitan Opera. Boito, Verdi's great librettist on *Otello* and *Falstaff*, took the demon by his horns and made him the principal character of his lone opera, a work that had to wait until 1969, in the Met's production featuring bass Norman Treigle (and, later, Samuel Ramey), before it would receive its just plaudits.

Whether Mephisto—also the subject of several Liszt waltzes for the piano, ranging from the virtuosic to the gnomic—wins his infernal bet with Faust, as he does at the end of both Marlowe's and Busoni's treatments, or loses to God, he is always a worthy antagonist. But this does not make him a hero; rather, by storytelling maxim, a hero can achieve greatness only when he goes up against a figure equal to or greater and more powerful than himself. The lowly hobbits of *The Lord of the Rings* must defeat the satanic Sauron; Siegfried must slay a fearsome dragon and then confront *Der Ring des Nibelungen*'s real anti-hero, Wotan—his own grandfather.

The would-be grandfather-slayers of the Frankfurt School, malcontents to a man, felt it their sworn duty to upend the old order. Heroes in their own minds, in order to do so they needed to create the satanic doctrine of political correctness, not to slay their enemy but to preemptively disarm him. As the military-affairs writer William S. Lind wrote in an essay based on his monograph *Political Correctness: A Short History of an Ideology*: "Political Correctness is the use of culture as a sharp weapon to enforce new norms and to stigmatize those who dissent from the new dispensation; to stigmatize those who insist on values that will impede the new 'PC' regime: free speech and objective intellectual inquiry."

Having abandoned the chimera of economic Marxism, the Frankfurt School was forced to embrace the Gramsci-Lukács "long march" paradigm, which logically concluded in a necessary, but stealthy, assault on the First Amendment. Like "tolerance," free speech was to be pleaded for only until it was no longer necessary to seek constitutional protection. Then it could be dispensed with. Satan's adoption of the form of the as-yet-uncursed Serpent, wheedling Eve in the Garden to take just one little bite, is all of a piece with political correctness's protective coloration as protected speech, the symbolism of the ur-Narrative in action.

The mainstreaming of pornography—Reich's theories brought to vivid life—in American culture began with *Deep Throat* and *The Devil in Miss Jones*, two pornographic films that won crucial legal victories in the mid-'70s on free-speech grounds. Pretty soon there were porn shops and peep shows everywhere; Travis Bickle even takes the girl he's ineptly wooing to one in *Taxi Driver*. Under the steadfast pounding of Critical Theory, what had once been criminal quickly enough became, for a time, chic, and over time, so acceptable as to be unremarkable. Today, hardcore porn is freely available on the Internet, and even public nudity is legal in some places.

Is this a good thing or a bad thing? Is it liberation or libertinism? The central argument of Camille Paglia's seminal study *Sexual Personae* is that when sexuality or any other taboo is heavily repressed, it does not disappear but goes underground. Certainly, mores change from age to age. The saucy sensuality of the eighteenth century—of the Enlightenment, but also of *Tom Jones* and *Memoirs of a Woman of Pleasure* (*Fanny Hill*)—gave way to the rather more straitlaced dress and manners of the Victorian period (which, in accordance with Paglia's theory, also produced volumes of choice literary pornography, such as *A Man with a Maid,* and which was also the time of Jack the Ripper). This duality, so human, is neither morally good nor bad. It is simply an acknowledgement of the dark side, with which humanity is constantly flirting—with which, as I've argued throughout, it *must* flirt in order to be fully human. Of saints we have few and of sinners, many. The rest of us fall in between, living tributes that vice pays to virtue.

Where Reich and others went wrong was in thinking that repression was a bad thing per se. Why should it be? Any artist or architect knows that rules are better than no rules and that creativity comes from operating within them, not outside them. There is very little creativity in pornography, only a theme and variations; like Kansas City in *Oklahoma!,* it's gone just about as far as it can go.

The campaigns to permit the publication of such literary classics as Joyce's *Ulysses,* Nabokov's *Lolita,* and Henry Miller's *Tropic of Cancer* were fully justified on artistic grounds; that these books also may have appealed to prurient (but how, one wonders) interest is part of their appeal. Many great works, including Shakespeare, have at various times been denounced by the Pecksniffs and Bowdlers as immoral or obscene. Erskine Caldwell's *God's Little Acre* was taken to court in New York City in 1933 for obscenity; the list of works banned in Boston included, at one time or another, *Leaves of Grass, Elmer Gantry, Manhattan Transfer, Lady Chatterley's Lover*, and *Naked Lunch*, among others. Whether any of these works coarsened society is debatable (they probably did), but in any case they were the creations of major authors in a way that, say, porn is not. The question for a moral society is where to draw the line; the assertion of an immoral or amoral society is that there is no line to be drawn.

Morality, however, is not law. There are many things that are immoral that are perfectly legal. In one sense, therefore, it is true that we don't legislate morality. Not that we can't; we can and do, drawing many aspects of our legal code from the Ten Commandments, such as "Thou shalt not murder," while ignoring for legal purposes the Decalogue's moral proscriptions again covetousness. This may be hypocrisy or it may be mere accommodation to earthy realities; we live with it.

Man is a complex creature, far more so than the angels. He is the only being who combines good and evil within the same shell casing, intermixed in every possible way; there is no one without the other. We have met the enemy, and he really is us.

Lytton Strachey's *Eminent Victorians* (1918)—short, bitchy biographical sketches of Cardinal Manning, Florence Nightingale, Thomas Arnold, and General George "Chinese" Gordon—contains a remarkable discussion of this very phenomenon in the chapter on Gordon at Khartoum. Not about Gordon, whose fervent religiosity comes in for a good deal of dismissive Strachey piss, but his bête noire, the British prime minister William Gladstone:

> *The old statesman was now entering upon the penultimate period of his enormous career.... Yet—such was the peculiar character of the man, and such the intensity of the feelings which he called forth—at this very moment, at the height of his popularity, he was distrusted and loathed; already an unparalleled animosity was gathering its forces against him.... "the elements" were "so mixed" in Mr. Gladstone that his bitterest enemies (and his enemies were never mild) and his warmest friends (and his*

*friends were never tepid) could justify, with equal plausibility, their
denunciations or their praises. What, then, was the truth?*

What indeed? It is hard for us today, with the passions of the late
Victorian age long since cooled, to think much of anything at all about
Gladstone. He is just another dusty figure in the passing parade of states-
man who once strutted upon the stage, making life-or-death decisions
that have, at best, only a lingering effect today. In Gordon's case, the
descendants of the Mahdi control Sudan even more surely than they did
in 1885, when they finally overran Gordon's fortifications. Was his sacrifice
in vain? Strachey continues:

> *In the physical universe there are no chimeras. But man is more various
> than nature; was Mr. Gladstone, perhaps, a chimera of the spirit? Did
> his very essence lie in the confusion of incompatibles?... His very egoism
> was simpleminded; through all the labyrinth of his passions there ran a
> single thread. But the centre of the labyrinth? Ah! the thread might lead
> there, through those wandering mazes, at last. Only, with the last corner
> turned, the last step taken, the explorer might find that he was looking
> down into the gulf of a crater. The flame shot out on every side, scorching
> and brilliant, but in the midst there was a darkness.*

This is an apt description of the problem of humanity in general. For
all the bluster, for all the sound and fury, is nothing at our center but a
darkness? Are we beings of almost infinite surface complexity, but with
a hollowed-out core? Are the flames of our existence just an illusion,
another of the Devil's jokes? Are we nothing more than black holes in
the fabric of the universe?

Our faith tells us no. Our literature tells us no. Our actions tell us no.
To believe in the absence of humanity at humanity's core is still to believe
in a god, but in an evil and unjust God who has created Man for sport—in
other words, a satanic God. Gordon himself reflected on this near the
end in a letter to his sister, Augusta. He was surrounded at Khartoum, his
hope in a British relief column rapidly fading, and very well aware that he
had sealed his own doom by refusing to evacuate the Egyptian garrison
in a timely manner and thus had condemned the people of Khartoum to
certain death. In a pause in the fighting, he wrote to her:

I decline to agree that the expedition comes for my relief; it comes for the relief of the garrisons, which I failed to accomplish. I expect Her Majesty's Government are in a precious rage with me for holding out and forcing their hand.... This may be the last letter you will receive from me, for we are on our last legs, owing to the delay of the expedition. However, God rules all, and as He will rule to His glory and our welfare. His will be done.

To Strachey—throwing rocks at Gordon's head from the safety of his sinecure as a charter member of the Bloomsbury Group (in a sense, Britain's own, home-grown Frankfurt School of cultural sappers and spoiled children)—Gordon's sacrifice was quixotic and inconceivable. *Eminent Victorians* appeared the same year the Great War ended; cynicism about national purpose was the order of the day in the wake of the fearful slaughter in the trenches to no apparent purpose. The cream of British manhood lay dead in Flanders' fields, while those unfit for military service eventually inherited the country; soon enough, they would manage to stumble into World War II, thus finishing off the British Empire they so loathed. Seen in retrospect, Churchill was the aberration (and Thatcher the throwback), Chamberlain and Atlee and Bevan the shapes of things to come. There could be no more heroes, because there was no future left to fight for.

As Gordon lay dying, a spear through his chest, descended upon by scimitar-wielding dervishes about to hack him to pieces, what went through his mind? Had God forsaken him? Had he fulfilled his fate and function upon the earth, and if so, what was it? Would Heaven be his reward, or would he find only Gladstone's darkness awaiting him on the other side? Obviously, these are things we cannot know. But even today, in the face of recrudescent Islam and a leftist high tide, some still honor his memory and his sacrifice; his statue still stands on the Embankment in London. On some profound level, we know that honoring him is the right thing to do, and that is a sign of a healthy society.

Yet Mephisto, the head greeter at the Ministry of Love, continues to demand his due as well. The same forces who would tear down the statue of Gordon with Marxist criticisms (imperialism, hegemony, etc.) wish not to erase his memory but to transform him into an anti-hero, a kind of white devil himself, piratically seeking plunder in Countries of Color. They cannot see him any other way, and yet they still make him an anti-hero, because their cause requires villains for anyone to take it seriously. Thus they cannot escape the central conundrum of the Battle in Heaven and its aftermath: Perhaps God simply desires an opponent. Perhaps Satan, for all his seductive power, is just another tomato can, a chump who hasn't figured out yet that he's supposed to throw the fight.

Certainly, Satan requires love as much as God does and is wounded when he doesn't get it. His brave bluster at the beginning of *Paradise Lost*—"better to reign in Hell than serve in Heaven"—is the boast of a loser. He is up and out of the Lake of Fire and through the Gates of Hell, pronto, ready to begin his long guerilla war against man and God. Here he is in Book Four, surly and petulant and brimming with false confidence as he confronts his former friend, now foe, the Archangel Gabriel:

> *Gabriel, thou hadst in Heav'n the esteem of wise,*
> *And such I held thee; but this question asked*
> *Puts me in doubt. Lives there who loves his pain?*
> *Who would not, finding way, break loose from Hell,*
> *Though thither doomed? Thou wouldst thyself, no doubt,*
> *And boldly venture to whatever place*
> *Farthest from pain, where thou might'st hope to change*
> *Torment with ease, and soonest recompense*
> *Dole with delight, which in this place I sought*
> . . . .
> *. . . Let him surer bar*
> *His Iron Gates, if he intends our stay*
> *In that dark durance . . .*

Call it what you will—the Devil's Pleasure Palace, Xanadu, the Venusberg, the land of the Sirens, the Ministry of Love, his own kingdom—Satan's residence is an unhappy place, and he would gladly trade it for ours. For as much pleasure as it gives him to torment us, in the end there can be no happy ending for him; like the rest of us, he is just a pawn in God's hands, except that his free will, unlike ours, is just another illusion. Even the Devil fails to "see how the Devil may joke."

One of the most contemptible of human beings is the man who constantly tries to fool you and trick you and cheat you out of what is rightfully yours. The mountebank is justly scorned by society, shunned and avoided whenever possible, jailed when not. The members of the Frankfurt School expended a great deal of squid ink in the defense of the indefensible—they were, proudly, cultural seditionists, operating in the no-man's-land between culture and law, advocating destruction and anarchy without ever quite calling for it. Yipping dogs in the manger, they chased the cars of the American caravan. Now that they've caught them, what?

"Under the rule of a repressive whole, liberty can be made into a powerful instrument of domination," wrote Marcuse in *One-Dimensional Man*. "The people recognize themselves in their commodities; they find their soul in their automobile, hi-fi-set, split-level home, kitchen equipment. The very mechanism which ties the individual to his society has changed, and social control is anchored in the new needs which it has produced."

This was published in 1964, in a decade that started, culturally, after the death of John F. Kennedy. This was a time when Marcuse's rhetoric might—might—have sounded plausible to the Baby Boomers (my generation) who had grown up in the security of the Eisenhower administration, only to be rudely thrust into the Age of Anxiety: nearly three years of the Kennedy administration's brinksmanship, including the Bay of Pigs disaster, the Berlin situation, the Vienna summit with Khrushchev, and the Cuban Missile Crisis. We learned to duck and cover, and images of nuclear tests on Bikini Atoll were a regular feature of our classroom instruction. The center, which had once seemed so secure, was falling apart.

But look more closely at Marcuse's argument and you can see immediately how simplistic and flawed it is. For one thing, it could only have been written by a resentful foreigner—worse, a German. German notions—especially postwar German notions—of creature comforts were, shall we say, severely restricted. Having been bombed back to the Stone Age by the Russians, the British, and the Americans, and being congenitally suspicious of urban environments in general, German Communists such as the Frankfurt School adherents hated and resented both American hegemony and American technology, which they viewed as soulless and vulgar. They could not make allowances for the bias of their own background: that the people, whom they theoretically championed, actually liked their cars and gadgets and homes; that

Americans, living in a country vastly larger than Germany, did not want to be confined to streetcars and trains, hemmed into small apartments in confined cities, and forced to live under the mentality of both war-time and postwar shortages. For them, philosophically, it was turtles all the way down—they had no understanding of the assumptions on which they grounded their theories.

Further, there's no lecturer like a German—one of their least endear-ing national characteristics. To live in Germany is to be subjected to near-constant, unsolicited hectoring about the state of the world, includ-ing the environment (*die Umwelt*), politics, America's cultural hegemony, and why crossing against the stoplight should be punishable by death. Within all the Frankfurt School writings swirls an arrogant incompre-hension of the American world, a resentment at having been forced to engage with it, and a passionate wish to be free of it, once and for all. Ingrates indeed.

Marcuse found easy prey on these shores. Many of his comrades returned home to Germany after the American Army had done their wet work for them, but Marcuse stayed, gleefully voiding poison into the American intellectual water supply. In 1972's *Counterrevolution and Revolt*, he wrote:

> *At the highest stage of capitalism, the most necessary revolution appears as the most unlikely one. Most necessary because the established system preserves itself only through the global destruction of resources, of nature, of human life, and the objective conditions* [nice touch of Marxist cant there] *for making an end to it prevail. Those conditions are: a social wealth sufficient to abolish poverty; the technical know-how to develop the available resources systematically* [more "scientific" jargon] *toward this goal; a ruling class* [yet more Marxist boilerplate] *which wastes, arrests, and annihilates the productive forces; the growth of anticapitalist forces in the Third World which reduce the reservoir of exploitation; and a vast working class which, separated from the control of the means of production, confronts a small, parasitic ruling class.*

Stipulated: This reads like a parody of every Communist cliché, not only from 1972 but from today. But it's not, and it indicates how success-fully the Unholy Left transferred its absurd obsessions into public policy in our own time. It's insane but extraordinarily potent, in the manner of true madness.

The proper response to this over-intellectualized twaddle is laughter. And therein lies the rub, for laughter—or, better expressed, disbelief that anyone could take this seriously—is what they count on. Surely, no one could take the idea of political correctness seriously, since it runs counter to every strain and fiber of the American character: How dare you tell me what I *can't* say? In its earliest incarnations, the PC code was considered so risible that it was even mocked by the libertarian Left, in the form of Bill Maher's television show, *Politically Incorrect*, and in books hawked at San Francisco's famous Beat bookstore City Lights, such as *Drinking, Smoking, and Screwing: Great Writers on Good Times* (1994). Here is this book's description, as provided by the publisher:

> *Before the notion of "political correctness" encroached on the ways people spoke, wrote, and conducted themselves in public and private, some of America's best writers embraced unsafe sex, excessive alcohol, and a good cigar. From the classically libidinous Henry Miller to the hilariously contemporary Fran Lebowitz,* Drinking, Smoking, and Screwing *includes novel excerpts, essays, poems, and short stories in a bawdy and thoroughly entertaining anthology with no warnings—and no apologies.*

Ha ha ha. Apologies aplenty now issue from the Left. Like the hapless Chinese and Cambodians in reeducation camps, they fall all over themselves to disavow their former behavior; surrounded by the darkness at noon, they have now seen the light and retroactively understood that their past actions—which were meant in support of the Revolution!—were misguided and probably corrupted by capitalist piggery. They throw themselves on the mercy of the People. "Trigger warnings" must now be posted on college campuses, lest someone stumble unawares across some sort of offense. Repeated consent must be given prior to and also throughout any sexual encounter, preferably in writing. And nobody in Hollywood drinks at lunch any more, much less smokes, which is now illegal, though the product itself, because of its position as a tax-cow, remains, for the moment, legal enough. How quickly the leftist paradigm, like Mephistopheles molting from a poodle into his own diabolical self in *Faust*, shifts shape.

In the Devil's Pleasure Palace, though filled with writhing naked nuns and fleshly temptations of every kind, there is no room for fun. Its pleasures, like those of the Cenobites in the 1987 film *Hellraiser,* lie in the infliction of pain. The flesh that shall be torn is ours. Jesus wept.

CHAPTER FOURTEEN

THE DEVIL IS IN THE DETAILS

The current struggle between Right and Left, like the conflict between occidental civilization and oriental Islam, is in part a battle over terms. The two sides do not speak a common language, nor, as we saw in Chapter Ten, do they take the same words to mean the same thing. "Peace" to an Islamic jihadist means the absence or submission of Christians, Jews, and all other infidels. It is, literally, the absence of conflict between *Dar al-Islam* and *Dar al-Harb*, between the world of perfect Islamic peace and the world of chaos and war, once the latter has been conquered. Similarly, the modern Left's ideas about "justice" have nothing to do with justice as most Americans traditionally understand it (blind, impartial, procedural) and everything to do with payback (social, economic, results-oriented). Both Muslims and leftists, in the furtherance of their aims, rely on their common enemy's good-natured misunderstanding.

Both, as noted, also proceed from a position of weakness, hoping, judo-like, to flip their stronger opponent by using his strengths against him—another characteristic of satanism, as Satan is always the weaker combatant against God. To take just one political example: In nearly every recent election, the Democrat-Media Complex has insisted, no matter what the electoral results, that what the American people are "really" (there's that word again) saying is that they want the two political parties to "work together." On the surface, this seems reasonable enough: Who could object to "bipartisan" cooperation on urgent matters of national security? But, like Marcuse's blather on capitalism, nothing about this bromide makes any sense.

I have coined the phrases "the Permanent Bipartisan Fusion Government" and "the Permanent Bipartisan Fusion Party" to describe this phenomenon. But what is "bipartisanship"? "Bipartisanship" is just another word for monochromatic government. Further, "working together," as currently practiced, means only one thing: that the party of the Right must abandon some of its bedrock principles to "compromise" with the party of the Left for the furtherance of some pet social program—and the only "compromise" will be over details of the program, not the idea itself. Thus the recent battle over national "health care." In reality, it's a tax increase in the service of a welfare scheme for largely subsidized recipients that benefits only a small fraction of the population at the expense of the many—a classic example of the Marxism dictum "from each according to his ability, to each according to his needs." Phrased like that, it never would have passed even a Democratic Congress; but disguised as "compassion," "insurance," and "health care," it just barely squeaked through by means of manipulation and outright deception, from the presidential level on down.

What earlier generations understood is that there can be no compromise with evil, only its unconditional (if temporary) surrender. The better elements of German society tried repeatedly to negotiate terms of surrender with the Western allies, to no avail. The Americans under President Truman understood that there could be no separate peace with the Bushido fanatics of Imperial Japan; indeed, once the emperor had accepted the terms of surrender of the Potsdam Declaration, there was a brief rebellion by some of his officers, the so-called Kyūjō Incident in mid-August 1945. But mindful of the Allies' promise that Japan would face prompt and utter destruction should it choose otherwise, the Empire of Japan sent its representatives to surrender two weeks later.

The lack of American success in subsequent wars—largely wars of choice, not necessity—has been instructive, because there have been no bedrock principles at stake. Korea was and remains a standoff, a failure of ongoing, eternal "diplomacy" that seeks no real end, only a continuance of process. Vietnam was no natural threat to the territories of the

United States, yet we lost 50,000 men there anyway in the service of an Ivy League theory about the "domino effect" of a Communist victory in Southeast Asia. The Cold War was played, by contrast, in deadly earnest, but mostly in the shadows, in the air, and under the seas. It was a Great Game between one side that played chess and another side that played poker; the latter won. Faced with what appeared to be certain economic defeat (entirely attributable to the inherent inadequacy of Marxist economic theory) and unused to the concept of bluffing one's ass off, the Soviets simply turned over their king and folded.

The Islamic wars since then have also been instructive, in the way of Dickens's Circumlocution Office in *Little Dorrit*: "Whatever was required to be done, the Circumlocution Office was beforehand with all the public departments in the art of perceiving—HOW NOT TO DO IT." Thus, the now all-but-forgotten first Gulf War, which ended in the expulsion of Iraq's Saddam Hussein from Kuwait, failed to change the balance of power in the Middle East, because the mission was HOW NOT TO CHANGE THINGS. The aftermath of 9/11 saw the quick defeat of the Taliban in Afghanistan, whence the attacks had been planned, but not the crushing of Saudi Arabia, whence most of the hijackers originated. Instead, the U.S. got bogged down in an ultimately fruitless war in Iraq and a Vietnam-like morass in Afghanistan.

The principles behind these Middle Eastern wars should have been simple: to inflict an Omdurman-like defeat on Islam post-9/11, one from which it would have taken a century or more to recover, if ever. But America's very own Circumlocution Office—otherwise known as the Department of State—intervened. For them, diplomacy is war by other means, which means full employment for the striped-pants set, who can always be counted on to find another reason WHY NOT TO CHANGE THINGS. The only victory came in the Cold War against the Soviets; when asked his strategy for winning the Cold War, Ronald Reagan replied, "We win, they lose." Patton couldn't have put it better.

But a principle, once hobbled, cannot be freed for a very long while. The Left seizes upon every rollback to demand a newer, fresher accommodation, all in the name of reason and compassion and tolerance and diversity and whatever the new buzzword of the day is. They never stop, they never sleep, they never quit. Constantly on the attack (as they must be, since they have nothing to defend), they constantly probe for weakness, for softness; frustrate them here and they will pop up there. Any inch forward is a victory, and tomorrow is another day.

In the face of this constant provocation, the Right has had almost no comeback. Why not? In part because the Left accuses the Right of what it itself, in fact, is either doing or planning to do; to use one of their favorite terms, they "project." A blank canvas, such as the mind of a young person, is one of their favorite things: everything to learn and nothing to unlearn. Only undermine the innate sense of morality—the ur-Narrative—and you're more than halfway there. Meanwhile, they constantly lob accusations of racism, sexism, ageism, homophobia, Islamophobia, whatever— the list is endless and constantly refreshed by the outrage of the day. It would be comic were the results not so tragic.

Still, the unwritten rule (enforced by a complicit media) is that no leftist provocation, however actually violent, can be reacted or responded to in kind, whereas any pushback from the Right is regarded as the second coming of Nazism. The Left has a need to feel oppressed, threatened, unloved; leftists are sure that a Christian theocracy is just around the corner, given half a chance, and they are utterly convinced that they can read the thoughts of conservatives and sense what they're planning to do.

As the novelist and journalist Tom Wolfe wrote in *Mauve Gloves and Madmen, Clutter and Vine* (1976): "He sounded like Jean-François Revel, a French socialist writer who talks about one of the great unexplained phenomena of modern astronomy: namely, that the dark night of fascism is always descending in the United States and yet lands only in Europe." Wolfe also quotes the German novelist Günther Grass: "You American intellectuals—you want so desperately to feel besieged and persecuted!"

Descendants of Rousseau, grandchildren of Gramsci and Lukács, children of Marcuse: Like little kids at a horror movie, they live for the imaginary threat, the frisson of danger, secure in the knowledge that nothing really bad is going to happen to them. They want to be the heroes of their own movies, even when they are only the extras in a bad remake of Fellini's *Satyricon*.

But, then, we all want to be heroes—that is the natural lot of man, and the subject of every boy's fantasy—but only one side will admit it, because only one side will admit the existence of heroism as a concept that exists outside literature, poetry, or the movies. It is something of a mystery why some leftist writers and filmmakers spend so much time denying the existence of heroism and then make a living by creating it, fictionally. Surely they cannot have that much contempt for their audience, because many of them are very, very good at it; their work has the resonance of authenticity, even if it is just fantasy. On some level, they must *believe* it.

Fantasy, however, is what we put on the page and up on the screen—fantasy, yes, but a fantasy that draws upon the deepest longings of the human heart, longings for love, glory, honor, family, friends, posterity. No matter how many times the Unholy Left derides these virtues, they continue to exist; no matter how many times the Left denies them, they pop back up; no matter how many times it tries to kill them, they live on, firing the imaginations of a whole new generation that, absent the sapping of the Critical Theorists, grows up *believing*. If this were not so, Disney would have been out of business decades ago; indeed, at the heart of nearly every Disney fable is the lesson that one must believe, against all external evidence to the contrary, in the rightness of one's chosen path.

Elementals, basics—these are the building blocks of culture, not the other way around. These are the essential themes, the innate beliefs, of everyone, and the Left cannot do away with them; they are too deeply ingrained. And they must come from *somewhere*.

Thus, principles matter. They are foundational, not arbitrary, as Critical Theory would have us believe. The Devil, the lawyer from Hell, may be in the details, but God establishes principles. If you don't believe it, ask any astronomer or scientist, even with his necessarily imperfect understanding of man and the universe, whether he detects an ordered hand or the Call of Cthulhu in the music of the spheres; many reject religion, but few advocate Chaos and Pandemonium. To defend a foundational principle is not arbitrary, it is mandatory.

Thus, no quarter. From the evidence above, it should be clear by now that both sides are Manichaean in their outlook. Neither, at this point, can give an inch, although one side constantly demands it, in the same of "compassion," "compromise," "fairness," "tolerance," or "Allah," as the spirit moves them. Details may be negotiated without affecting principles on either side, but details must never be primary. That way lies death by bureaucracy, something that, ironically, helped kill the Soviet Union and that promises to be the death of the United States unless it is pruned back in time. Jesus did not promise that clerks would inherit the earth.

Therefore, there can be no such thing as "progressivism," the once-and-future label under which society's sappers have chosen to take refuge. Instead, there is only regression to an ugly and sordid future that, satanically, squeezes the humanity out of the human, sometimes literally. As Mary McCarthy said of the American Communist writer Lillian Hellman: "Every word she writes is a lie, including 'and' and 'the.'" (The witticism provoked a $2.5 million libel suit—an Oscar Wilde moment for Hellman, fatally damaging to her overblown reputation.)

Why on earth is the Unholy Left trying to re-create the Garden of Eden, something whose existence they passionately deny, both literally and symbolically? Welcome to the dystopia of numerous futures imperfect—not just *1984* but *Brave New World, Fahrenheit 451, Atlas Shrugged,* Kurt Vonnegut's "Harrison Bergeron," et al., not to mention countless motion pictures, among them *Brazil, The Matrix,* and *Dark City.* Futures all too easily imagined and innately feared, like snakes.

This regression is accomplished by death through a thousand details, regulations, and bureaucratic boilerplate, administered by drones whose only function is the administration of process: everything within the Circumlocution Bureau, nothing outside the Circumlocution Bureau, and with a liberal application of molasses to gum up the works just to make sure nothing does work. They care nothing for humanity, and in that they fully partake of the spirit of Mephisto—amoral, callous, deceitful. As Faust shouts when he finally realizes, too late, with Gretchen condemned to death and languishing in prison, the depth of the Devil's depravity:

FAUST
Dog! Abominable monster! Transform him, oh Infinite Spirit! Transform this reptile again into his dog-shape, as he often pleased nightly, trotting up before me, growling at the feet of the harmless wand'rer, and hanging upon his shoulders when he fell. Change him back into his favorite shape, that he may crawl upon his belly in the sand before me, that I might trample him, the cast-out, under foot!

MEPHISTOPHELES
Now we are already again at the end of our joke, where the mind goes mad for you humans. Why did you make this common cause with us if you can't

see it through? You want to fly, but are unsure because you're dizzy? Did we force ourselves upon you, or you upon us?

Scales fall hard, even those of serpents, but they do fall.

Is this the future we want for our children, should we choose to have any? Is this the present we want for ourselves? Best to reject not only the Left's prescriptions for a "better"—a fundamentally transformed—America, but the very terms of their argument. Up is down. Black is white. Freedom is slavery. War is peace. And ignorance is what they count on. Nothing is what it seems at the Devil's Pleasure Palace, especially the pleasure.

"Did we force ourselves upon you, or you upon us?" What a question.

CHAPTER FIFTEEN

OIKOPHOBES AND XENOPHILES

In his first homily as pope, Francis invoked the saying of Léon Bloy: "Anyone who does not pray to the Lord prays to the devil." Then he got even blunter: "When we do not profess Jesus Christ, we profess the worldliness of the devil, a demonic worldliness." The first Jesuit pope was proclaiming his profound disinterest in the political divisions of our day in order to concentrate on the essential dichotomy of human existence in a world that either does or does not believe in God.

Can one believe in nothing, as some atheists would have it? As G.K. Chesterton apparently never quite said (the aphorism seems derived from several different writings, including his *Father Brown* stories): "The man who no longer believes in God does not believe in nothing; rather, he will believe in anything." The Satan of *Paradise Lost* very much does believe in something: the necessity of revenge, a desire so great it overcomes even his lust for Eve's perfect female body. Like the flames of Hell, it consumes him without killing him; it literally fires him to effect his vast plot against mankind. Much of today's Unholy Left seems motivated by the same emotion: revenge on the country that gave them either birth or shelter. They are at once oikophobes (fearing their home) and xenophiles (loving what is foreign)—particularly untrustworthy specimens of humanity.

The Left's is not a classic Third World revenge, best expressed by Inigo Montoya in *The Princess Bride*: "You killed my father. Prepare to die." Instead, it seeks a larger, dare one say, "comprehensive" target: a revenge on a society that remains distressingly what it is and that adamantly refuses to become what, by their lights, it *should* be. At root, their beef is not with Man but with God; even if they refuse to admit he exists, they still want to fight him anyway.

As refugees both luxuriating in and resenting their outsider status, the wise men of the Frankfurt School were infuriated by the non-state control of Hollywood and the national and local media they encountered in New York, New Jersey, and California. They scorned what they dubbed the "culture industry" and seethed with contemptuous rage against a land that cared very little for what they thought. Except of course for academia.

Most of today's "vilenesses various" (in J.P. Donleavy's phrase from *The Unexpurgated Code*) derive from this deep-seated resentment. P.J. O'Rourke's famous characterization of the Left—"a philosophy of sniveling brats"—is spot-on. As Mephistopheles observes in Marlowe's *Doctor Faustus*: "*Solamen miseris, socios habuisse doloris.*" ("It is a comfort to the wretched to have companions in misery.") For those of us who came of age during the tumultuous 1960s, who saw said sniveling brats trade in their knee pants for the tie-dyed jeans and ponchos of Woodstock, for those of us who never joined them in their posturing anarchy and supererogatory celebrations of self, the Left has been a continuing mystery, perhaps most especially in its remarkable success at making a parasitic living from a society it claims to despise. Like the bank robber Willie Sutton, modern leftists went where the money was: at Gramsci's behest, into academia; prompted by Adorno's ire, into the "culture industry"; and at Marx's insistence, into the machinery of the state.

And there they have stayed ever since, fifty years on and counting. The irony is remarkable: a group of self-styled revolutionaries constantly reliving the glory days of their youth and professing fealty to ideas a century older than they are. The government programs they cherish date from the Roosevelt administration; never mind that schemes such as Social Security and Medicare, fraudulently conceived at the outset, are careening toward auto-destruction. Never mind that the leviathan state espoused by the "progressive" wings of both political parties is itself fundamentally regressive in every sense: sclerotic, unworkable, infeasible, and (something they will never admit) immoral. They are Dorian Gray inverted and writ large in the Baby Boomer generation: inwardly still youthful (indeed adolescent) in thought and outlook, but outwardly wrinkled, decrepit, corrupted, doomed. Until this wing of the Boomers shuffles offstage and into that black nothingness it so desperately claims to embrace (but against which it will fight to the end, with the best doctors and medical technology its money and yours can buy), the country will continue to be afflicted by their reductive, jejune, hand-me-down Marxist philosophy.

What will it take to disabuse the rest of America? We have a partial answer before us—and in recent history. As it happens, I spent much of the period between February 1985 and the summer of 1991 behind the Iron Curtain, in what was then the Soviet Union and the Warsaw Pact nations. From the time I arrived, it was evident to me that the socialist system could not last. Its "internal contradictions" were not merely theoretical, like the West's, but visible and grotesque. Its "liberated" women had been reduced to little more than prostitutes, sexually available for the price of dinner or a new dress. In the Soviet Union, if you were a man in need of female companionship, it came to you: All you had to do was wait for a woman in an elevator to offer to visit you in your room or, even easier, wait for the chambermaids to knock on your door, with delicacies boosted from the kitchen and themselves as the sweeteners. The old Soviet Union was Reich's sexually liberated paradise come to life, and all the scars on the women's bodies from multiple abortions spoke of its mutilations and death toll.

The men, meanwhile, were seemingly disinterested members of the economic-justice proletariat, but you couldn't find a taxi driver in Moscow; the official "living wage" fares weren't worth the trouble to start the engine. Far easier for you to hold up one or two fingers (signifying how many packets of smuggled-in Marlboros—the de facto currency—you were willing to pay for a ride) and get a lift immediately, to anywhere you wanted, no questions asked. An added bonus: Very often, the civilian driver would be carrying a load of fenced contraband, including caviar, vodka, and, at times, weapons.

These men and women were not examples of the failure of the Soviet system; they were exemplars of the superiority of capitalism and the Christian West's desire for personal freedom (contrary to George W. Bush's claim, it is, alas, not universal). In the fun-house mirror that was the old Soviet Union, citizens learned a devilish lesson: Vice is virtue. And they profited from the lesson, as best they could, until at last the entire rotten edifice buckled.

Why the Soviet Union so suddenly collapsed at the end of 1991 is a puzzle that has occupied scholars and apologists ever since. Yet it is no mystery to anyone who was there. "A house divided against itself cannot stand," said Lincoln. Far more so than the U.S., the U.S.S.R. was beset by the cognitive dissonance arising from the conflict between its proclaimed ideals and the brute force with which they were implemented. Everybody knew it, except the Western intellectuals and mainstream journalists, who insisted, right up to the end, that the Soviet Union was the "other super-power," the idealized (if not actually ideal) alternative to the American experiment. The evidence was right in front of their faces: The Soviet Union was a society that could barely build a functioning toilet; it was afflicted by severe housing shortages (it was customary for parents of marriageable children to retire discreetly to the bedroom of a two-room flat in order to let the young folks have sex in the living room; failing that, couples had sex in the backs of cars or in the local graveyard); it tested the seaworthiness of its deep-water subs by sending a few underwater to measure at what depth their hulls cratered and their crews died.

The clue that the end was near came in the summer of 1989, when the Hungarians—faced with a crush of East Germans trying to flee one of their few legally allowed vacation spots—decided to open the border with Austria on August 19. There had been a gesture in that direction a couple of months earlier, when the Austrian foreign minister and his Hungarian counterpart symbolically clipped a section of barbed wire that had divided the two formerly united provinces of the old Austro-Hungarian Empire. But on that day, as the East German "Ossies" first forced their way through whatever remained of the old Soviet-imposed fortifications, something that had not happened since the erection of the Berlin Wall actually did happen: nothing. Nobody stopped them. Nobody shot at them. Nobody killed them. In the face of freedom, and their willingness to risk their lives for it, the death cult of Communism had fallen impotently silent. Again, why?

For one thing, the Communist system had become so economically moribund that it could no longer afford even to keep its prison fences in working order. It took money—real money, "hard currency," *valuta*—to buy materials the system could not supply. For the Hungarians and the other satellite nations on the fortified border with the West, that expense had more and more been rolled off on them during the Motherland's long, slow twilight. Finally, they had had enough. As Margaret Thatcher famously said, more or less: "The problem with socialism is that eventually you run out of other people's money." (She actually said: "Socialist governments traditionally do make a financial mess. They always run out of other people's money.")

Many of what we used to call the "captive nations" lay within television-signal reach of the West. In East Germany, only the Saxon city of Dresden was beyond immediate Western cultural influence, and its people were derided by their fellow Ossies as ignorant buffoons. Throughout Eastern Europe and even in Moscow, a brisk trade in bootleg Western jeans and rock albums had long been in place, but restive populations wanted the real thing, plus (as we soon learned after the Wall fell) fresh fruit, bananas, and porn. Adorno's feared "culture industry" had done its work well.

Who were these heroes? The names of the border guards that day are largely lost to history, but they were the Men Who Didn't Shoot, who did not contribute to the death toll that hardened the postwar division of Europe, who finally just said no to Satan. Unlike Michael Corleone, they meant it.

To stand at the Berlin Wall near the Brandenburg Gate before the *Mauerfall*, the fall of the Wall, was to see, on the Western side, rows of markers, each one in memoriam of some brave East German who had tried and failed to breach the "Anti-Fascist Protection Barrier." Not far away, as the Wall doglegged behind it, stood the dead hulk of the Reichstag, so symbolic of both German strength and German savagery, abandoned along with the *"Dem Deutschen Volke"* commemorated in the famous dedication above the doors: to the German people. And who could forget the defining image of the end of the war in Europe:

the Russian soldier atop the Reichstag, waving the Soviet flag over the bombed-out ruins of Berlin?

Few would have expected that the fierce Soviets would simply give up, allow the Wall to fall, and freely remove their troops. After all, they had been hell-bent on revenge for what they saw as Germany's treachery in launching Operation Barbarossa in 1941, when Germany invaded the Soviet Union in defiance of the Molotov-Ribbentrop pact of 1939, which had partitioned Poland and given the Baltic states over to the Russian Bear. But give up the Soviets surely did. There came a time, even for them, the victors in what Stalin called the Great Patriotic War (they were fighting for country, not Communism), when further killing wasn't worth the price it took on their souls. The Devil may never sicken of slaughter, but humans do.

I recall in particular one hot summer afternoon on the Potsdamer Platz: July 21, 1990. The occasion was a live performance of Pink Floyd's *The Wall*, a rock opera suddenly current again. My review of the concert, which ran in the August 3, 1990, issue of *Entertainment Weekly*, began like this:

> You couldn't go anywhere in Berlin on July 21 without bumping into The Wall.... On this hot Saturday afternoon, Potsdamer Platz, for 28 years a bleak no-man's-land known as the Death Strip that separated the two Berlins, was transformed into a 35-acre German Woodstock. All morning, a crowd estimated at more than 200,000 had gathered outside the temporary wire fences, and at 2:30 P.M. the gates opened and the people started thronging in. Quickly, they formed a mass that stretched from the old Wilhelmstrasse across the square to the Berlin Philharmonic's concert hall, the Philharmonie.

You can find my full review of the concert—which also featured the Hooters, members of The Band, Sinéad O'Connor, Joni Mitchell, and a host of others—online on the magazine's website, but perhaps the conclusion is worth quoting:

> The day after the show, the curious were poking through the concert debris. A few tents were still pitched, harboring sleeping hippies. Some youths sat by the side of the road, dazed from their exertions of the night

before when, after the concert, Berlin was one big party town. A young boy with a shopping cart happily wheeled away a souvenir: one of the Styrofoam bricks, nearly as big as he was.

A lifetime ago, the Woodstock Generation thought it could change the world with a flower and a three-chord song, a dream that died in a hail of bullets in Vietnam and Kent State and Memphis and Los Angeles. Now, 21 years later, their sons and daughters had gathered, 200,000 strong, and by their presence made the eloquent point that maybe the Woodstockers were right all along.

It is interesting to note that as workers were excavating the site, not simply for the concert venue but for the new, commercial Potzdamer Platz that was slated for construction, they came across an old SS bunker, an unexploded Soviet bomb, and small arms and ammunition, some of the last relics of the war. And then those, too, were gone and the musicians took over.

I spent much of that day wandering around the spot where Hitler had spent his last hours in the *Führerbunker*, aware that the advancing Soviets were drawing ever nearer, and finally shooting himself, like Brünnhilde throwing herself upon Siegfried's burning bier, a drama queen to the end. All around me were Soviet soldiers, their presence purposeless, their mission once accomplished, now failed. I got together with a Russian "journalist" and an East German whom I had first met under official circumstances in East Berlin back in 1985, who is now an old and dear friend, and we repaired to a nearby pub for some cold beers. I made them buy. We drank a toast to the end of the Cold War, and to whatever was coming next.

Like the Soviets and the East Germans, Gramsci's long march must and will finally fail when Alinsky's children are inevitably co-opted by the "culture industry" that Adorno warned them about, when they give up and give in. It's difficult to retain revolutionary fervor and high dudgeon for very long. The red-diaper babies—quintessential imported oikophobes and xenophiles (certainly, Russsophiles)—of the 1930s managed to do it even as they grew old and fat on the spoils of the capitalist system they still railed about to their dying day. One thing you could say about them: If the cognitive dissonance of their lives and beliefs ever bothered them, they didn't let it show. They retained their animus against

America—and their fondness for a political system they knew they would never have to suffer under—to the bitter end. But their children and grandchildren are another story.

There is an old saying: "from shirtsleeves to shirtsleeves in three generations." That's the length of time any American institution lasts between its founding by a man of vision (Joseph P. Kennedy, Carlo Gambino, Henry Luce, to name at random three family enterprises, only two of them criminal) and its demolition by inadequate and unworthy heirs, who wreck it with their foolish business decisions. The Unholy Left and its institutions are not immune from these ironclad, deterministic historical forces (pure Marxism in action, when you stop to think about it).

Their prolonged assault on American politics and culture—which, for purposes of discussion, we might date from the anti-Constitution Woodrow Wilson administration—has been steadfast and unwavering. But no political victory is ever permanent, as the Soviet example shows. No military victory is ever permanent, either. The Left's ascendancy in the U.S. culminated in the election of a frankly socialist candidate, but two terms of exposure to him and his leftist ideals have resulted in a vast revulsion against "the fundamental transformation" of the United States he promised to deliver. Because the high ground of academia, the media, and pop culture is still occupied by fellow travelers (and their spouses, neighbors, friends, and intimates), the Left's recent losses have been partly hidden. Conservatives might not like to hear this, but until the day the *New York Times*—the die-hard house organ of American progressivism—admits on its front page that it has been consistently wrong for more than a half-century, the Academic-Media Complex will not be disabused of its long-held, devilish illusions.

We have seen earlier how most of these illusions are based on what "ought" to be, rather than what is. Indeed, a refusal to accept reality is, for leftists, a form of heroism. Yet it is not; with the possible exception of Don Quixote, there is nothing heroic about mental defectiveness, emotional immaturity, and a cowardice that hides behind the skirts of doubletalk. But this is what the Left offers to an apparently inexhaustible supply of impressionable, often materially comfortable young people in need of a cause. The Democratic Party, which was seized by radicals between 1968 and 1972, has evolved into a party made up entirely of factions: the youth vote, the black vote, the Hispanic vote, the single-women's vote. It has no center and is now largely confined to the two seaboards and a swath of the upper Midwest. Historically disposed to social do-gooder-ism, the latter is only now becoming aware of the consequences of its one-size-fits-all Protestantism—something made visible, for instance, by the burgeoning Somali population of Minnesota, with its concomitant jihadi subculture. For Democrats, it doesn't matter if the center cannot hold, since there is no center, just a never-ending quest for more aggrieved "minorities" with which to fan the flames of resentment and deliver the payback the Left earnestly desires.

Viewed in military terms, conservatives should be rolling up the progressives rather easily. They are essentially confined to the tribal homelands, where they should be quarantined until the ruinous poison of their governing philosophy has run its course: the busted budgets; the enormous dependence on the public sector; the political internalization of organized crime (a hallmark of big cities since Tammany); crushing taxation; ever more social programs piled onto earlier failures; tight, expensive housing; and de facto racial and economic segregation in their principal cities.

But of course they cannot be confined, which makes them akin to the predatory, parasitic aliens from *Independence Day* (as conservative a motion picture as *High Noon*) who move from planet to planet, despoiling everything in their wake until their host orb gives up the ghost and it is time for them to move on and seek fresh victims. When the president of the United States, in temporary mind-meld with one of the monsters, asks, in true liberal fashion, "What do you want us to do?" in the hopes that we can all just get along, the beast hisses: "*Die.*"

Is death really an option, even for the Left? What happens when there is no longer a cause for which to "fight"? (Like Satan, the Left must always have something to "fight," lest it be rendered impotent, because its driving force, as we've seen, stems not from philosophy but emotion—hatred, resentment, envy, and malcontentment.) Some thought that the disintegration of the Soviet Union signaled "the end of history," and in fact the Left was quiescent for a spell after the self-immolation of the U.S.S.R. and the Warsaw Pact nations. Even leftists, snark-mongers that they are, had no comeback to the economic and moral revolution that began with the fall of the Wall and continued to the events of September 11, 2001, when a new and perhaps even more potent ancient evil re-announced itself in the form of four hijacked American airliners. And then the Left found a new enemy to love.

We are engaged, as Lincoln noted, in a great civil war, this one not yet fought with weapons, but with ideas. In the Left's attempt to "fundamentally transform" the United States of America, it has used every other weapon in its arsenal, from indoctrination to fabrication, from "moral" suasion based on no morality at all to an unapologetic celebration of hedonism and sybaritism embodied by Reich and Marcuse, Leary and Hefner. To its everlasting shame, it has convinced women to murder their own babies in the name of "rights": Adam Gopnik, an otherwise fine writer for the *New Yorker,* has called abortion "one of the greatest moral achievements in human history—the full emancipation of women." The Left has convinced black Americans, on the Orwellian theory that freedom is slavery, to flock to the banner of the party of slavery, segregation, secularism, and sedition in search of freedom from slavery. It has convinced generations of college students that their country was founded in Original Sin (which the Left otherwise rejects). Furthermore, it has taught that this Original Sin can never be eradicated or expiated, since there cannot be a Redeemer; the only recourse is the self-abnegation or total annihilation of the Principal Enemy, which just so happens to be (as Pogo famously observed) us. By embracing the Cause, they are saved, indeed elevated above the constraints of morals, as their goal is just, and they are freed to make holy war upon the sinful, wicked, damned folks back in Dubuque or Topeka.

None of this is going to happen, not as long as one free man still breathes. For freedom is akin to the light in the darkness: A single exemplar represents total defeat for the other side. Darkness can never be complete until the eradication of the last light, a task beyond even the superhuman capabilities of Satan. Marxists such as Lukács were adamant in their belief that Western civilization needed to be destroyed before true "justice" could arrive. And while the Left relies on youth's innate "liberalism," conservatives need to appeal to some of youth's other typical characteristics, including its skepticism about dogma, its belief in its own heroism and immortality, and its profound sense of self-interest.

In other words, conservatives should focus on selling the old virtuous wine—those virtues that have fueled every myth since the time of Homer—in new, improved, "revolutionary" bottles. One "scientific" fact the permanent revolutionary Left cannot escape is that eventually the rebels becomes the establishment, and revolutionary theory requires constant revolution in order to keep moving forward. It is a Serpent, unable to fuck Eve, eating its tail.

Some "revolutionary" parties, such as Mexico's aptly named "Institutional Revolutionary Party," a member of the Socialist International, rely on Marxist anti-Narrative to keep their voters in a perpetual state of economic fear while subjecting them to economic misery—on the theory that things could always be worse. Others, such as the Democrats, continue to reinforce their own narrative via the use of the popular media. The majority of leftist and mainstream journalists (a redundancy) subscribe, however consciously or unconsciously, to the following beliefs, which drive how they select or ignore stories: The U.S. is incorrigibly racist; racism is often hard to detect but always present; racism plays a role in nearly every news story, especially when it's not at all clear that it does. Call it the Holy Ghost theory of racism, explained by the secular version of Original Sin.

Journalists also reflexively subscribe to cultural-Marxist notions of class; they have internalized them so thoroughly that they no longer even think about them. Just about any story can be framed through the grid of race or class, especially that staple of television news, crime stories. The idea that crime is a function of poverty or the legacy of slavery (which ended in 1865), or that it results from some combination of other social ailments, is axiomatic. That the residue of Evil should also be evil is beyond their comprehension, since the only evil they will admit to is that of their ideological opponents. That Evil could be external is impossible, since there is no other explanation beyond the "scientific" for any human phenomena.

The third leg of the late twentieth century's cultural-Marxist stool is "gender," originally conceived of as liberating the oppressed proletariat of women from their male oppressors (into the nirvana of careerism and lesbianism, they frankly admitted). When the returns on women as mascots began diminishing, gays became the cause du jour; and with little other than same-sex marriage in the cards for gays, "trans" people have now become the new object of pity society must be coerced to love. Once they've had their day, some yet smaller, more outré group—polygamists? pedophiles? animal fanciers?—will be picked out and their hurt feelings at the larger society's considering their lusts bizarre will be engraved on the cudgel with which the institution of the family will continue to be beaten bloody.

The extraordinary effrontery of this philosophy deserves to be more widely mocked than it is, snark generally being a tool of the Left and not the Right. But consider: For the Unholy Left's philosophy to be correct, we must reject the experience and empirical evidence of thousands of years of human history in favor of a relatively recent "intellectual" construction that arrogantly assigned all virtue to itself, demonized its opposition, and went about creating a new Garden of Eden here on earth, with man- and womankind at its center, as long as they were having sex. Preferably "safe," non-reproductive sex.

Not only, therefore, must we apparently reject the principal tenets of organized religion, most of which share the same basic concepts, variously understood. We must also reject a folk storytelling tradition that is even older than the principal faiths. We must, in short, reject *everything* that we have previously believed about ourselves that our ancestors taught us. Tradition is the democracy of the dead, as the saying goes, and that democracy must be overthrown in favor of our momentary whims, with an *Ermächtigungsgesetz* ("enabling law") that criminalizes even the memory of doing things differently. We must discard out of hand the experience of earlier generations, all deemed superstitious idiots in continuous thrall to some kind of primitive mental illness or superstition, with only a few bright lights (within the upside-down, Bizarro World context of the Left) such as Rousseau and Marx to dispel the darkness of macho mythos and repressive Judeo-Christian sexual morality. Only just be free, they sing like the Sirens to Odysseus, like Mephisto, promising infinite knowledge to Faust and everlasting happiness to the sexually repressed but delivering only slavery, disease, and death. You shall be like gods, they promise the rotting corpses.

How can conservatism not sell a political program of Freedom, Liberty, and Leave Me Alone to the youth of America and elsewhere? These are heroic verities that have sustained the Republic since its inception—and precisely the truths that have come under the most sustained attack from Critical Theory. Freedom is "really" slavery. "Liberty" is illusory, as we are all subject to Marxist political-historical forces against which the individual counts for nothing. And Leave Me Alone—the crucial principle of the American Revolution—is simply antisocial self-ishness. Far safer to be confined to a yoke, free from the terrors that lie just beyond the campfire, and serving your fellow man.

Fear is what they sell, fear of the unknown. Heroism is what we should be selling, heroism in the face of the unknown. No matter how they may try to reframe the heroes of myth and legend, it is impossible for them to hammer heroes from Ulysses to Dirty Harry into a Marxist cosmology. Our heroes are too individualistic, too contrarian; they don't care what the world thinks of them, they only want to do what is right. Were we once more to unleash our shared, innate notions of heroism upon the Unholy and Unheroic Left, we would crush them, see them driven before us and hear the lamentations of their women (to paraphrase the immortal words of the fictional Conan the Barbarian, themselves John Milius's paraphrase of a purported aphorism of Genghis Khan's). Their cruelty is their strength, but it is their cowardice that will be their undoing.

CHAPTER SIXTEEN

GOOD-BYE TO ALL THAT

We have, intellectually, come to the dead end of Critical Theory. It may stumble around, like Frankenstein's monster, seeking revenge on a world it feels has wronged it, but the theories set in place by the Frankfurt School have played themselves out intellectually; now they are merely dogma. Although the divine–demonic struggle for mankind's soul is not yet over (nor can it ever be, until the Last Trump), the high tide of cultural sedition represented by the Institute for Social Research has passed. The brutal facts have had their way with it, and now, it is just a matter of purging Critical Theory from the institutions through which it marched for so many years and that today represent (like their redefinition of patriotism) the last refuge of scoundrels.

That no good has come from the Left's relentless assault on Western culture is beyond dispute. Not a single American institution has benefited from progressives' "analysis." The most common riposte is for them to point to the civil rights movement of the 1960s, which remains for many aging modern leftists the signal memory of their youth. That their participation in it is largely a fantasy, like their attendance at Woodstock, doesn't matter; their need to be on the "right side of history" allows them to be the heroes of their own story. Even a leftist or a Communist needs to feel that he or she has made a difference *for the better*, when better is usually the last thing they were aiming for, except in the broadest

theoretical sense. The civil rights movement—their one ostensible triumph—was largely a story of the center of American politics: The old
liberals for whom the New Left had nothing but contempt united with
boring Republicans to defang racist Southern Democrats. But that matters not a whit to them. If it was good, it was a deed of the Left; if it was
a deed of the Left, it was good.

The idea of "progress," a version of Marx's historical inevitability, is
central to the Left's mythos. Having imported the concept along with a
grab bag of statist policies from Bismarck's Germany in the first decade
of the twentieth century, the Left embraced the label of "progressivism"—
effectively, anti-constitutionalism, which held that America's founding
document was the antiquated stricture that kept the enlightened scientific
functionaries of the age from hurrying society toward Progress.

Woodrow Wilson was the great champion of early-twentieth-century
Progressivism, though he comprehensively delegitimized it with the public when he took up dictatorial War Socialism. Indeed, his duplicitousness
in bringing the U.S. into World War I discredited Progressivism—or at
least its name—with a group of mostly literary intellectuals who adopted,
with some historical illiteracy, the sobriquet "liberals" in the 1920s.
When these "liberals" gained power in the 1930s, they immediately set
about recycling their favorite aspects of Wilsonian Progressivism and
Bismarckian welfare-statism, adding in the sexy new doctrines of Italian
Fascism and National Socialism (which had yet to remove its mask,
revealing the Jew-devouring Moloch beneath).

These New Dealers, like their Progressive predecessors (in fact, many
were the very same individuals), disliked the civil society formed by our
constitutional system (Sinclair Lewis's famous *Babbitt* remains the classic anti-middle-class polemic). They attempted to abrogate its limiting
mechanisms whenever possible, as FDR did when he threatened to pack
the Supreme Court. Later, in the 1960s, '70s, and '80s, they took refuge
behind those aspects of the Constitution that suited their "revolutionary"
purposes, especially those amendments in the Bill of Rights that gave
them safe harbor as they erected their program of "tolerance" of "dissent."
Positing by fiat, without ever quite explaining why, a set of new "values"
that mostly were anti-values, they demanded that the larger society conform to their minority wishes. They indicted that society incrementally,
attacking its history ("racist"), its religious culture ("Christianist"), its

very existence ("colonialist"). But call them "Marxist" and listen to them squeal; by their lights, any attack on them is illegitimate. It has been an unequal debate between unequal sides, both intellectually and morally, in which the minority report argues from its own authority, arbitrarily denies legitimacy to the majority, and counts on the gullibility of the American public and its sense of fair play and sympathy for the underdog not to notice the difference. But even evil things must, thankfully, come to an end, especially when their sole prop is a self-flattering claim to intellectual superiority.

In the early 1960s, a Communist (Trotskyite) front organization in the U.S. called the Fair Play for Cuba Committee was supported by a parade of leftists, including the writers Norman Mailer and James Baldwin, and the Beat poets Allen Ginsberg and Lawrence Ferlinghetti. Its most notorious member was a New Orleans–born defector to the Soviet Union named Lee Harvey Oswald, who had returned from a short stay in Minsk with his Russian wife.

Who could be against "fair play?" That's un-American! Journalistic convention helped, for it was axiomatic that there must be two sides to every story (whether one was true was a matter of "judgment" and not for the reporter to decide). Living in the Land of No Consequences that was America before the Kennedy assassination, and before the new waves of immigration from non-European countries, most Americans at the time could not conceive that anything essential about the nation could ever be changed; so a little good will toward even the delusional would be tolerated in the name of fair play.

But young men are dangerous, because they are young men. They are soldiers and criminals, inventive artists and moral monsters, capable of astounding heroism and utter brutality. It's no accident that the young men Mephistopheles bewitches in *Faust* in the *Auerbachs Keller* (the second-oldest restaurant in Leipzig) are students, the future leaders of German society, the "intellectuals." Mephisto, however, does not appeal to their intellectual vanity; rather, he tests them with coarse, bestial pleasures and punishes them with fire for their gullibility.

Lee Oswald, only 24 when he died, was a dangerous young man who changed the course of American history with three shots from a mail-order Mannlicher-Carcano rifle. Shortly before he died, he translated Prince Yeletsky's aria "*Ya vas lyublyu, lyublyu bezmerno*" ("I love you, love you immeasurably") from Tchaikovsky's opera *The Queen of Spades* and left it for his Russian wife, Marina, to find:

> *I love you,*
> *Love you immeasurably.*
> *I cannot imagine life without you.*
> *I am ready right now to perform a heroic deed*
> *Of unprecedented prowess for your sake.*
> *Oh, darling, confide in me!*

Not even a leftist like Oswald could deny the power of illusion, or its oft-beneficial effects. Illusion was such a powerful force acting upon him that he got it into his confused mind that a heroic deed had to be done, and shooting the president of the United States would be it. (Many assassins are driven by love, like John Hinckley, who shot President Reagan to impress an actress he had never met.) Illusion is the very stuff of Hollywood—although "Hollywood" itself is an illusion, as anybody who has ever worked there quickly comes to understand. Illusion is part of storytelling, and storytelling, as we have seen, is innate. But illusion is only the surface of storytelling, not its heart. Its heart is Truth.

Note that it was Pilate, the Roman governor of Judea, who introduced the notion of the uncertainty of Truth. (He, not the Jews, is also the weak man who passively condemns Jesus to death.) If we can argue about what the truth is, then we can argue about anything. That is what the Left has counted on since Rousseau. It is the essence of the Frankfurt School's program. When anything is subject to debate, then everything is; and when that thing is something as essential as Truth, then nothing is sacred.

But that is precisely the point. The sacred verities of Western civilization did not survive the hellish trenches of the First World War. The period 1914–1918 was the time when culture fractured, when the eternal verities that had built a civilization from the Holy Roman Empire to the Edwardian era came apart—over a family squabble among three members of Queen Victoria's extended family. In the end, it was a destructive, internecine war of cousin against cousin, a family tragedy, much like Wagner's *Ring*. Phylogeny recapitulates ontogeny.

Nowhere was this family tragedy more vividly illustrated than in poet Robert von Ranke Graves's memoir of the Great War, *Good-Bye to All That*, written after his return from the trenches and published in 1929. Graves was Anglo-Irish on his father's side and minor German nobility on his mother's; nevertheless, like the cream of young British men, he went to war against his Hun cousins willingly, enlisting in the Royal Welch Fusiliers and seeing action at the Somme, where he was badly wounded.

World War I has not received the attention it deserves in American popular culture. This is partly because the war was very controversial among Americans on the home front: At the time of the war, the largest ethnic minority in America was German (as it continues to be, depending on how one counts the peoples of the British Isles), and the sudden possibility that the nation's largest "minority" could be seditious had a profound effect on Wilsonian America. Fear of Germans led to such oddities as "Liberty cabbage" and "French toast," the new names for sauerkraut and what had hitherto been "German toast." A more serious consequence was Prohibition, the revenge of Protestant America on the more recently arrived German and Irish Catholics—the "drinking class" of Oscar Wilde's famous aphorism—and their Jewish liquor-selling enablers. Whereas World War II offers a handy program of Nazi and Japanese villains and British and American heroes, World War I has murky, familial, Wagnerian, even biblical origins: Who, exactly, begat whom? And who forced himself on whom?

Graves understandably reacted to the disillusioning horrors of the Great War, with its unholy, useless carnage—the Devil's Charnel House disguised as the Pleasure Palace of the Arc of History. There was precious little individual heroism in World War I (for the Americans, it was the Tennessee country boy, Sergeant Alvin York, the conscientious objector turned Medal of Honor winner), just the endless grind of the trenches, random death, pointless charges. (One is also tempted to add, impiously, the great line from the final season of *Blackadder*: "the endless poetry!") What nobility there was died at the point of fixed bayonets in no-man's-land. But let Graves tell the story:

There had been bayonet fighting in the wood. There was a man of the South Wales Borderers and one of the Lehr regiment who had succeeded in bayoneting each other simultaneously. A survivor of the fighting told me later that he had seen a young soldier of the Fourteenth Royal Welch

bayoneting a German in parade-ground style, automatically exclaiming
as he had been taught: "In, out, on guard." He said that it was the oddest
thing he had heard in France.

By the book. And yet that was how you did it in a Dickensian world
of HOW NOT TO DO IT. To put it in slightly more modern terms, those
steps would be: in, up, sideways (to the heart), out. And then watch him
die as you get ready to kill the next bastard in line. Unless he killed you
first. Someone was always dying for King or Kaiser.

These words sound cruel, and they are. Death is always cruel;
inflicting it depends on whether you have the stomach for it. Our
enemies today do not flinch at cruelty—they behead little girls—but we
do. Americans are not innately cruel; unlike the German forces on the
Eastern Front in World War II, we do not send flying squads of mobile
killers ahead of our lines to eliminate "undesirables." We do not, as a
matter of national policy, unlike the Russians in World War II or the
Muslims today, send troops to rape, loot, and pillage as instruments
of the state, to corrupt the blood of the subject peoples and turn their
children into us. We do not line up the severed heads of our enemies
on the ground for a photo-op.

In other words, we have standards—observed in the breach, perhaps,
but standards nonetheless. The history of America, unlike the history of
Europe and elsewhere, is in fact one of magnanimity, although coupled
with righteous anger when necessary, when attacked, when challenged on
moral grounds. Standards, not behavioral impulses, are what set us apart
from the chimps, who have only the latter, no matter how much projec-
tion and anthropomorphic wishful thinking we might direct their way.
Call it happenstance. Or call it the Breath of God, which gave *Ur-Vater*
Adam life and brought forth *Ur-Mutter* Eve to make us fully human. So
which myth would you rather believe?

But righteous anger is now forbidden as the relic of an earlier time, as
if only the anger were at issue, not righteousness. In the world of Critical
Theory, there is no righteousness except the angry righteousness of
Lucifer; there is no enormity we need address except imaginary outrages.
And those outrages are endless. As Ted Kennedy famously said, "the work
goes on, the cause endures, the hope still lives, and the dream shall never
die"—the leftist manifesto, in a few phrases.

No more chilling words have been spoken in modern American history. "The cause endures"? What cause? Certainly not the constitutional cause of fidelity to America's founding documents. Speaking in a code he was sure his audience would understand (a "dog whistle"), Kennedy telegraphed to his convention-center audience in New York City in 1980 that the Unholy Left was not about to give up, that *la Causa*—as the Communists fighting in the Spanish Civil War so proudly proclaimed in the run-up to World War II—would go on until the Manichaean conflict was at last resolved. It was a war cry that few on the Right heard, drowned out by the crushing defeat Reagan inflicted on Jimmy Carter shortly thereafter.

It is time to say good-bye to all that, to the philosophical detritus of post–World War II America, to the second Age of Anxiety, to being frightened of signs and portents and shadows and dog whistles, to the bands of illusions, to the negation of our entire cultural patrimony. Out of the goodness of its heart, America welcomed vipers into its breast and then raised a second generation of its own snakelets. It embraced Chesterton's heedless fence-cutters, bent on mindless destruction. Eden, just as it did in *Paradise Lost*, gave way to Chaos.

In Milton, Eve's rapture upon tasting the forbidden fruit ("Greedily she engorged without restraint / And knew not eating death") foreshadows Brünnhilde's call to the Light in Act Three of Wagner's *Siegfried*: "*Heil dir, Sonne! Heil dir, Licht!*" she cries, after the hero has awakened her with a deeply sexual kiss. Wagner surrounded his heroine with magic fire created by Loge, an ally of the gods; God sent Raphael and Gabriel to protect Adam and Eve, a job at which they signally failed. After tasting the fruit of the Tree of Knowledge, Milton's Eve rhapsodizes:

> . . . *henceforth my early care,*
> *Not without song, each morning, and due praise,*
> *Shall tend thee, and the fertile burden ease*
> *Of thy full branches, offered free to all;*
> *Till, dieted by thee, I grow mature*
> *In knowledge, as the Gods who all things know.*

Brünnhilde's awakening also signals her descent from demi-goddess to human woman; she consummates it by having sex with Siegfried (it's his first time, too); their knowledge of each other is carnal. Eve's revelation is at first spiritual, but when Adam joins her (because he cannot bear to be without her), their first act is to make love. Sex, in the work of these two great artists, is what makes us fully human.

But sex comes second—in *Paradise Lost* it is the transcendence of the spirit, not the concupiscence of the flesh. What comes first is the violence, the prolonged Battle in Heaven, the various thefts and murders that mark the first half of the *Ring*. The angels and the Germanic gods are a violent bunch, but humanity does not kill until after the expulsion from the Garden. Sex and violence, Eros and Thanatos.

It's no accident, then, that the assault on American culture has come precisely in these two areas: the diminishment of sex (its "liberation") and the, so to speak, violent War on Violence. For the Left, there is nothing more abhorrent than violence; even the hint of it ought to be actionable. Unless they are the ones doing the attacking, violence is always unacceptable, especially when used against them. Their bodies are their own private, personal temples.

Much as Lukács had hoped, the result of this sex reversal has been to emasculate and feminize males and turn women into ersatz men. With the masculinization of women, unsurprisingly, birthrates have dropped; and the entry of women into the workforce has resulted in, practically, the halving of men's income, since it now takes two incomes to provide a standard of living equivalent to what the middle class enjoyed in the scorned 1950s and '60s—and which generally supported far larger families.

Innovation, once the hallmark of American society, has slowed dramatically except in the areas of medicine and consumer electronics. Personal computers and other devices have changed the way we work, and advances in medical science have prolonged lives and reduced suffering. At the same time, though, infectious diseases thought wiped out generations ago have made a comeback, in part owing to a newly primitive, superstitious fear of vaccines—a fear that Americans for much of the twentieth century would have regarded as insane, since their children had been saved from polio thanks to Jonas Salk.

America put a man on the moon in 1969; it cannot do so today. Neither could the Hoover Dam be built, nor, for that matter, the Interstate Highway System. Gulliver is immobile, pegged to the ground.

The supersonic jetliner has come and gone, and air travel is noticeably meaner. The first seventy years of the twentieth century took the country from the horse and buggy to the Apollo project. What has been achieved, comparably, since then?

Innovation is first cousin to its uglier relative, bellicosity. From the warlike impulse comes the "primitive" need for triumph, the desire to impress women in battle, the need to raise strong sons and protect daughters. We once saw children as part of a family's storehouse of wealth, a protection against old age and an investment in the future of the bloodline and the species, not burdens or biological inconveniences to be terminated on a whim. Today such notions are dismissed with snorts of derision, and for much of the upper middle class—the kind of people who read the lifestyle sections of the *New York Times*—children are simply ornaments, a "choice," not a necessity. For the Left of the future, one's existence depends entirely on the whims of one's parents. By killing their unborn, they become like gods.

To change the nature of the sexual relationship—and, latterly, to add new variations to it—and to saltpeter out of the males their natural instinct to fight, which includes their natural instinct to win, to build, to succeed, to create (including artistically), is a prescription for "fundamental transformation," and not in a good way. Its proponents rely on the natural tendency of the young to see "change" as always good, to view "dissent" as always both moral and correct, and to always root for the rebels against the Empire.

Thus, as we've seen, the Unholy Left, with satanic facility, manipulates language in the furtherance of its aims. Starting with the proposition that "liberal" or "progressive" equals good and "conservative" equals bad, they merrily apply the "conservative" label to *their own movements* once they go bad. Note, for instance, their dogmatic reluctance to use the full name of the Nazi Party: the National *Socialist* German *Workers'* Party. The Nazis enthusiastically employed as many heroic images of the Toiling Proletariat—hammers swinging, factory wheels turning, bosomy peasant girls saluting the rising sun—as did the Soviet Communists. But, insists the Left, they had nothing whatsoever to do with each other—beyond their iconography, their anti-capitalism, their philosophical affinity, their political alliance, and their willingness to employ violence in the name of the state.

The sclerotic bureaucracy of fat old Slavic men in greatcoats and plastic shoes standing atop the Lenin Mausoleum and feebly waving at the military parade on Red Square (an image that personified the end of the Soviet Union) was invariably referred to by the leftist media as "hard-line" or "conservative." (The missing noun for these free-floating adjectives was "Communists," but that would spoil the story.) The theocratic mullahs in Iran, who overthrew the secular government of the Shah and today murder women and homosexuals with impunity, are similarly characterized by the media sloths. So is the Taliban, savage cultural vandals with little interest in preserving any vestige of that country's pre-Islamic past, called "conservative." And the heirs of Mao in China as well.

Gramsci and Lukács were right: Better to tunnel under the walls of the American Dream and detonate it from below than try to storm Heaven. This they learned from Satan himself, who failed at the latter task—as did Marx—but succeeded to a limited extent in the former. Despite my Irish-Catholic background, it amuses me to think that, at the Last Judgment, Hell will be liberated of its human souls, no matter what their earthly crimes, and they too shall ascend to Heaven, having done their time. Call it a final flip of the divine bird to Lucifer, the only real criminal in the entire ur-Narrative; after all, why should God concede even a single soul to his only rival, especially after the Son's Descent into Hell? It would be the manly, not to say the human, thing to do. And what a wow ending to the longest-running tale ever told.

Still, as Teddy said, the work goes on. (Kennedy's final, desperate, dying plea to Pope Benedict XVI—"I am writing with deep humility to ask that you pray for me . . . I've always tried to be a faithful Catholic"— was perhaps politely shunted to the circular file.) Our task on earth is never complete, it can only be handed off to the next generation; Adam and Eve saw to that, and we owe them a debt of gratitude. *Ils ne passeront pas.* "They shall not pass," said the French general, Robert Nivelle, at Verdun, in the closest thing to Hell on Earth mankind has ever experienced. (J.R.R. Tolkien, a veteran of that hell, put a close paraphrase of that declaration in the mouth of his angelic Gandalf, when the wizard forbade the arch-demon Balrog passage across the Bridge of Khazad-Dûm.)

Facing overwhelming odds at Thermopylae, the Greeks under the Spartan king Leonidas responded to Persian demands that they surrender their weapons with these words for the ages: "*Molōn labe.*" "Come and take them." Confronting Islamic demands to "submit" to a satanic barbarism masquerading as an "Abrahamic faith," Roland and other Christian warriors refused. Receiving German demands for surrender at the Battle of Bastogne, General Anthony McAuliffe replied, classically: "Nuts."

He could have said something earthier, but "nuts" is plenty earthy enough. "Nuts" means balls, testicles; McAuliffe and his surrounded soldiers at the Bulge fought on as, unknown to them, Patton's Third Army, spearheaded by the Fourth Armored Division, sped toward its rendezvous with destiny and glory. The root word of "testify" could not have been more appropriate.

Or politically incorrect. Warriors do not seek to understand the motivations of their enemies or to treat them with "respect." They kill them, and they keep on killing them until those enemies either are all dead or cannot fight anymore. The progress of modern warfare, whose logic was evident in the firebombing of Germany and Japan, and in the use of atomic weapons to end the war, has cruelly made civilian destruction inevitable. It was the looming threat behind the Cold War, the punch line of *Dr. Strangelove*, in the discussion of an "acceptable" rate of casualties in a nuclear exchange with the Soviet Union, should it come to that. "Ten to twenty million killed, tops," exclaims George C. Scott's General Buck Turgidson in *Strangelove*'s famous War Room scene, "depending on the breaks."

Scott's character was written and played as a bellicose buffoon, a safe depiction in the environment of 1964 America; the reasonable character, by contrast, was meant to be the ineffectual, Adlai Stevenson-esque figure of President Merkin Muffley, although the two double entendres in his name made their own commentary on the character's manliness. Balls were out, pussies were in; and the Vietnam War was about to begin, although we'd never pursue victory fully in earnest. It was the first war deliberately fought first to tie and then to lose. There have been others since.

As American society became ever more solipsistic and fearful—ever more protective of its nuts, as it were, and thus ever more unmanly and unregenerative—it played directly into the armchair-general mitts of the Frankfurt School philosophers, for whom (in the words of the late Washington Redskins head coach, George Allen) the future was always now. Still, the philosophers fled Europe rather than stay and fight. Only Walter Benjamin committed suicide in the border town of Portbou, Spain, rather than fall into German hands as he tried to escape via Varian Fry's trans-Pyrenean underground railroad in 1940. Yet even his epitaph reads, "There is no document of civilization which is not at the same time a document of barbarism"—a typical Frankfurter sentiment combined with a cheap twist of phrase, one more worthy of Dr. Frank N. Furter in *The Rocky Horror Show* than a German intellectual of the Frankfurt School, but there it is.

Don Quixotes of the mind, their philosophy giving unholy birth to the "sniveling brats" of the contemporary nasty, sneering Left, gibing at both the traditionally masculine and feminine virtues and appurtenances, desperately trying to relegate the ur-Narrative to the realm of secondary myth and legend, to bedtime stories for the gonzo Bonzos of postwar America: Such was the Frankfurt School. Having seized academia, they left a legacy in the cancerous growth of "studies" departments (gender, race, queer, whatever) that infest the modern university at the expense of classical learning. They have turned prominent institutions of what used to be called "higher learning" into reeducation camps of lower learning, populating them with "diversity" commissars and political officers, blunt fists in tweed jackets, sucking taxpayer money to fuel their own employment, forcing the larger population to subsidize their own theory of destruction.

I have termed this ongoing political war between Left and Right the "Cold Civil War," except that, until perhaps recently, it is a civil war that only one side understood it was fighting. In this it most closely resembles the declared war of Islam on the West, and the half-hearted, undeclared war that the West is endlessly, purposelessly, fighting against Islam in Mesopotamia and Afghanistan. Wars cannot be won without a clear understanding of what might constitute victory, as both General Gordon and Field Marshal Kitchener would have understood. "There can be only one," the immortal swordsmen say in *Highlander* as they go about the grim business of beheading each other. Even a B movie gets that right.

And so the United States, as the twenty-first century gets fully under way, finds itself in the position of the two combatants in Robert

Graves's vivid Great War image—the two bayoneteers locked in mutual death and rigor mortis, literally transfixed by each other, united eternally in the comradeship of hatred. Only one camp, however, has the additional elements of duty, honor, and country on its side. Only one side defends its women and children. Only one side fights to preserve instead of destroy, to honor instead of mock, to improve instead of tear down—to maintain the fence between civilization and barbarism, and to ask "Why?" instead of "Why not?" That knowledge, hard won, is both ancient and ongoing:

> *...The angel last replied:—*
> *"This having learnt, thou hast attained the sum*
> *Of wisdom; hope no higher*
> . . . .
> *... Only add*
> *Deeds to thy knowledge answerable, add Faith,*
> *Add virtue, Patience, Temperance, add Love,*
> *By name to come called Charity, the soul*
> *Of all the rest: then wilt thou not be loath*
> *To leave this Paradise, but shall possess*
> *A Paradise within thee, happier far."*
>
> — *Paradise Lost*, Book Twelve

Thus does the Unholy Left return to its crumbling *Teufels Lustschloss* and take up residence within—like Wotan in Valhalla, impotently watching the flames leap and the walls tumble, in silent vigil for the end it has so long awaited, so long feared, so devoutly desired. A philosophy of nihilism, according to the ur-Narrative, must and will end nihilistically.

The rest of us, though cast out of the Garden, yet attend to the sacred texts and heed the stories in our hearts. Having witnessed the Archangel Michael as, with fiery sword, he banished the ur-Father and ur-Mother from Eden, we can still see the eternal Cherubim guarding the gates, disporting themselves among St. Michael's magic fire, secure in the knowledge, and the hope, of our return.

The world was all before them, where to choose
Their place of rest, and Providence their guide:
They, hand in hand, with wandering steps and slow,
Through Eden took their solitary way.

And, in that moment of grief and loss, humanity was born, to begin its long journey home.

ACKNOWLEDGMENTS

The author would like to thank the following people for their invaluable help, encouragement, and suggestions during the creation and writing of this book, including Roger Kimball, Molly Powell, Jack Fowler, Tracy Scoggins, the people of Holy Family Chapel, Elena Kurtz, and Mr. and Mrs. Robert Maxhimer. Special thanks to Bill Walsh.

INDEX